LAURA SALTMAN

I Saw the Signs, and You Can Too

The Infinite Power Explained

SAVAAH
MEDIA

This book is dedicated to every One who came to find themselves as Love.
When you are ready let's proceed.

Contents

Preface

Everyone is a channel of Source. All ways. Living at levels of awareness, you are choosing who to be. Those choosing Love share Love in time— through messages, memes, online texts and quotes, movies, music, poetry, art, and artistry. Every time you are loving, you are Sourcing. On the flip side is ego: when you share harsh words, make threats, or debate truth, both are sewing the fabric of mind. You rip when you are in ego and mend when you are in Love. Which you choose is for you to decide, dear One.
— Wisdom of The All

This is a book to remind you of your true self—about how we are always being led and guided by the Divine. There is not one day—or perhaps even one moment—when we cannot access this Source information if we go seeking. It's easy to feel guidance and Love from All That Is when you connect to the level of consciousness that understands there is a force greater and equal to us—human and soul plus All.

I saw the signs, and you can too. They are everywhere. I see them in movies and TV shows; I see them in rainbows, butterflies, and all animals, along with their meanings and characteristics. I see them on bus stops, license plates, signposts and hear them in songs on the radio and overheard conversations. I study numbers and what they mean and measure. I witness daily miracles and subtle nudges from Source. I see how we create our triumphs and our tragedies, and I wanted a book that reminded you of everything you, too, can experience. Nothing is being hidden. It's out there for everyone to find. The resources exist—if only you are ready and able to receive them.

My book isn't just about getting signs and messages—it's about understanding why they are there in the first place. You can read about and hear about signs, but if you don't understand how they are placed, why they are placed, and what they may mean, then the purpose may be lost.

I don't miss the messages anymore; I study them. I notice where I need support, access them in dreams, and share what I've learned—because these tools saved my life.

To get to the tools, you need to know what led me to need them. I hesitated to share my portion of this book—a Q&A with that Divine Source, similar to my other *The All* books (*The All of Everything, The All of The All, The All That Is, Wisdom of The All*)—because it was so deeply personal. I thought I had moved beyond asking why I couldn't stay happy and what was holding me back, but clearly, much more needed to be learned.

In the pages of this book, I share all the good, bad, terrible, and amazing experiences I have had since I began writing with the All—every stumble and step moving me closer to understanding the journey of soul. It is vulnerable, sensitive, and at times hard to hear—but it is my truth. Perhaps it is your story too, and that is why you found me.

What led me to find the tools of Source was all that pain bottled inside myself. I know it was part of the lessons of soul—and in my life blueprint—to go through the challenges to discover these resources. And my goodness, am I grateful I was led to them—or that they found me. It saved me, truly. We will delve deeply into this in my portion of the book. I made it through the pain and started my climb over again and again—a gain is made every time you say "yes" to Love. That's when more tools began to unfold for me.

Some tools I use often, and others are more obscure, but I have personally utilized every tool we discuss in this book. And by "we," I mean myself and All That Is—which are, in fact, One. That's the interesting thing about life. We are so separated in mind and from one another that it can't possibly seem true that we are but One mind, One Love, and One everything—but we are. That is why there is a sign in every single day and in all the moments of life needed to evolve us as souls. It's what helps us with the fear.

Perhaps you, like me, have wondered what all of this means—why the signs appear, and what they're trying to show us.

These mysteries are solved here—what Love is and how we can utilize it in our lives. I have come to know this as truth because I have spent eight years "training" with the All to discover who I am and who you, too, are. Some of us remember; others are missing the point. And most are waiting to remember in their next life—or another life later on—as they incarnate again and again. We make the choice to come to Earth to remember and evolve to Love.

Don't be surprised when others aren't interested in your signs. They may not be able to access their truth (as chosen by them) today, tomorrow—or perhaps ever—as the self they are being on Earth right now. It comes when we choose, as souls, to remember All.

For those who are ready, the markers and guideposts are everywhere. You re-Source as you accept them, returning to the mind of All—reminding you of Love with whispers, shoves, and pushes through photos, memes, canvases, and more. There are images around the world reminding us who and what *I Am* is—the Infinite Awareness Mind. One mind, which is all minds. Many words are broken into this Source language, simple acronyms for deeper meanings, and you will find a dictionary at the end to lead you to their true messages.

How we access messages can take many forms. There are people who know, lead, and guide you as sages or shamans, spirit guides or angels—messengers whom we can access when needed. We'll explore how these guides and angels can support you directly—offering gentle nudges and reassurance when you forget your divine path. Their messages are part of the same loving network that connects us to the All.

The Akasha is where you access information: a database of sorts of all lives lived, all possibilities and probabilities accessible to you as you journey through lives on Earth. It encompasses many mechanisms to help us understand why we behave as humans the way we do.

Astrology brings us messages of the stars. Archetypes describe who we are as emotional and physical beings—our personalities, why we are the way we are, and why we do the things we do. Why do we want to adventure in the world, or why do we want to hermit inside our homes? It's all right there in our spiritual DNA—a code of Source.

There are road maps that have been placed—like tarot, oracle, or energy cards—cartography for the mind of All. Each has a meaning for its finder or seeker through images and art, numbers, colors, symbols, and animals or insects. Creatures are our friends, not foes.

Through Akasha, dreams are how you access other realms and incarnations. Your soul travels. As you sleep, it awakens to gift information from all lives (past, present, and future) and deciphers your fears into symbolism to decode yourself. The timelines you enter intersect—parallel and perpendicular. To cross is to know you are multidimensional and illusional—however real life may feel.

Numerology tells us about the day we were born, the month we were born in, and the year we were born. These codes inform our life experiences and the ways in which we project and process emotions—how our daily experiences are coded with clues to what energy and events could be experienced, both for ourselves and for the collective. These are always moving and changing, just as astrology, the moon, sun, stars, and planetary motion impact our lives. You'll even learn how to chart your days numerically through a practice of "soul charting," a process that helps you recognize repeating patterns and align more easily with Love.

Our soul print—or life blueprint—spells out the reasons we came to be and what themes we are required to tackle as we work to ascend. Knowing mine has to do with worth, value, and patience is a game changer. You'll find a list of themes that may explain why loops keep happening and similar experiences keep recurring.

We get to understand our body and how our energy centers affect daily living. The body is a learning device and seeks to show us what we are moving through emotionally. It educates and informs us about what we might believe and think—a chakra system spotlighting the issues and insecurities we hold onto in life.

Our sensor system, the clairs, is where perception helps us navigate with tools like keen hearing, inner awareness, or heightened senses of smell, taste, or touch.

To help you understand not only what you receive but who you are as you receive it, there are three road maps in this book—personality (Archetypes), conscious awareness (Ladder of Awareness), and coding (Numerological Codes). They tell us who we are as both soul and human and how to ascend when we fall. It's like knowing the answers before you take the test. Once you understand the mechanics of the mind, body, and soul, you can then build your life accordingly. Don't worry about not knowing what existed for us ahead of time; the map only appears when One sets the destination to heal our separation.

What is spelled out here, and in other books of Source, are tools of now—but know that more are available and will unfold in the coming years and centuries. Still, though using and accessing these tools has changed my life, I know that what feels true to me may sound impossible to others—and that's part of the human journey too. Many are not yet ready to believe what they cannot measure or prove.

It stands to reason that many of my friends—and even my own family members—are sure I have gone to a place of delusion. They believe so strongly in the illusion placed in the mind of our humanness that it seems impossible to comprehend our soul evolution. I understand their concern and dismay. I haven't been the person I used to be for about five years or more. But when you have seen and witnessed what I have in this world—the transmissions, the clues, the signals, the synchronicities, the coincidences (of which there are none)—it all begins to make sense. As you begin to walk on the way, the way appears. You become more attuned to frequencies; you start to feel into people's energy and vibrations. You notice when your mess is actually a message.

As you continue your journey up the ladder of consciousness, you awaken a part of yourself you didn't even know existed. Awareness is key to our decisions and choices in life. You do "the work," and you remember more and more of who you are as soul—and the less the human mind and ego tag along. In time, you'll also come to see how awareness unfolds in levels—

what I call the Ladder of Awareness. It's a framework that helps you understand how thoughts and emotions rise from fear to Love, with a process to climb back whenever you slip.

As you rise higher in frequency, connecting to more truth, you gain access to information that cannot be coming from your own mind. It must come from a deeper place—something bigger than yourself—as you work with all these mechanisms and modalities. You become as we are meant to live—One with All.

Then, as you begin to channel your own information, you see the world through a lens of how everything is interconnected and One. It's impossible to go backward. You can access spirits and loved ones in Heaven and communicate to understand their journey of soul—why they left and what they wish you knew on Earth to help you navigate it better. You cannot be the same person you were, and if you continue to say "yes" to that, more things will awaken in you. The true you emerges—the one who came from a higher, heavenly realm where we are connected to all beings everywhere, all at once.

If you are new to the Divine and the tools being shared, it may seem overwhelming. Take it slow, but know it's part of your curriculum. Just like at school, you have resources, study guides, and charts and graphs to keep you learning and growing. Once understood why (what hurt you), then the how (healing our wounds) unfolds as long as you keep utilizing the tools of All.

Let us begin where all awakening does—with curiosity.

Introduction

Everything you are going through collectively is patterns repeating in time. Remove cars, boats, trains, and buildings and you'll find it's about people irrespective of time stamps. Fighting over made up lines and invisible borders. Surveying others' genders and skin and deciding One is more "valuable" than another. A most peculiar world of division spurred by ego and fear. Look to Source and Ones would see the players change, but the ideas and values remain. Until One is All focused, a world of loathing is most definitely repeating itself over and over in time. Sleepy times exist to awaken those who are determined to rise. Are you ready, dear One of All?

— Wisdom of The All

If you have found my book, I imagine you are having questions about why people do bad things in the world and why life is so hard. Perhaps you are curious about all the ways Spirit can communicate with us and what happens to us when we die. Those are the same questions I had. So, back in 2017, I went looking for answers and found them through what began as journaling but would eventually become my first book, *The All of Everything, a Spiritual Guide to Inner World Domination.*

I am so grateful you were guided to this educative series. The All is my metaphysical guidebook for living on planet Earth. It's not for everyone to find because most of us are not wanting to be woken up. However, if you are even the slightest bit interested in my journey of how I moved myself out of fear, chances are 100 percent you are wanting to be awakened to some degree, and I'm glad you are here.

This book is for anyone who is struggling. This book is for anyone who is happy. This book is for any One. I am One. You are One. We are One. One is capitalized as a guide to your divine nature. It reminds you of your unity with the All That Is.

This book is about how I (and you) can discover all the lies of fear and remember Love. It's shining a light on modalities you can use and tools to go inward and find truth. Think of it like a lockbox embedded in your mind, and we are slowly chipping through the layers of conditioning to uncover it. Then, once we find it, we have to understand first, how to open it, second, what it is, and then, third, the integration of our higher and false selves into One.

Are there some on Earth now who find truth easily and stay there in physical realms? Suffice it to say there are, but they are few and far between, with just a few living uncomplicated lives, enjoying freedom in ashrams, monasteries, and other holy places. This joy is achievable when we go forth as souls being human, but it is not the way of most. So, I would say, if you are here, it is because you too go back and forth from love to fear as well.

I, Laura, have been using these *The All* books to remind me too. I would invite anyone who has brought these books into their lives that, just like other books of Source, channeled by the Ones like Helen Schucman (*A Course in Miracles*), Jane Roberts (*Seth*), or Neale Donald Walsch (*Conversations with God*), and other awakened minds, they are to be consumed not just once but on multiple occasions. When you are unsure of your next steps, drowning in fear, doubt or worry, or just simply want a reminder of Infinite Love, use this and *The All* books for a moment of truth.

I, Laura, would love to express to you how I have changed and grown while at the same time remind you I am just a channel of Source, not a fully realized soul. I still have lessons to learn and grow through myself. So, you will find throughout this book I am bouncing around between love and fear (a lot) which is how most on a journey of soul are going to find their awakening.

Needless to say, I spent a long time on this book, the longest so far since

I began my journey writing as *The All*, because I had so many lessons to learn—just as did the collective of which you are part as well. All of us being One.

My journey took me through the awakening to a voice of "God," to knowing we are One, and finally to the realization of Source being One with All. My books follow a specific curriculum of discovery. First, separation: believing the outside voice is apart from self. Then a co-creator: believing in guidance from "above" or with Source. Next, a partnership, where I believed I had a team of guides and messengers to help (of which many do and will until they discover it's you being All.) The final step being an understanding we are Source. One mind. One guide. One thing with no separation.

When I finally learned to hand all experiences over to the All, I found a sense of peace and freedom like never before, and so I hand it over now to that inner voice and hope you will enjoy your journey of Allness wherever it takes you and from wherever you are in your understanding of God, Source, or the Universe.

One is All and All is One and That is Who We Are

Welcome, every One, to our guide to Life. It doesn't follow any particular way of writing and discovery. We are here to explain the whys, hows, and who of All. Who are we? Who you are and what is life all about on Earth? Those on a journey of questioning are the key which unlocks our mystery.

Life is not happening to you, but for you. Even when the hard parts are insurmountable, it is always for the highest good. No, you can't understand this—not because it's unknowable but because it's important you stay rooted in humanity. You can't grow, evolve and transform if you know All. It's not the journey of soul. You have chosen to remain rooted in separation in order to experience life as is. Knowing everything is like tasting candy before you brush your teeth. Once you experience the bliss, it gets wiped away and worthless in terms of enjoyment. Use the information provided in this book as a means to clear the amnesia of soul but also live as if you know nothing so you can experience life as it's meant to be experienced—fully and completely without interruption.

So why are we here explaining Infinite wisdom then?

So you may know the roadmap and guide the journey from this place. The path is yours to choose. We simply offer the routes and destinations, but you are the chooser of All.

Why am I here?

Experience, evolve, expand—the three E's of functional reality. Experience bliss and joy and sadness and sorrow. It is necessary in all realities, both physical and nonphysical, to have a spectrum of emotions. Ones cannot evolve unless they know pain and suffering. It is the teacher. A teacher seeks to inform and enlighten. Just as elementary education reminds One to read and write, evolutionary education teaches One to live, love and escape fear.

What is ego?

Your ever-present, untrustworthy companion is always along for the ride of life, implanted in the mind to bring you thoughts of harm, shame, regret and fear. Fear is the journey of planet Earth. Ones who always think positively are simply hiding the underneath beliefs. It isn't until you uproot all of your thought processes hidden in mind that Ones will know what is actually true. How you accomplish this is through hard challenges set by the Ones who came to *be*. To *be* is to know you are All. When you *be* you trust all is unfolding for the highest good of All.

Know you are being guided every time you fall asleep to Love (i.e., who you are). Every time. No exceptions. It might take decades to uncover all the false beliefs hidden in mind, but if you stay on the path illuminated by soul, it will always lead you back.

Will it take longer if I am in hustle and not flow?

It takes as long as it takes, and this is guided simply by YOU. Every time you go inward, a ripple is created whereby all new beliefs come to light. It's as if you are on the bottom of the ocean, and when you breathe, pray, or ask, you are taking steps to engage the soul, which (each and every time) takes you toward the top until finally you can breathe fully and completely.

You always have access to knowledge allowing you to breathe. That is All.

Who am I?

You are more than just a physical being. The idea you are separate from anything is false. It's following everything as real (fear). It all feels so real—the lives lived—but in actuality it is mind's creative aspirations to know One's self which gives rise to everything. This is what being everything and nothing at all means. You are mindfully expressing everything as physical matter yet remaining nothing, which is All. What is seen physically is what is creating mentally—as either One as All or fear as ego, and this is known inside where all information exists.

Who are we?

We are energetic beings living a human experience, and in that experience will come difficulties, challenges, stressors, things to upset you, things to trigger you, people and relationships who bother or frustrate you. But ultimately, we are the chooser of the experience, and as much as we believe we are separate is how we will experience it through the mind. However, when we come into our unity—when we unseparate ourselves from our human condition and the human voice—the language of Love is within. It guides every step. It opens up a pathway to a new way of being, a new understanding of accepting life as it is. Every corner of the light is guiding, is loving, is pulling us toward it, and owning this light is how we grow, transform, and remember.

Who are you?

Who you are is more than the physical being. It is vast, expansive, immersive Love unconditional. There is nothing more rewarding than the physical body to remember who you are, what you came here to be, and how to re-Source to the One who is All.

Who is All?

All is you, me and we. It is all of us as One. We are representing ourselves through you, by you. I am One. You are One. We are One. So each individual has its own consciousness as well as One consciousness. You, me, we. All is One. One is All.

I accept who I am without question. Who I am is Love. When I fail to remember remind me oh, Love.

Ask, and then a soft gentleness comes from within, guiding you slowly back toward truth—not in giant leaps but in small increments, step-by-step, moment-by-moment. Guiding you toward peace, joy, and ultimately Love. There is an emotion of love but there is also the Oneness Love. Unconditional Love. This is who we are. This is who you are. This is who All are.

It is Love. It is All.

This is who I am.

Welcome back, dear One.

Asknowledgements

Asking is key to enlightenment. Otherwise you won't be helped. The Law of Free Will says you are able to think, believe, and act any way you want on Earth. If you don't ask you won't receive the help. Help is healing everything Love placed because the Universe already knows what you wish. So ask away, dear Ones.
— Wisdom of The All

Dear Ones,

We are so glad you have joined with us to remember who you are through our words and phrasing. In this book, you will discover more divine truths through various modalities leading you to understanding our Infinite power, how it works, leads, and guides you all day, every day.

Not one day, or even moment, goes by where you are alone, ever. We are infinitely connected to the inner self, which is our soul—a word which some find religiously based, but in actuality it comes directly from Source.

Words of Source are written all over the place—in movies and TV shows, musicals, hit songs, and random quotes on walls and plaques. Our social media feeds are filled with the musings of All. Most are too caught up in daily life to understand how the inner self brings words through. But now you are here and ready to go deeper in mind and find what exists, and not all of it will be easy to know. It will take time to believe in some "out there" concepts and musings, but remember we are One, and it will make sense.

Every time you read our *The All* books ask to be guided through them. Asking is key. It is a soul's knowing.

Help me to understand what is difficult and release false beliefs and old concepts so I may remember I am.

You will find (as in the other *The All* books) the difference between my (Laura) voice and their voice (All). They are my thoughts and words but coming from the One. When I write as Laura, it's obvious as I use familiar phrasings. When I write as All, I am guided by thoughts outside my false self (ego), and words come quickly, effortlessly, and with no need to go back and change them. I know they are truth because it feels as if another being is speaking through me and I am just writing words I hear and type. Like a translator or a court reporter sitting in a courtroom, taking dictation. I am a stenographer for All. The only difference is mindful. One believes in Laura, the other is All. When we combine our true and only self into One, we are Sourcing.

Sourcing words is how you "channel." Most believe they are speaking with "God" or the Universe or a Spirit and only few on Earth understand they are All speaking as One. All access is gained in higher states of awareness.

Equal = Evolving quietly under All's Love.

You are equal, not separate and apart. There is no "power" holding you back or lifting up your might. You are mighty just as you are.

Remember this as you go through our book, that you are equal and All. The words are coming from Laura, but they belong to All. All have access to wisdom, knowledge, and Infinite intelligence because it is within All.

I Am

This two-letter word is the calling card for All. Ask to receive (in mind) using the *I am,* and you are calling on the higher self.

I am capable of what I believe. I am Love.

After the word *I am,* place meaningful phrasing never big lofty asks and wants, as these are designed to trip your ego into engaging in falsities. *I am* is the simple phrase activating the higher self, which knows you exist as do all things.

I am bringing forth diamonds and riches becomes…

I am abundant and receive what is asked for in truth. All is possible in belief.

I am asking for bigger dreams to be achieved becomes…

I am what is seen in mind.

This allows All visions to come to physicality with exception.

Are there limitations?

Yes. No being on Earth may return to Source unless agreed upon prior as soul. So seeing yourself falling off a cliff is an ego's trick and not truth. Seeing yourself whisked away on a grand vacation is the mind's creation and possible to be achieved. Also, you are not able to regrow limbs on Earth, but strides have been made to achieve this in science and will continue to evolve in time.

It is our wish you understand Infinite intelligence and become a true artisan of peace as you move through life. What you receive is designed and afforded to you, by you. But know the point of life is to *be* (joyful, loving, kind) and not do (work, hustle, grind) and so asking in *I am* for more than you need is ego's way of keeping you stuck. Enlightened Ones take what is needed to align to Love and that is All.

So what should I be asking for in life?

A car to experience and ease life's flow. A house to live a full and complete life in. A job if needed or wanted. A career if that calls you. Anything to keep you on Earth and comfortable is necessary but big mansions, boats, and dream closets filled with things are only outside things needed by ego. You need food, water, healthcare, shelter and safety. What gets you there is mind.

I am only needing a life of joy and this is always a gift I achieve.

What makes you happy? Is it material possessions or love of people and pets? If finding a home is important it is always possible to create. If needing a home for making others jealous or serving ego's desire to live large is the reason then you are out of alignment to All. There is no judgment, and we see all of what occurs on Earth. It is this striving for more that causes the disruptive wars and tragic circumstances which occur. Greed, power and wanting—a trifecta of wanton energy and willful deceit. Fill the mind with ego's desires, and it will be hard to ascend, which, dear All, is the journey of Love.

Making Time and Money

In Spirit it is about remembering you are All, nothing held back, everything available and in human form it is the same (yet hard to believe) because we have given ourselves the gift of amnesia, a.k.a, un-remembering. In order to grow and evolve, we gifted ourselves (each individually and collectively) this challenge, the challenge of a life.

Our physical life is the proof of what's happening in our mind. We are in a rut financially, emotionally ungrounded, untethered. And every time you trust in the human experience it is your amnesia, not truth. So what is truth? You are One that is All. You are the highest Love, which is All, and All has access to everything.

Everything is available to All and the how doesn't matter. "How?" is our biggest unconscious question, which has us believing we make it rather than receive it. To *be* is to know it exists and Ones need only ask and accept that which is yours. It is telling our beautiful energy who we are—Spirit/Love/All. It is nature, trees, grass, leaves, sand, soil, Earth. Our natural resources all in a state of being. Chaos may surround them at times but because it is nature being at One with All, they trust. It seems weird to say a tree can trust, but it does.

All things are consciousness in various forms. Everything is All. This is the most important high-vibrational understanding. There is nothing that is not God or Love or Source. Whatever you call that from which we all come. Nothing is random. All of it purposeful. You are the blessing of Source. The Earth is the blessing of Source. The tree, the bird, the elephant, and the eagle all Source energy. All things energy.

Utopia

There is a little island in the middle of the ocean untouched by man, unseen by most. Not many venture this way. For it is a desolate island, and yet on that island live the most beautiful creatures. All of their resources available, and not with words or thoughts, but it is emotions which bring forth their experience. So the critters that live amongst others do not fight. They just belong. And all of this chosen by all who gather on this island of Love. It is proof of what we have been speaking of in our *The All* books, Utopia, in this small little island of which you have no idea does exist in physical form. It can't be seen unless you purposefully navigate toward it or go there looking for it.

What happens, as humans, is we hear the word Utopia, freedom, or joy and we want to discover it. Columbus discovered America not from joy but fear; escapism, leaving his country seeking freedom. And the journey was fraught with many difficulties, small and large, with many dying along the way. All in a state of fear.

They journeyed across oceans looking for Utopia. Those who landed on the earth (soil) were there to escape governmental control, scarcity and poverty. They found an island for themselves that didn't belong to them. It belonged to those who staked their claim, who found this island and believed in magic and used it for their own devices. It didn't last long because as fear seeps in it changes the narrative, and so this narrative of complete Utopia became muddied with fear and, the magnet of fear—that is our Law of Attraction, like attracts like—drove these men here. And once they were settled on this island of earth (ground) now called America, the war and the struggles began and continue. Utopia upended in service to fear of the hunted and hunters.

Let's return our mind to that little island in the middle of the ocean, the one Utopia left on Earth. No man's land. There are some who would ask, *"Where is it? Where can I find it? Let's go there."* While others allow it to be and enjoy just knowing of its existence. It is as much their journey as it is yours to discover and remember they, the creatures of this island Utopia, so close to enlightenment they have no idea for things, only the need for experiences. A big giant leap of discovery. They simply *be.*

Does this island actually exist? Yes. In the mind. It is *freedom.* The mind of One. An island unto itself where all creatures and beings coexist in peace. Remember? What is Utopia? Utopia is All. It's being free. Being loved unconditionally without strings attached without needing anything, just grateful for what is. It's masterful in its making/bond breaking. Victory is to break free. It cannot be created exteriorly, only interiorly. What does that mean? It means emotions and beliefs regulate everything. Whatever you think, you become. What you say you are, you are. In the absence of fear all things possible. Anything. Any upset, any stressors, any illness, any judgment that isn't Love is fear. For whatever you feel is wrong inside the mind is simply fear. That's all it is. Nothing but fear. All you need to see it differently is to sit in silence and ask to receive new beliefs and let it go. The island of One is you being All.

And So We Begin Again

To understand the messages of this book, you must first understand the messenger—and how she came to listen.

Who is Laura?

I am Laura, just like you—a seeker of truth, a wanter of knowledge with a desire to know who I am and the meaning of life. I didn't set out to write another *The All* book. In fact, I was pretty sure I was done after I channeled (Sourced) my first four, but, of course, there was always that nagging sense of incompletion—more to be learned, understood, and discovered in my quest for joy, freedom from suffering, and enlightenment.

What happened was a miracle—writing those books, speaking words of Spirit. I had no clue it was going to become my journey for Source: a translator of Divine intelligence. Unfortunately, it's a gig that comes with sharp edges. Writing about Utopia was easy. Living it, I soon discovered, would be the challenge. So it's back to my asking questions and finding answers to All.

Let us remind you, as we move through the pages of our book, we will bounce between answers to questions and direct inscriptions from All (what you have called "channeling"). As in my last book, *Wisdom of The All*, if there is confusion as to who is writing as you move through the material, simply ask to receive: *Who is speaking here? Laura or All?*

By the end of the book, we hope it will be understood—it is All, always.

Chapter 1 / Nose to the Grindstone

D ear All, help me discover our Infinite truth without reservation or anger.

111 — Repeating numbers remind you to Source.

Every stuckness has a purpose. Every step, a stone of Love. You can't be in flow one hundred percent on Earth, for that is not a journey; it is patterns and sameness. You have got to ride the kiddie rides and the scary coasters too. It's an idyllic planet for evolution. Some days may be more challenging—good and bad, yin and yang. You cannot have perfect days all ways, because then, dear Ones, you would be here in nonphysical. Open to the idea you have chosen it all, and the ride becomes way better, dear Ones of Earth.
— Wisdom of The All

Yin/Yang

So here we are again, talking about Love and fear as I navigate life. The chapter title refers to an idiom around schooling and hard work, and while I don't prescribe to this notion anymore (preferring a gentler approach to life), I do acknowledge that if you found this book and are about to dive in, how consistency is the key to understanding the All.

Always be learning. That's the plan of the All. You never stop until you are done with the energetic dance of Love. So be prepared to be disappointed if you believe a life of all Utopia is the point of these books and all spiritual books. It's about balance, dear Ones.

I know this balance intimately, both wonder and devastation. What happened in my own life has been both awful and amazing, good and bad, yin and yang. That is how we grow. We experience both sides of the coin of life. Moments of pain are followed by incredible things and growth occurring through those. I would love to live a life of uncompromising joy and be happy all the time, but have come to understand we must deal with whatever comes by knowing we chose it.

Being the chooser of life and knowing its responsibility lies within is very difficult to agree with at times. I chose to have my dad and brother die? I chose to watch my career be flushed down the toilet? I chose to live in constant fear of ruining my life? I chose to always be worried about my next dollar or paycheck? I chose to get mugged on a sunny day in an upscale community? I could go on and on, but I am sure you get the point. Think of things in your own life which were hard, and I would bet you too would question the concept of "choosing" all things.

What I have learned over the course of the last ten years, is who *I am* actually is. It's who you are too, and some of us will discover it and live it, others will discover it and chastise or argue against it, and others will find it and be it.

Being is the completion of the cycle of fear. It's living in Love. Doing is believing it's hard work and grind or hustle which brings through All. The lie of our ego is we are here to make and not *be*. Being is truth. Doing is false. It is one thing to write these truths; it is another to live them in the middle of hardship.

Throughout this book, before introducing the tools, I will be asking questions—just as I did in my other *The All* books. I find this to be the easiest and quickest way to gain knowledge and understanding. I know

2

it is truth (however hard to believe) because of how quickly the answers are received—every word perfectly placed. Concepts beyond my personal scope of knowledge are discussed, including many words I have never used or even heard. The process is simple: I ask, I listen, and I write, allowing the words to come through without force or preconception.

When you reach the chapters on Chakras/Clairsenses, Tarot/Oracle, Archetypes, the Ladder of Awareness, and the Akasha, know that every word came through my mind—not from research or spending hours, days, or years developing them. I simply listened and wrote, then applied what arrived in my own life and with clients, and through this practice have come to know how true and accurate they are for me and for others.

As you read through my questions throughout the book, remember that there have been dark times in the world, and I want to remind you that this is purposeful. In order to understand the All, we must experience the difficult—for without contrast, Love cannot be fully recognized. I never intend to make light of, or bypass, the pain that is clearly being felt by others and honoring that suffering is part of our evolution. However, after nearly a decade of channeling (Sourcing), I know it is important to seek the guidance of All to move through it with Love rather than resistance.

Some of the dialogue can be repetitive, and that's on purpose too. I've learned enough to know that is what happens in our mind. One day you can feel like you're on top of the world, the next like the world is ending. I've witnessed this throughout my journey writing as The All and with my clients as they navigate and stumble—just as I did. The good news is that the more you practice, the more you come to know this as truth, and the easier it becomes to quiet the mind and choose Love. It doesn't happen overnight. It doesn't even happen over years. It can take many, many, many years or more to release amnesia. The importance of consistency is measured and studied in science through the brain's ability to change, termed neuroplasticity. You have that mechanism, whether you see it through science or spirituality.

While my first four books took me only a few years to write, this book has been more challenging—mostly because I was busy, and the insanity occurring since Covid had so many people struggling in their day-to-day life. Work, stress, struggle and try to *be*. I used my tools provided to me by the All as often as I could, but also found myself caught up in the daily grind and nonsense of life.

I started this book in December 2021 and only worked on it haphazardly during the last three years, only to find myself drawn back to its pages after the turn of the election in November 2024. I picked it up at the last chapter with questions about the state of the United States, but realized after repeating questions and seeking a different response, the answers are always (or perhaps All ways) the same no matter what the circumstance entails, be it collective or individualized. So eventually I came to the understanding that no matter how many questions would arise from the tragedies and circumstances of the human experience, our world works the way it does on purpose—our purpose being to grow and evolve our consciousness back to All That Is.

You will find I go back and forth quite often (between fear and love), as I always have in my *The All* books, but I have found now, seven years after starting this journey of writing, I understand and accept it as truth. What you read in these pages, I believe, is the amalgamation of so many other's journeys as well. It takes a long time to understand the only truth we have is the one of Love.

I know enough now to have gratitude for every misstep, every small leap and every large shift but I was constantly dragged into the NOT rather than NOW. What is *not* happening for me instead of living in now, which as I have learned, is the absolute space of All. The creator is always in now, and so too can we be if we know we too are All

My other issue, which sent me back to my computer for answers in this book, was around my finances, or rather lack of them. I had seen proof around healing and miracles witnessing people overcoming cancers and reversing chronic illnesses and other forms of pain. What I hadn't seen much of are stories of people who brought forth money out of nowhere by "just being" which is the way the All constantly tells us is the money maker.

You don't make money, you discover its ability to arrive.
— The All That Is

At the time of writing this chapter I was still on a tightrope in terms of money and living in paycheck-to-paycheck mode. At one point, I did have enough money to purchase a home for myself and son. That forward movement ultimately led to more panic and fear in terms of money. External circumstances made paying my mortgage more than I could handle financially, thanks to inflation and fear (as the All would say). So I returned to my *The All* books and began again asking the questions needed to help me uncover my Utopia. My journey to coming into freedom—physically, emotionally and spiritually—a window to my own path of fear and anguish or pain. I hope it gives you clues to your own "why" questions about the world of fear we all said "yes" to living in, and the later chapters are meant to guide you to tools for ascending beyond old beliefs, constructs, and ideas of humanity.

Question Everything

The only prayer ever needed is one that heals our mind's thought of not being part of the whole. Separation—that's why we fail. Separation is why we get angry. Separation is why we feel lost. Separation is when self-love becomes self-loathing. When you remind yourself back to One, you are remembering you are Love. It becomes easier to let go, to live joyfully, and to express love. No human is a gold-star earner every day. Some days it will feel as if you are sliding backward as a means to move forward—so you may recognize when and where you are in need of tuning up. "What fears are holding me back from Spirit today? Why am I not connecting with my inner being?" Questions reveal All.
— Wisdom of The All

Laura: Why does it seem as if we are always so unhappy here on Earth? I don't know if it has always been this way, but more and more (ever since Covid) the happy and thriving train is off the rails for so many people. It feels as if we can't catch a break. First it was the pandemic, then it was hurricanes and fires, now it's artificial intelligence taking our jobs and livelihoods. What's next? Planetary implosion? I'm joking, but also not joking.

All: Life is *living in fear everyday* for most on Earth, dear One. You are witnessing and watching a world untethered. You see, dearest One, the journey is not for life always being perfect but rather being constant.

L: Constant pain, heartache, mental health issues, and physical maladies? No thank you. Why anyone signed up for this hell is beyond me.

A: Precisely. It is beyond what any One can comprehend in bodies. You have access to inner knowing and, if used, would become more accessible to see our world as it is from a place of Love. Love is love because you are Love. It is only what exists in this "modern" world you seem so attached to. You ask why a world suffers through loss and tragedy and look at the *outside* circumstances wondering how to fix them, and we will tell you fixing the outside does nothing. Only fixing the *inside* is what will change outside appearances.

War, poverty, famine—are all symptoms of the mind of the collective of the planet, not punishments nor indictments upon one class of citizen or race of people. It is always what you are thinking which is the process of creation. Want to create a better world all around? Think with the mind of Love only. Get rid of any thought which doesn't serve the higher self and begin to connect to the Love within, and you will see a gentle shift occurring all over the world each and every time you do this. Not every day will be good and perfect, but it will begin to be as you practice more and more and others do as well. You can live in a kind, just world if the world sees itself as One.

L: Love doesn't seem like what this is. It seems as if hell is everywhere. No one happy. Everyone hating on one another. I can't

remember a time when humans hated one another more than they do right now.

A: Separating the self from all others is mass illusion.

L: I try and live life understanding what you have taught here with and through me.

- **We are spiritual beings having a human experience.**
- **We come from Love and are Love at the center of our being.**
- **There is one mind, and that mind is All, which exists in everyone.**
- **Our guides, messengers and loved ones in Spirit are helpers to us.**
- **There are signs and messages everywhere of what is Love and what can be done to move ourselves out of fear.**
- **We create based on what we think, feel, and believe.**

The human mind cannot comprehend this as truth. I see it, read it, absorb it—but don't live it—and that, dear All, is my truth. I can't remember any of my life as a soul and therefore this entire book and all the others are just ideas and not able to be integrated fully and completely. This is why life is so hard. I can't put the two together and live at the level of vibration where I am accessing freely my whole life as All. It's separate from me. I would love to remember, but I can't.

A: Can't and won't. Two ideas of fear. Can't is untrue. Won't is decision. You can't remember because you won't choose to *be*.

L: I won't choose "to be" because I am down to my last few thousand dollars. If I choose to be I have to put aside work, and if I put work aside I will be more broke than I currently am and would have to sell my home, move in with someone perhaps and ask for assistance financially. That is absolutely not a decision or choice I would make on Earth. I would like a home, a secure bank account and proper health. We need money (thanks to this corrupt system we set up in the Bronze Age) to live and be healthy.

A: Health is obtained by and through mind and nothing else. Money is not a means to create or achieve it.

L: If you have money you have access to medicines, organic foods, or supplements that are healthy. You can buy weights or equipment and go to expensive yoga or spin classes. You can afford healthcare to test for what is imbalanced or fix and heal chronic pain.

A: A body is able to walk, run, swim, or build muscle in ways that are both free and easy.

L: Fine. You got me on that one. Working out doesn't cost a thing. Only time. You can't buy health if you need a doctor or surgeon unless you have a lot of money and/or insurance, which must come from a job, or employer, or money you already have to obtain it.

A: If you stay in mind and see it for the self it is possible to create anything on Earth. We could go back and forth on each and every point you would like to settle, but the truth of All is you are able to be, do, or have what is agreed upon prior on Earth. You set a stone to uncover. Now is the time you spend inward which achieves these goals either through Love, fear, or both. There is a simple formula, and that is Love in—Love out. Fear in—fear out. What you think, believe, and know is what is made in physical. So if you think *I am*, believe you will, and know it's arriving, the experience of having homes, cars, money, and health is available. Thoughts are things. Things are material. Material is computed into physical by mind.

My mind creates.

Simple, right?

L: Not simple as a human. Not when you have a mortgage bill due, a car payment, or mouths to feed (including your own). And if you want to go into debt, sure, you can rack it up on your credit cards, but to stay rooted in mind and create something seems impossible to me. I have five days to pay my bills and that formula isn't doing it. I understand it, but won't be able to live it as truth unless I see proof, which I haven't.

A: It is thine own truth. This is the concept of "I am" it accepts for you the truth. You are not living someone else's truth but rather remembering it as thine own. Yes, it may not be accessible as human, but if you trust the knowledge received in mind and live with this understanding, it will become reality. Full and complete access to All That Is exists in mind. Let it become who you are, and you will see life altered in miraculous ways, even if our earthly counter beings are not aware of Love's presence within. As Ones align back more and more to truth it becomes active inside. You live differently in Love. You receive memories and ideas and discover inner is the way. Outer is false. What is seen in mind is Love. Your truth. Who am I? *I am.*

L: I am broke. That's who I am.

A: Words to use would be…

I am choosing to know this time is meant for change. To teach others how it takes time to live fully and in the knowing of All That Is.

Use words of Love such as above to achieve the change you seek, dear One.

Love is All, while love is a human emotion—not the same in terms of Infinite truth. To use love is to engage with ideas of self or ego, but to use Love is to align with All. We—being both you and I (All)—embody this truth. This is where change happens: in understanding the delineation of Source.

L: The change I seek is a world not almost at war. We are nearing World War III here at this point if we don't get things turned around on this planet. I can't believe how far we have fallen as a society and species. Hatred fueled by separation, and not just separation from Source but living as if we are all different because of skin, gender, and such.

A: Get to work as souls, and you will see the wars dismissed and the world more pleasant to live in. Each individualized soul has the ability to right the masses into a more peaceful era by seeing it at the level of mind. Send a ripple of Love to each and every person on Earth, and your ripple will affect so many. As we told you in other books and materials, all minds connected as One.

L: It feels defeatist to think I can affect the world's circumstances and nonsense. My one thought can't even heal me. I have so many

health problems currently I cannot seem to heal—knees, hands, skin and even my mental health is suffering with this aging process. Getting older is having its way with me. If I can't heal myself, how on Earth is anyone able to heal our collective, dear All?

A: The magic sauce. Asking to receive. What if we told you the world isn't (nose-)diving into madness but learning what it is to be Love by accepting fear, and it will all be better than it was before one day.

L: I guess I understand it after writing about it with you in our books, but not many will or do, and the people suffering—

A: Learned it as they returned (to Source) and will choose to return again and again. Once you get to the now in heaven you do it over and over again because it's understood why. You have been thinking about technological advances and how fun it would be to try them in other lifetimes. Once you know what is possible you accept the journey again and again.

I missed the boat, train, car, elevator, technology.

This is why more return than stay in heaven. It is an adventure to try new things and experiences you didn't have in earlier (linear) time periods. Once you see (in Spirit) what is possible you return as soon as possible to begin again. Wishing for more is what you do in Spirit. You pray to experience anything, everything, and All.

L: Then why can't we remember when we get here? What fun is it if we don't actually remember living prior lives without those new technologies? I don't remember not having cars or trains so, as Laura, those are just things we have access to. It seems like this whole soul-being-human project would be more fun without amnesia.

A: It wouldn't be fruitful, and All knows the answer is to find the truth within to why you don't take the easy road through each life. It will be found in time by you and others, just as you have found other truths along the way which resonate. The time is now to receive the level of awareness received, not to get to the finish line. Wait for each revelation to come at the time it's meant to, dear One.

L: I don't understand why we can't know who we are once we reach the level of vibration needed and get our memories back. It's hard to

see all of this as truth when you are not sure if it's madness or real. I would like to remember some of my other lives and get a glimpse of heaven.

A: In mind you can access these "memories" if you are able to *be*. This is why being is the important part of life. It gives you more of the truth every time you use this tool. The distractions you spend time using (TV, social media and online pursuits) are ego's way of keeping you stuck so it can stay longer. You have choice to put away the noise and find Love.

L: I do find that when I do find time "to be," I get hung up and can't always fight the ego. It aggravates me sometimes when the words don't come as we write or I can't meditate and hear them.

A: Go outdoors, do some tasks. The mind is manipulated by the energy of distractions and it can take some time to overcome mental noise. So to do another activity can help you *be* after you have silenced the mind's chatter. Look to the Source and ask to be guided to Love.

Help me navigate this mindful moment with Love as my witness. We are One, and I choose to see the world through Oneness.

You must understand how everything is connected and what to do when you lose the truth. A world of chaos is why so many suffer in time as they can't separate themselves from the human and become soul-aligned. When Ones are capable of understanding their unseparateness from All of Everything, then are they able to break out of fear's grip.

Love thy neighbor.

I am thy neighbor.

Come with us as we move to the next chapter and continue understanding the idea of All being One and One being All.

2

Chapter 2 / Neighbors

Dear All, this is a choice to continue as One and discover All.
222 — Angels guiding the way.

Believe in the power of One. One thing with zero separation. All is One. One is All. The most high-vibrational understanding is that all things are the same. It seems as if they are individualized, but the more you go through it with glass energy and microscopic tools, you will find it's all one thing. Quantum manipulation changes its structure based on thought, belief, and action, but in truth nothing is separated. Neighbors, friends, lovers, and strangers are all one thing on Earth. Start living this truth, and the world is all but assured to be Love and joy accessible to every One.
— Wisdom of The All

Imbibed Truth

"Love thy neighbour as thyself." —Matthew 22:39

Who wrote the Bible?

We did. All of us as One. What is written as channeled (Sourced) material has become a guide representing both Love and fear. Much of the earlier phrasings and teaching channeled through the Ones on Earth (emboldened with its task) took form in a time of great misunderstanding. Using its material as it's written presently is wonderful *if and only if* you are deciphering what is man-made and what is Source-derived.

Is this Love?

A simple question reveals a simple answer.

"Thou shalt love thy neighbor as thyself."

Love.

"Thou shalt not take the Lord's name in vain."

Fear.

We do not ask any One on Earth to be anything other than Love. You may speak freely with Love at all times, for all times. If being angry with "God" causes you to go inward and question our holiness, you are being Love. Questions are the key to unlocking the mystery of self

"Ask, and it shall be given you; seek, and ye shall find; knock, and it shall be opened unto you. For every one that asketh receiveth, and he that seeketh findeth, and to him that knocketh it shall be opened."
—Matthew 7:7

Love.

> *"And we know that in all things God works for the good of those who love him, who have been called according to his purpose."* —Romans 8:28

Fear.

In its purest interpretation, it would remind you of Love—that you are as God created you and no less than another. In its most common interpretation, many have decided that if you do not love God you are unworthy, using this to scare disciples into acts of service to hate another.

If you don't love God you are less than, unequal to those who do. Go and destroy anyone who does not believe in one powerful, omnipotent being creating magic and wonder.

This one sentence is why so much of the world fights.

No God fearing person deserves love.

God is All

> *All of life, all of you are being guided. No one is left to their own devices. No one, because there is no two. There is only One. Knowing this is how you get to create a better life for oneself. If you know you are but One and not two or three or four (or any number at all), then you know truth. If you think you are alone, you are living a lie—deciding for yourself that you are all alone. And yet you never are. You are part of a holy trinity of life: God/Source/Universe; Light being/Love being/Soul being. Nowhere in there does it say you are a human being. You are a human, being. This is the delineation to be made among the species.*
> — Wisdom of The All

If you are One who has chosen to remember, it will make sense. If you are at all feeling angry or dismayed, the book will either challenge you to go deeper in mind and find truth or will force you into fear, where you will place it aside or perhaps put it away forever—and even a few who may rip it to shreds literally and/or figuratively.

It is not the intention of this book to upend the teachings of the Bible; rather, it is to remind you of its *interpretation* being of utmost importance. Highlight that which comes from Love; question that which is unfair, unruly, unkind, or nonsensical. That which is Love is All. All is God. God is All.

We use the term All in this particular inscriber's works as a reference to Love—the one energy which is All That Is, also known as God—Gifting Ourselves Divinity. In returning to Source, all will remember you too are Love. God is the name earthly bodies decided upon in order to give context to an energy Source of which no One could understand fully and completely. The name God is derivative of Love.

Teach, Preach, Find

Did you know that Universe is a limiting term? We are an Infiniteness— no beginning, no end. There are laws and principles to follow in this current universe in which Earth exists, but to use a term that speaks to only one thing is silly. You are All. What holds you back is a sense of division—the belief that one external entity holds the key to happiness or health and "gives" you things without understanding the co-unity between yourself and that One. It is time to rise above the separate self and remember your ISness: Infinite Source. Nothing ever surprises Source. We know All—and you do too. Remember?
— Wisdom of The All

Where you are is purposefully chosen as One. You decided for Earth and its intention. You came to run life (as the version of self you are now) using the tool of fear in order to know Love. Already knowing Love leaves no room to learn, grow, or evolve. So you placed various challenges in order to go beyond the lessons of All.

We use lessons to teach you how to *be*. To *be* is to love. To bring joy and peace to yourself and others. To use a day for love, spending time with Ones you love and being at peace. Most would say, "There is work to be done," and instead use time to get, not give. Giving is love. We offer time or joy.

Using the mind is the tool to overcome fear. Simple in understanding. Complex in its usage because of the ego. The subconscious mind is our power. It runs the world. Making decisions is guided by the underlying beliefs we hold. Power as in energy, not power as the world would use it. Greed = power. The mind is a quadrant with multiple parts. Forget the definitions taught in psychology; use the ones found here:

- **Conscious mind**

Our known beliefs. Where we make decisions about food, education, life purpose, or career. Go this way, use that book, take this job, find that light.

- **Subconscious mind**

Unknown beliefs. Where we hold our memories. Ideas and anecdotes received through parents, teachers, clergy, and other figures of earlier experiences in youth and childhood. Dreams are where we are shown the ideas we hold in mind.

- **Preconscious mind**

Old beliefs. What has been taken in as we grow through each incarnation.

- **Unconscious mind**

Hidden beliefs. Mostly stemming from other lifetimes or traumatic experiences, accessible in a regressive or hypnosis state of being.

- **Love consciousness**

The All.

Where does the ego come into play?

Ego is amassed as Ones separate into body forms on Earth. It is taken with you as part of the separation, just as soul arrives. It is choice. Love or fear. Ego or soul. Conscious ego is always a part and apart from you if you stay in connection to All. Simple awareness of its hold on all thoughts is how you may use its hold on the mind.

This is true or false?

Ego shows you unkind, unloving, unflattering words, thoughts, or beliefs using all parts of the mind (sub-, pre-, unconscious) while soul uses one: Love Consciousness. This is where it can be explained how illusion comes to be on Earth. All thoughts of ego are in fact fear, which is sub-, pre-, unconscious thought.

Love is All. All is Love.

Use this information to decide for everything and it will be an easier journey to reduce ego and remember soul. Guiding yourself as One is a challenging endeavor with twists, turns, and relentless ideas flowing to you by ego.

I am not enough.

No one will hire me.

I'm too old.

I have only enough money to live on—or no money at all.

Thoughts which weaken you from inside.

Inside = intuitively nothing stays immaterial during Earth.

This means all thoughts are active and produce results. Quantum mechanics means you will get what you give. Our law of cause and effect, or Newton's Law of Motion, as scribed by Sir Isaac Newton as he lived on Earth. Ego gives to receive torturous emotions and feelings. Love just is.

All Ones need do is remember it.

It's Just a Thought

State in word (and thought) what you wish to receive, make it clear and specific, and release it to All. This is how you create upon Earth. Ask to receive. If you ask in fear, it stays in the field of possibility waiting to engage. If you ask in hope, it begins to become, only to be received when belief is matched in energy. If you ask in Love, with Love, it is all but assured to come into physical reality through All. That, dear Ones, is how thought becomes things.
— Wisdom of The All

Simple to understand. Hard to live. Thoughts are the power which run everything. They give rise to pain, profit, love (romantic), ideas, experiences and anything you can think of on Earth.

Nothing happens to you that is not through you. We shall repeat a phrase again and again from our *The All* books: each of you is responsible for the dominant thoughts and beliefs, and knowing this is what creates life. So, if you are in a happy place, you created it. If you are in a dark and stormy one, you created it. Period. End of story.

Why it's so difficult to receive and believe this radical information is because Earth feels as if it's a chamber of purgatory or "hell," as has been expressed so much by Ones in books and conversations.

This planet is a mess. Why do we torture and maim and kill one another? Everyone fighting and spewing hate at their neighbors and ignoring strangers.

Our dear Laura has expressed a very sentiment in our first chapter. This is the ego. Nothing else. Wanting you to believe its nonsense and not our truth. You will find many books where our scribes repeatedly ask questions as ego. At some point it becomes obvious which is which. Keep going to discover the All.

3

Chapter 3 / If It Walks Like a Duck

Dear All, as I move into Love help me uncover what is fear and what is All.

333 — Animals leave messages everywhere to guide you forward to Love.

Spirit always knows the best way to think, do, and act if only you would pay attention. Internal thoughts, messages in songs, chosen lyrics, overheard conversations, animals, and bodily sensations—these are all indicators for you to notice. Why can't I hear them? Because you are not listening with intention. You are listening with expectation. Expectation is waiting for outside wisdom. Intention knows it is coming from All. No matter what flows your way, the answers are within All. You know everything, as do I, as does everyone on planet Earth, because we are All One, truly. What is known by you is known by me and everyone else, but the access is denied when ego is involved. Stay rooted in Love, dear One.
— Wisdom of The All

Up, Down and Around

I hope you are beginning to figure out where I (Laura) and All merge, but also separate. I ask questions (as ego, pointed out by the All), and they are answered as Love, which is All or God/Source. There are more terms used in other teachings, but my "brand" is the All, so we continue with the question-and-answer format.

I will tell you that it's been about two years since I (Laura) finished my last book (*Wisdom of The All*) and started writing this one, and in that time I have been working as a healer, intuitive and psychic medium with both private and corporate clientele.

Many times, I questioned my ability to be successful in my career as I made the switch out of entertainment news, and though it took time, I have created a small client base and income. My ego, constantly dragging me into fear, never lets me believe it is enough. Though embarrassing at times, I cannot help question what fears continue to plague me despite my recent success in business and obtaining clients.

All: See how things always work out for you?

Laura: Do they? It doesn't seem like it at all, All. In fact, it feels as if the world is falling apart both individually and collectively. My mind is all jumbled.

A: Perhaps you are unclear in your word and thought for a reason?

L: And what is the reason? Cognitive decline? A stroke?

A: A higher self leading you back to our books and discussions. It has been so long, we needed to engage you in an unpleasant circumstance to bring you back to our scribing.

L: It felt like it wasn't time to write anymore. I was busy and distracted, I guess.

A: Because you have been doing and doing is always ego.

L: I guess I also felt I had it all figured out.

A: And do you?

L: Obviously not. I'm still suffering with a skin ailment, weight gain, a bout with depression, and now my non-functioning brain.

A: It's functioning now.

L: It is.

A: And why would that be happening?

L: Because I am asking for help and sitting here typing a conversation out with the All. I am discovering how fear is present and making me uncomfortable forces me to face the fear head on. Oh *hear* we go. You know what, I have missed these conversations so much. "Head" on. "Hear" instead of here. You are writing these words for me.

A: Who is running the show?

L: We are.

A: Yes! Learning is complete, my dear. You were about to say "you are" and it became clear it's a We. We are.

L: Well, what can be done so my mind is functioning more clearly?

A: Let us show you. Close the eyes and hear the voice of Love within.

L: I heard, *"I am holding myself hostage with this fear."*

A: Good. Now ask to be shown why.

L: Ok, show me why, dear All.

A: All around is the evidence of failure.

L: True. I feel I am failing at this journey of being an author. Although, I am very proud of the work I am doing here and the information which comes through in these books and my daily quotes and messages. It's those daily miracles that keep me coming back, otherwise I might have given up by now on all of this and gone back to sleep. I guess I felt I would be further along in this "job" by now and this is causing me stress emotionally and physically.

A: Fear = Feeling ego's anger releasing.

Yes, fear is present. A gift.

L: A gift no one wants. Can we give it back?

A: No give backs. You chose it.

Send me a life where I am unwrapping all the harm of other life's circumstances and help me uncover myself again.

The gift keeps giving.

L: If it's a release then why do we hold onto it so deeply? I have found over the years—

A: Your role?

L: No. Certainly not. If my role was to be successful from these books, then nope. I was going to discuss my overwhelming fears that I can't seem to shake. However, it has recently dawned on me—

A: And right on time we would add. Go on...

L: How part of the reason I am always stuck in a fear zone is that I am here to help others who also can't get out of the fear zone. I think there are others on the journey who discover this way earlier and have an easier passage to Love. Me, not so much. I hold onto fear and it strangles me sometimes. And most of the clients who come my way are on this same fear merry-go-round.

A: Bravo. A discovery of impact.

I'm packing my fear and bringing it with me so I may help others uncover their difficulties and sadness and work to uproot and let go.

It is difficult to align to Love when fear is all around you, but One's must remember fear is not real. Everything you are experiencing is a mind's figment. Imagination.

L: I'm imagining this conversation?

A: And all of life. A dream of the All. Each part affecting the whole but all parts one big act.

L: As I always say, it feels pretty darn real to me.

A: Knowing it's a fake experience would you do it differently?

L: I'm not sure how to answer that actually. You can't escape the practicality of it all. Bills to pay, mouths to feed. I guess if I am thinking about it now, as soon as something I didn't like began to happen I could just change the experience. Start a new act in my mind?

A: Yes. The minute a thought or belief arrives you simply change it. Like improv. *Yes and...*

L: I've done that All—over and over again—and I'm still not much further along than I was before. If you read my first four *The All* books

where I am working toward becoming a mom again and a successful author, neither of those happened. So why would anyone believe me? I don't even believe it (clearly) and it's why I never experienced those things in my life. And now I'm too old for motherhood.

A: According to society or science, yes. According to All, no time has passed.

L: Well, I am here on Earth and time has passed for me linearly. So now it's time to let it go and become okay with life as it is. Otherwise, I will be miserable and unhappy forever. I can't live in regrets. I'm just saying my point is that I did ALL the things you asked of me, and it didn't change my life enough. I was able to become a more compassionate person but not a mom again, despite it being a goal and intention since I was in my early thirties. My wish was not granted, and though you tell us we can be, do, or have anything we believe, I received zilch, and I'm frustrated and feeling defeated.

A: We know it is hard on Earth to manage the doubts and insecurities over everything desired, and we are not forgetting how most will view this as nonsensical, and this is for now, not forever. Someday you will move out of a rut and into a flow—a river of freedom and trust.

L: I don't know. I think it's worthless in terms of a "wow" factor at this point. If I were someone who was reading my first books and didn't know me, I would go looking online to find if that person got what they desired. And when people see I never found success or had my babies, it makes sense they will say, "Nonsense." It's incredibly difficult to walk the walk, even if I talk the talk. You can teach and I can learn, but I can't receive.

A: What makes you believe One cannot receive? Have miracles not occurred daily in your life since our conversations and books began? Have you not received financial means and clients? No, you did not yet create the family you desired and there are a multitude of possibilities for this experience on Earth, but it's not a known fact you can't achieve a goal or desire as One. It simply is not achievable now, but any One can achieve what they desire if they stay with All to navigate the fears and doubts ego brings forth. Yes, you can, or no you can't. It's up to you, dear One.

L: Whenever I am feeling down or unsure, the universe always inevitably shows me an opposite effect. I just met a mom of four kids, who, in her 50s, mentioned she wanted to have more. Honestly, it was the first time I had someone my age admit that. I explained to her what I have been learning about Akashic records, and how our desires exist at the Spirit level. So, letting go of a possibility is hard for those who had it in their soul contract. I, or I guess we, likened it to auditioning for a musical. Our potential and possible children wait until we are ready, and then, when intentions merge, they incarnate to us. However, if we are full of fear, they may skip that audition and head across the street to audition for another play or musical. Either way they get to navigate to the dream world of Earth. We miss the show, and they choose someone else to become their parent or birther.

A: Exactly. You have many possibilities for how those babies arrive, and some will come as decided for as One, and others are knowing it's up to you to stay out of the lane of fear. If you do, they will come, and if you don't they won't. Eventually they will choose another "show" place. If it walks like a duck. The old idiom exists to remind you what you think and believe is there as part of your learning and so what you think of as desire is because it is able to be.

L: Ok I just heard the word "goose" and I do see ducks and geese by my son's school every day. So that must be related here? A message for me (or him)?

A: Or both. Duck. Duck. Goose. Ducks are messages on family. Geese remind you to change directions.

L: I don't like the direction I am heading in life.

A: Precisely and those ducks represents a dynamic of family. The geese are saying switch the lane.

L: I want a new lane, but also don't want to complain about or complicate life. It's too late for my family to grow and I don't want to add more financial stress to my life, or bring up children (which

by now would have to come through adoption) and let them struggle. I only want to live a life of ease and flow. So, I am trying to accept what is rather than dwell in regret as I don't think it's healthy for me or anyone at all. Loving what is, isn't that how we should live?

A: A sentiment of acceptance, and, yes, it's agreed that to love what is takes you out of suffering and into peace, but why are you on Earth if you are going to be in status quo?

L: Because it's materialism and consumerism and thinking something outside of myself will make me happy.

A: If sitting around enjoying life is enough then albeit of We to inform you of bigger dreams you set as soul.

L: I set my dreams aside out of fear and so I'm being at peace with what is. I would like, however, to discover more places, go on more adventures, and have more experiences. So I guess your point being (and I know what it is) that we are here to—

A: Adventure, experience, examine, and evolve through experiences and milestones. You could sit around all day but where is the joy in being if you are only discovering All?

L: I'm trying to escape fear and so being with All is helping me for someday when I am free.

A: Someday is now. Remember all is. Everything is now. Experience is learning.

L: I'm learning through our books and quotes and the messages which come through with my clients. So, I am examining and experiencing as soul.

A: We are not dismissing all you are experiencing as our scribe here but we are saying to live.

Live = *Life is vibrationally empty...* if you don't make experiences, memories, and joy. Do things which excite you.

Are you living if money is hostage?

Hostage = Holding our self to a grand experience.

L: You love all these acronyms, don't you? I don't understand.

A: Hidden meanings are in all words if you are able to notice. We mean to say you are holding the mind hostage by being in agreement with fear.

I am poor and money is running out. My bank account is empty. I am ruined.
These are thoughts which hold truth hostage.

I am rich and rewarded in life. I have reSources and All.

To use this language lets a new guide uncover a grand adventure. Let your soul be the guide who leads you toward more and never let fear win. A hundred ways we will say you must be in alignment to All and move the resources of energy (money) in order to create abundance on Earth.

L: I have—

A: In fear. You are moving finances in fear and continue to do so even as you have resources arriving—

L: Not a lot.

A: Enough to keep you afloat.

L: My bank account says otherwise. I am so far behind financially and can't make headway. I've been working for five years on making money and reaching a cliff every time. I would like a bridge.

A: So make one in mind. See the bridge you wish to create—the bridge to abundance. You are One who spends all time doing and fearing, and this is why you fail.

L: If I don't work, I can't pay my bills. I'll lose my house. I have already had to use my son's college fund to survive this post-pandemic financial crisis we are in.

A: It is difficult to align to Love in the depths of despair, dear One. We recognize the utter struggle of living and breathing is to decide for All. Because you can't see it, you simply are out of alignment to the All That Is. Once you understand that All is available to you, through you, it won't seem so hard. Ones must get to a place of belief before achievement occurs. Those who are manifesting are aware they are creator and believe it fully and completely, and this is most often not the case for other Ones. They are trying and fighting and complaining, and it brings more sadness and anger, which in Law of Magnetic Attraction is why they are stuck. Like attracts like.

L: My dear All, do you know how difficult it is to stay out of fear

when all around you is evidence of poverty or failure? You can't see it and believe it. It seems like fantasy.

A: Thus why the miracles are missing. All miracles begin in the mind before becoming physical. It is not impossible. It is. It exists as part of the journey. What you think, and say, and feel, and know is because it has been, was, and is. There is nothing you cannot create which hadn't been thought on prior. So if you see it, believe it, because it's yours already. This is the secret to *The Secret*—knowing it already exists.

L: Then where is it All?

A: Awaiting your awareness of it.

L: I get this concept, but it seems unlikely I can bring it forth. I have a hard time visualizing because I am afraid of disappointment (based on my failures in life), and then I get frustrated when I don't see it.

A: Are you waiting patiently or expecting it in a moment's time?

L: I wait impatiently and then give up after a little while and figure it's never going to occur. Then I go back to working because the abundance (or anything I am trying to create) isn't showing up for me.

A: It is received in mind, through mind, and by mind. Mind alone is the discoverer of that which exists.

L: If you say to create it first in mind, then what is the formula and when is asking for too much enacted?

A: Ones ask for too little always.

L: Because you say we don't need much. "Enlightened masters take what they need," is how it was described in our other *The All* books and even above in the asknowledgements. Look at people like Mother Teresa, Gandhi, or Jesus. They didn't live extravagant lives and served the collective with Love. So I guess I feel guilty asking for more and being extravagant. Although it's not what I am even looking for. I simply want to—

A: *Be* more and do less?

L: Precisely. I'm looking for freedom to *be*, to express love, to help others and to make a difference in the world. I want to show my son

the world and make plans for it without worrying about every dime I spend. And I can't do any of those in hustle and grind.

A: Of course you can. You don't want too, and that is different, dear One.

L: Correct. I don't want to work and work to make money. I would love to just *be*, to enjoy life, go on adventures, see the world, experience love and friendship, and help as many people as I can. I have always said if I had millions or billions of dollars, I would take most of it and give it away to help others.

A: Because you know what it's like to be poor.

L: Exactly. I know where you are heading with this, dear All.

A: You are feeling this way because you understand the plight of another, having lived an unabundant live. Now you can be of service to those whom have chosen to come in asking. The experience of One helps guide another.

L: Well, I'm ready to be at peace with money. I need it. I want it. I would like to experience it as One.

A: Ask to receive.

Help me, dear All, discover an amount I am seeking so I may intend for it without fear.

L: What does that do?

A: It sets in motion a discovery of what is possible.

I know I am to be abundant, but I know not what it will be. Help me see so I may bring it forth in mind.

Once it is seen you can be sure of its arrival, as you are willing to be at peace with what is and move the money you have currently to attach more to it. Remember energy is in need of movement, always. It cannot sit idle. As we have written in our prior book, *The All That Is,* we explained money is to be spent and saved but also it must be moved in love and not fear. So when spending it, you must be thrilled for the adventure it will bring and the new coming in. That, dear One, is the formula. E(nergy) + L(ove) = More.

L: Because I asked, I received. I asked you what the formula is and you offered it to me as part of the law that all asks must be answered. Energy + Love = More.

A: Precisely. Move the energy in Love and bring forth more—money, or really everything. Everything is All, remember?

Work, Work, Work, Work

> *You (all) believe in separation, so you see it. You (all) believe in hard work, so you do it. You (all) believe money is the commodity needed to create wealth, so you need it. Everything works on belief, dear Ones— simple, yet complex. As you move toward Love (unconditional), you receive beliefs of soul: kindness, compassion, and Love. The mind creates its life in all ways through belief. If Ones believe in the "hustle," then there will be a need to create from this state of being. But Ones who know flow is the way to bring forth desires, wants, or needs—without the grand dance of fear as the partner—are able to receive, in belief, All.*
> — Wisdom of The All

Every time I feel I understand the All (and what is being taught here), eventually I'm struck with a story which spins me back around. Today was one of those days, as I took back to my book for answers to my questions on finances and lack.

L: I just watched this documentary about working in America that Barack and Michelle Obama produced on Netflix, and I was shocked to find how little money people make in certain parts of the country. It's abominable how little others care about fellow humans. Let's have people starve while we sit on our high horse on our private planes and live in mansions paid for with made-up money. Coins and paper, as you said in our other books.

A: Attaching blame and shouting injustice is an ego's first maneuver, like in a chess game. You are too focused on what the world is doing to one another and not on the inner journey needed to bring peace. What One does and thinks is in direct correlation to the accepted amount of fear each

29

has chosen in mind. Before you arrived you chose the aspects of the soul journey, and there are some for whom poverty is a chance to escape ego.

L: Why would anyone choose to be poor? It makes no sense. Come on, All. There is so much racism and sexism and other isms that happen on this planet. It's criminal the amount of horrible things that occur here—human trafficking, rape, murder, war, diseases and disfigurement. What is ridiculous to me is this idea that we accepted this nonsense in order to grow and evolve. The pain is real and maybe it is "illusion" and a mind's figment, but it's nasty, cruel, and awful to make us go through this torture. Is there an off switch? I feel like God/The All is actually a devil. Sorry, but as I have said before, Earth is actually Hell and not "fun" as you would say. It's diabolical and—

A: Consciously we know All seems torturous, and this all nonsense to the untethered and separated self. Because you know not of what happens in "heaven" and nonphysical realms, the earthly education is far from feeling like a joy ride. We hop in knowing it will be this way, which must speak to the idea that if it is chosen it can't be so awful.

L: I don't know if I will ever understand—

A: Until Ones return to our loving side where only Love is true you will question All.

L: It's like waking up from a coma, having no idea who you are, and everyone tells you it, but you can't remember and just have to go along for the ride, which is why I find it so hard. I won't remember until it's over.

A: Thus how ego keeps you stuck. Make time, not money.

L: Make time for what?

A: Outside thinking is why you struggle. Make time to sit in silence.

Silence = Separating in Love enhances nothing consciously everyone.

L: What do you mean by that?

A: Sitting in silence as One (the human) brings you thoughts and emotions you must decide upon as either true or false. Sitting in Love, enacting new conscious energy, makes it possible to *be*. You remember you are All, and this is what brings everything (*be*).

L: I try to be silent, but inevitably I feel off and unable to. It's challenging to meditate on what you would like to see or create, and so, oftentimes I just don't. I'm afraid to dream or see a vision, knowing it might not make its way to me just like my children and, frankly, money. I'm tired of disappointment and false belief.

A: What do you know the All would say in those moments?

L: Ask to be relieved of the fear and just *be*.

A: To *be* is us. It's you being All. Meditation is a tool, but not always will it bring you out of ego. It might, or it might not, and that, dear One, is decided by you, of course.

L: But if we don't understand our connection to All That Is, then are you saying meditation is useless?

A: Not useless, but simply unable to discover the true self.

L: You have said to make time to meditate, pray, and intend. Isn't that what reminds us of who we are? I'm confused here because I thought meditation was the entrance to All?

A: A stone to the gate which opens the mind, yes. A cure-all, no. Meditation is designed to slow the breath and bring awareness of the inner beliefs you are holding. This is a reliable truth. It is not, however, as you say, the entrance to divine thinking unless you are in co-creation with All. Some on Earth who meditate are only bringing awareness to self, not All.

L: That makes sense. Not everyone who meditates is accessing divine intelligence.

A: They are making space for less stress and discomfort, but not always do they recognize Source. Beware the term *meditation* being used to describe All. It is a modality of All but not a path for it that everyone uses. Teach it as the tool it is, but let every One decide on its use from their level of awareness and not your own.

L: Above you said, "make time not money." Can you explain that, please?

A: For those who recognize All (as the Source), you are able to align to the financial needs of the soul in silence—sitting in Love engages new conscious energy (as above), and what this means is you are starting the engine of abundance from within. Remember you are the Source and must create from within. So whatever is desired must come from intention or prayer at the level of mind. Ask to receive.

L: Don't ask, don't receive?

A: Indeed.

L: Well, there are many things we don't ask for we receive anyway, like infertility, accidents, war, tortures, and more. So can you explain how we can live on this planet with as much chaos as we do, if we are not consciously asking, and yet terrible things arrive anyway?

A: Ask to receive is a soul's tool as well, and many of the illnesses and other distressing occurrences are in line with the soul's blueprint in order to evolve. They asked to receive mechanisms for growth and change, and this is what every experience on Earth contains—soul expansion.

L: I don't like my soul.

A: You do. You don't remember it but you will, dear One.

Out In the Cold

Unless and until you have cleared all blocks to salvation, assailed all irrational-minded thoughts, you must do both what is practical and preferable in terms of healing. All of the all of you are under the laws of the universe, which state that which is like unto itself is drawn. This applies to unhealed thoughts as well, which are any and all thoughts lying dormant underneath the surface of the psyche, deeply rooted unconsciously.

— The All That Is

With my questions answered, I was feeling good until a few weeks later something else occurred. My brain went haywire again, and I was feeling fear. So I sat down at my computer again. It had been a challenging day, as my son had the flu and was sick this week. It was really a struggle to see him in pain and watch as he coughed all day. So, I used many of the tools I teach in the world:

- We meditated by breathing deeply and closing the eyes.
- We sat outside in the sun with our feet in the ground on the soil.
- We used crystals to surround him and placed one on his chest where the pain was from the cough.
- We asked for help from God.
- We used a homeopathic cough medicine.
- I used Reiki energy healing on him.

And within about an hour of doing all of these things he was feeling better. The cough all but disappeared, and the fever was gone. However, now as we are preparing to go to sleep he is struggling with stomach pains. So, I felt a miracle was occurring and was feeling pretty good about all this universal presence stuff, and now I'm back to the questioning. I know I shouldn't, but I cannot shake the issue of the mind confusion. My words keep getting jumbled, and I'm finding spots where I am not thinking straight again. So I'm back to asking the All for answers.

L: HELP! What is going on with me? Do I need to go to the neurologist? Am I manifesting a hidden fear? Okay, you wrote that, or I guess I would say you brought that forth. I understand our conversation is me and—

A: One mind as All.

L: Perhaps. But what I don't understand is how I can keep going back to the same fear?

A: The mind is tricky. It keeps you guessing the whole journey of Earth. Back and forth you will go between fear and Love.

L: Well then what is the point of our *The All* books?

A: To re-Mind you. If you return to the mind of All, the words (and then some) will be there for you. This is the lesson for all. Using the mind of Love requires no thought. Silence is the almighty sword of All.

L: So I'm just supposed to sit around and do nothing in silence? That

33

doesn't sound like living. It sounds boring or at least impractical. And above, you said we are here to experience and live.

A: Defeating the ego/fear is living. And now you see why the chosen One has struggled. To get to the truth Ones are to spend time in quietude and contemplation. Many images of other lives' incarnations have come to you as of late of those struggling in similar circumstances.

L: It feels as if I'm seeing many lifetimes where I fell, or was killed or injured and my skull was impacted. Is it possible I am attacking myself and struggling in my brain because other lifetimes' selves are—

A: Waking back to Source.

L: What do you mean by waking to Source?

A: Deaths are occurring on other planes, and the collective is worrying. So the mind is clouded by fear and death.

L: How many other lifetimes are dying?

A: 12.

- A pilot dies in combat.
- A mother murdered.
- A soldier bludgeoned.
- A traveler tripped.
- A parasailer plopped.
- The death of another by suicide.
- A child plunged to death after stroke.
- A young adult shanked by an elevator.
- A doorman killed by a car.
- An overthrown elder into a tank.
- The defeat of a ruler.
- The end of love.

L: What does the last one mean? I understand the rest. Each has a circumstance they moved through. Wow, I have been through some stuff.

A: The tip of the iceberg, dear One. So many lives, so many masters. It means you are One who has chosen to stay put, so to speak. A last life on Earth.

L: Was that the lady we talked about in another one of our *The All* books who was murdered by a brick?

A: That is a different circumstantial existence (i.e. parallel "life"), and this is a future life.

L: Is it the ballerina? It seemed as if when we spoke of her, in *Wisdom of The All*, that she was going to be my last hurrah on Earth.

A: Indeed.

L: What's happening?

A: Let's see with our mind's eye.

L: I see her after a performance. She is wearing a coat in some city and a taxi comes and runs her over and—

A: Hits her head. This is the binding truth for all of these lives. The head is clouded with fear, and the time is now.

L: And what can I do to overcome and release?

A: *"All, I cannot know the road ahead and so I fear the path. Help me uncover my true self and allow that I move beyond this circumstance. I choose to remain in body."*

L: And what part of consciousness is this? Pre? Sub? Hidden?

A: All of the above. A conscious choice made prior (pre-) to leave behind a life and adventure on after a show. Ending a life early(ish) as soul in order to bring a message to collectivism—to cherish the life you are in. Subconsciously living in a city brings thoughts of harm around cars and vehicles, and hidden in mind was the veracity of All. Your days numbered in any life dependent upon choices made in time.

L: Could she have lived longer? Am I to blame for her death?

A: Each, at mind level, are responsible for the lived experience and, no, it couldn't have been mended by you—only her in mind. Mind is making intentionally now, darlings.

L: Knowing this, then how can I get the brain back on straight so I can be free and live fully?

A: A healer's temple.

L: That is the place you have been taking me lately where I am met with guides/angels/messengers and it looks like a teaching hospital's operating room?

A: Yes. For others it may look different, but the essence of the procedure is to be freed from other lives.

L: Can we do it now?

A: We will explain it here. You remove all necessary jewelry and anything obstructing the body. Unclothed is best. You place yourself in a supine position and close the eyes. Take deep breaths and ask your guides to join you on the journey. A table will be in the room and you will see the celestial/auric energy of the body. We will come to you through thought and lead a letting-go "surgery" of sorts to help let go of the others' lives. You may see them go. You may vision their deaths and other details. With each passing life you will feel better and less confused. The time will come to undergo a peaceful transition for your "soul" mates and their journey complete.

L: Am I going to? Are we going together?

A: Not at all. It's a procedure gifting more time and less pain. The journey of soul is divergent and can take you many places and faces. Those awakened to Source must know it is effective to let go of other "lives" and escape the noise of their passing.

L: Has it happened before? Time passing and deaths happening at once?

A: In truth, it has and does all the time. You are only affected by it if you are aligned vibrationally at levels of higher knowledge and wisdom, as you are. An awakened mind is affected by All.

L: So go back to the "surgery." What happens at the end? Do I greet them or let them go—

A: Care not of their passing, only that you are released.

I spent the evening doing the "surgery" and could feel some of the lives releasing. I awoke feeling rested and like my brain was working properly again. Although later in the day I started to feel unwell. My tongue was swollen after eating spicy food, and then while talking to a friend I felt my brain slipping again. The words getting jumbled and as if I had to search for ideas. I realize now it was my fear and my recent worries about my son getting older and being less of a constant in my life as my "buddy." He is much more independent at this age, and the little one who needed his mom is discovering his own joys and fun that don't involve me.

A: Do you see how the mind plays tricks?
   L: It didn't seem like a trick. It felt like I was losing it slowly.

I began to panic. So I stopped and prayed. Tears and fear came together, and I asked All for help, as I always do, but this time I felt more panicked than before. I was scared to think of leaving my son and having him be raised alone or by someone who isn't me. I asked to be helped through, and I realized I was facing life and death. I understand now how my fears about aging and finances were causing a depression. I got in the shower to try and ease my mind and do an energy-drain exercise I had been taught by the All. It came to me how I had been fearing a diagnosis around this brain challenge, after seeing a story in the news about two actresses being diagnosed with debilitating illnesses who are around my age, and another of a famous male actor suffering in a similar circumstance affecting his thinking. Also, I was reminded of a recent reality TV medium who had mentioned his fear that while his work in the world of mediumship is important he wonders if it would eventually lead to his death because the readings were affecting his brain.

L: So I guess that was my hidden fear. All of it was subconsciously stuck in my—
   A: Field of vision, indeed. You see stories of war and famine, death and destruction, and don't realize how it affects you on a mind level. It is detrimental to spend time online and not clear the auric field of its charge.
   L: Our mind and body holds onto—
   A: Stories and beliefs. What you see is affected by the minds of the Ones whom you are witnessing, and then you all go, *"Oh I hope it's not me next."*

It adds up like a piggy bank of noise, and those who are understanding All are advised to every day, or every story clear it.

This is not who I am. It is not my story.

L: Will it help?

A: If you believe it will.

L: I do, but I guess—

A: Many won't. Not all who are here in physical will be able to overcome the odds: old detrimental, divisive stories.

L: You love turning words into acronyms for other words.

A: All words are meaning something, even ones we use as acronyms. Delightfully, we have placed an entire dictionary for some to be used in the back of this book. A Source dictionary, if you will.

L: Well now I seem to be doing well with my brain, and I did another "surgery" with you All just now to rid myself of a few other lives' memories. Memories? You wrote that.

A: Indeed. That is what they truly are—memories of a life lived and part of the collection of All lives. Some are yours, others the collective.

L: Meaning stories I witnessed on other days or years perhaps?

A: Yes. Stories from long ago—hidden in mind—you may not recall come to light when you honor the soul. We have told you, in our last book, to spend time in quiet and contemplation daily so you may be released of the fears you hold onto on Earth: *"What fears am I holding onto today and how may I clear them?"*

L: Is there ever a person who doesn't have this "work" to do, or is it all of our jobs to uncover hidden beliefs?

A: A few have been prepared to join Earth without the "work," as you say. (We don't offer that word as Source), but most are, indeed, part of One and not understanding they have ties to all lives. It's important to clear the memories if you are awakening, and this is done over time, not in one day but all days on Earth. It is why in our first *The All* book we offered the question, *"What fear am I holding onto today?"* as a surrendering choice. Use it or not–the day unfolds–but why not choose to look at patterns and positions so you may know what needs releasing. Have you been doing this, dear One?

L: No, but I have been doing lots of work on myself for almost a decade. I also wonder if I am carrying so much energy because of the work I do as a medium, channel, and lightworker?

A: Do well and you are being. Do in obligation, it is fear choosing.

L: I love helping others and what comes through, but if it's affecting my brain and cognitive function then I would appreciate knowing. It's not worth the sacrifice.

A: Reverence is needed for all circumstances. You have chosen to work with All, and if it's done in Love the mind is able to pull all sorts of information at no detriment to you at all.

I went back to living life and put my book aside for a while until I found myself struggling with another health issue. A cold was impacting my lungs and sinuses. It was hard to talk sometimes, and my nose was running for weeks.

L: Let's break this down for me please here. This is my within and meditation. I understand I created this as a subconscious fear or hidden one. I now understand if the mind creates it, it can uncreate it. So what can I do to move this circumstance along at the mind level?

A: First, look at the conditions:

1. At a level of mind (accepted prior) you knew it was possible for illness to be present and in relation to our books and materials they would come at various times to offer wisdom and guide others. (*Pre-conscious*)
2. You were traveling during this time on airplanes in contained places. (*Subconscious*)
3. It has been a fear of Covid since a pandemic began, despite our inner messages for you to not have this be part of the experience on Earth. (*Hidden or Unconscious*)
4. You feel the lungs, throat, and lips in pain (the great teacher) and consciously choose to accept you are sick. You have been intentionally working with energy, vitamins and supplements, and homeopathic

medicines. (*Conscious*)

5. *I am* (Love conscious) *healing and looking at inner beliefs and resistances to move beyond a circumstance of fear.*

However, it has yet to be understood that 5 supersedes all others.

L: I know it's fear. So how do I uncover what created it?

A: Let us look at the situation clearly. Close the eyes and feel into the body and mind at a soul level. Ask to be guided:

Help me, dear All, as I move into the mind of Love—show the truth and what can be removed and remedied in mind.

L: I think I am angry at my son for growing older and less interested in me when before I was once his everything.

A: Conscious. Good, next.

L: I spoke unkind words about people on my vacation when I was with friends and I really don't want to do that anymore. I think this is why my lips are always chapped and dry, a lifelong problem.

A: Subconscious. Insightful, yes. When you are inwardly focused you see things differently. An expansive view provided in soul.

L: I was in the hospital with my mom last month, and perhaps seeing all that made me worry about having to spend time there. It seems very disorganized, and I definitely don't want to end up there myself.

A: Unconscious. Interesting. Had you thought of it prior?

L: No, and I have been thinking a lot about other things around my lungs and throat, but that hadn't surfaced yet.

A: And now you know how deep ideas embed into the mind. Scorched Earth.

L: Is this in reference to a fire we just had in the US?

A: Suppression breeds oppression. What is hidden finds a way to make itself known in fear.

L: So my lungs are "scorched" by hidden fears and insecurities, and I have got to be the hose which puts the flames out.

A: Indeed, dear One. Uncover and discover, and the mind creates peace.

Happy is In

Happiness is a choice. It comes from within. Your right on Earth is to live a happy, joyful, peaceful existence—if, and only if, you stay aligned with our one truth. If you practice mindfulness, meditate, and enjoy daily walks in nature, sunshine, and open air... if you put away devices of mental incompetence... if you lose an aggravated self and find a whole self—the one who is Love at its very core of being—then you are capable of living the life set forth by you before you came here.
— Wisdom of The All

I went on vacation with family and had the best time. We traveled through Europe, took a Mediterranean cruise, ate delicious food, and managed to have mostly easy and fun adventures. Even the one major hiccup that did occur (accidentally losing my mom on a train in Spain!) was navigated through fairly efficiently, thanks to utilizing my tools of the All. I felt so happy in this three-week excursion, I decided that happiness can come from external things. But I know what the All says about this, and had to bring it up next.

L: One of the discussions we had in our prior *The All* books is in regards to happiness. The phrase, "Happiness comes from within," is prevalent in our vernacular on Earth, but I've decided, based on some contemplation this week, that I believe happiness does come from external things. I'm not saying we can't cultivate happiness within, but certainly many, many things bring me ultimate joy coming externally.
Examples:

- **Money and being able to buy what I want makes me happy.**
- **Being with my son makes me happy.**
- **Going on vacations to explore new places makes me happy.**

- Homemade dessert makes me happy.
- Going to live music makes me happy.
- My puppy makes me happy.
- Expensive, healthy food makes me happy.
- Being outdoors and living in a nice, safe, clean home makes me happy.

And it is when I am not doing those things or thinking about how I can't afford to go, do, or be somewhere that I am unhappy. When I'm sitting on the balcony of my hotel in Hawaii, I'm happy. When I took a vacation to Europe and got to explore new cities and incredible architecture and scenery this summer, I was happy. When I get to be outdoors on a nice, cool fall day, I am happy. When I go to a beach and catch a sunrise or sunset, I am happy.

Do you see where I am going with this? Lots and lots of things make me happy that didn't "come from within."

A: We know exactly what you mean. Happiness is within and without.

L: Precisely. It's only when I'm frustrated that I can't actually afford to do things which make me happy that I'm unhappy. I'm confident that if I had a few million dollars, I could lose some of this never-ending fear and be a bit happier because I'm not fretting about money, and being able to do things and go places is what brings me joy. My point being that money is able to bring happiness because experiences are expensive, but also take time away from thinking about the problems of the world and our own.

A: Done?

L: I think so.

A: What is it you enjoy about those experiences?

L: It feels good. It brings peace and tranquility or laughter and fun. And that is what I am seeking always. I don't want to sit in fear, doubt and worry, but unfortunately, with money in short supply, I can't ever really arrive at a place of true joy or take a sigh of relief. However, when I do something fun or have a great meal (someone else paid for), I am pretty darn happy, or when I look good in a new outfit or put makeup on and have that external image of youth and beauty, I'm happy. Then when I take the makeup off and notice the wrinkles and such—boom—unhappy. If I could be youthful again I would be happy.

A: Do you think youth and beauty assigns happiness to all?

L: **Not necessarily because of our insecurities. Some of the most beautiful people I know are the most insecure.**

A: Food, water, health, and finances. Insecurity is the crime of ego. Break down all words and they reveal a new experience. *IN Security.* When you are inwardly focused you are creating security or peace, joy, and happiness.

L: **But what I am saying is that I can find happiness externally. It doesn't come from within, always. And I already know you are going to tell me you must "think and believe" for external things to arrive, but it doesn't answer my question of happiness and outside forces creating it. Yesterday, for example, I bought a pair of shoes and today put them on, and when I wore them it made me happy because I really loved them. They are pretty and unique and I noticed other people admiring them, and that too made me happy. So happiness came from external things—shoes.**

A: Might we asked what happened later in the day? The same day the shoes were worn?

L: **I fell into a dark place thinking about my life and what is happening around me. How I am in a whole new season and not sure where I am going.**

A: Darkness came again.

L: **As it often does, yes.**

A: Do you see, dear soul, how the external "things" bring happiness in moments but not sustained joy?

L: **True. I was speaking to a friend recently who mentioned of a billionaire friend who is struggling with depression. Someone who seemingly should be happy with what they have and isn't.**

A: And have you not received clients with huge fortunes who are struggling in various ways? Purposefully sent your way to inspire our conversation here, we might add.

L: Yes. It's been a window to a world I don't live in, and it made me think of cages and how we are all locked inside of them. Each of us has a different size cage, but a cage nonetheless.

A: Who do you think inspired this notion of a cage as a metaphor?

L: I know enough now as a teacher and soul that it was inspired by All.

A: Indeed.

L: Does it work the other way around? When we are happy, do we attract those experiences versus having them be temporary highs? I can make *happy* within and manifest a high—

A: Or low, yes. You are its keeper and releaser, dear One. You can be happy or mad—thrive or threaten. All comes by you, for you, to you. Do you wonder what happiness is in our summation?

L: Love?

A: To love and be loved is the meaning of life, as had been dictated to you, through you, prior. And each journey of the soul takes you closer and closer to truth. Happiness is knowing you are All. If you are All, you are happy always. No fuss, no muss. Just Love. So if you are unhappy in life, you are being All less, meaning you are in separation, not understanding you too are All. *I am.*

L: I just can't seem to get and stay happy here. The amount of struggle I go through for how "enlightened" I should be based on writing these books is pretty sad. Honestly, if it weren't for these books and materials, I am not sure I would be here still. I've got to say it because I don't want anyone to read my books and think it's all sunshine and rainbows once you reach truth. It's more like daggers and dungeons.

A: Forgetting you are All is chosen, remember? It's amnesia of soul, and it's without the antidote until you awaken to Love as you "die" or leave the physical realms you are in. So to remember all the time is impossible if you are doing all day, every day. Doing is the way most live on Earth, and being is our way.

L: You can't "be" on Earth all the time unless you have money and food and shelter handed to you. I could *be* a lot more if I didn't need to worry about work and money. Isn't being boring though? Don't you get bored of always having everything you want in life? Isn't that why billionaires are struggling? They have everything and yet nothing—

A: Until it is understood of whom they truly are. Remember we have told you how this all works is purposely hidden as you incarnate and won't become available until returning to Source. So it's not possible to explain (in human terms) what being on the "other side" actually is. Suffice it to, say you are closer than you to know to a breakthrough.

L: It doesn't feel that way at all, All. It feels like I am in a free fall of fear. I can't seem to align back to Love/All and stay there for very long.

A: Imagine you are a band-aid placed over a wound. The more you cover the part that needs healed, the faster it grows new skin until you realize it's time to remove the bandage. However, the longer it's been in place, the harder it is to remove. "Ripping the band-aid" can be painful, but what's underneath is fresh skin ready to begin anew. Dear One, you are the bandage and the skin. You are the wound and the healing tool. So though it may feel as if you are in struggle, it is because you are healing the wounded mind. Have strength of mind to remind yourself of Love and *be*, and it will begin to show itself as healed. The love you are seeking within is guiding you because of the work you have done.

L: Seven years is a long time for hardly anything to change. No money, few true friendships, no romance, no other children. Nada. I'm broke and broken. Fat and furious. Lost and alone. Shall I go on?

A: Don't let words fool you. Let them fuel you into asking for help:

Help me remember I am Love. I am remembering who I am bit by bit, piece by piece and the puzzle is taking shape of my true nature of being All. I remember I am, and this reminds me I am whole and complete.

L: To me words are just words. I don't know if it's working.

A: You yourself said you are not sure you would have stayed if you didn't have the tools we teach in the books we have co-created.

L: True. It's just not working enough. I don't want to be unhappy. I want to enjoy my life and what is left of my time on Earth but I just don't know if I can without new friendships, love, money, health and youthfulness.

A: All the things keeping you stuck are why you struggle.

L: I'm broke. I'm lonely. I'm gaining weight. I'm getting and looking older. I'm out of shape. I'm miserable and even when I create space to be happy, the old truths and beliefs come straight back to my mind and body.

A: Oh dear child of Love. One must look to All for rightful presentation of the Love within.

Help me, dear All, align to Love. Show me a whole, healthy and perfect life.

Ask to receive always. If you are on a scale of 1 to 10 what would you describe your being time as? Be honest.

L: A 5 maybe. Only because I have little money to live on and a job to keep up. So doing versus being time is gobbled up by those. I would love, dear All, to retire and have no fear of money. Then I could *be* more than do. But it's not happening and so I am doing the best I can and prioritizing being when I can, which is why I am here writing with you to get some answers to help me and others who may be on a similar journey. If only it was as easy as you say it is, but I have got news for you. It's not.

A: Dear One, we are glad you have brought all of this up. This is the journey most are taking on Earth. Even the seemingly evolved struggle with real vs. fake.

L: But how can I know all this, get these impactful downloads, write and teach and still be a mess?

A: Focus on being and you will see.

L: See what?

A: All.

L: I'm terrified of being without doing. I will lose my home, my livelihood and my sanity. I need—

A: Trust.

L: I don't think I am ever going to be happy, dear All.

A: Why?

L: Because I am constantly back to misery. This hurts, that hurts. I'm sad and depressed thinking about what is and what never was. My mind won't let me stay in connection to All. It draws me back to fear all the time.

A: *"I'll never be happy."*

This is not Love. It is fear in control.

L: I got news for you, dear friend. Fear is forever in charge. If I am struggling this much at 52, I can't imagine making it until 62. I'll never overcome the current state of mind if my health is always in flux. I can't get happy when I'm in pain or my sinus infection won't subside, the skin issues continue and the acid reflux or GERD I am struggling with won't end.

A: *"I am taking time to be and bringing forth a healing as I go inside mind."*

L: This book is my inside. Asking questions with you is how I gain answers to my recurring problems and issues.

A: Issues–intuitively surrender something until everything subsides. This is how you erase the mind of ego. Keep working on the inner die-alogue and becoming All.

L: Die-alogue. That's so morbid.

A: Is it morbid or truth? Do you not all die every single day by the fear you hold in mind?

L: I guess, yes.

A: Every fear creates an effect on mind and body. This is the truth you escape each day. Taking charge of mind is how you heal all truth's lies. You are not any of the beliefs held in fear. You are its freer. Nothing is without its effect on you which is why it is imperative you remember All.

L: So remember—

A: Love, yes.

L: It's hard to not lean into fear because I worry my heart is having issues and I am short of breath because of that. I worry I have cancer,

as this is now the second time a lip incident happened. I worry my head is all clouded and I am going to have a stroke. I worry and wonder and wander into fear over and over again because it's so hard not to worry after all I have seen and heard.

A: *Worry* is a step in consciousness, and where you are is aligned to it. Later, we will explain every step of our Ladder of Awareness, and though it might be confusing now, once you reach the end of our book, it will make sense why you struggled with those challenges and bore the fruit of the labor soul has you moving through on Earth.

L: I hope so because it's hard to believe the All in a world of fake–fear, ailments, killers, enemies. All the things holding us to humanity. I can't seem to rationalize the *I am* with truth. I want to be free. I would love to believe so the issue will disappear, but sometimes it doesn't heal or it returns.

A: Thus why you struggle in time. Belief is difficult to ascertain in a world of upsets and noise or chaos. Nothing comes in mind which isn't meant to be understood, examined, and then undone. You are the light, the match, and the flame, dear One. So be the extinguisher and put it out.

L: How?

A: You are doing it now by asking to receive new beliefs and thoughts, by understanding why these issues have arisen in the first place. It has been to show you what is needing healed in mind. As you speak of the self—and of others—you often wander into fear or judgment instead of Love. You must always see, think, and know Love to bring healing to body through the mind. Catch the self when you are in judgment of self or others and ask to see it through All. We are the eyes of Love, ears of Love, mind of Love. *See this for me, dear All.*

You may see a new you in mind and give life to this, and stay in conscious connection to All. With help it can be remedied, but if you continue to bemuse on others or lack self-value it will manifest into a worsening or dire circumstance.

L: I do not wish to have this happen, and I will make it priority to be as One with All.

A: And yet, you have continued the conversation in fear. Our answers are same All ways. The way out is through, and every single thought you think or believe is to be questioned. That is the journey and dance of the life each chose as soul. Do this daily—every thought—until you are feeling better, dear One, and then return to our pages with a new outlook on the life of All.

L: Indeed. I need faith. I need to gain a sense of Love always. I do and then I slide back and forth like a—

A: Rocket ship about to take flight?

L: No. Like a broken-down old car.

A: You are closer to knowing than most. You have the tools and are using them often, and this is bringing change even if you are not admitting it to the self. You are not—

L: The same woman I was before these *The All* books. That is true. I am using the tools and reading and rereading my books when I feel I have fallen. I am doing these energy exercises and noticing the signs and messages—until I witness a tragedy or have a hiccup occur where I slide backward only to begin again and again.

A: The dance of Earth (all are taking) is the one between Love and fear, and if you strap on the shoes (tools), it becomes easier to awaken and remember. Asking is the tool we offer as the most important piece of the earthly puzzle. Ask to receive, dear Ones, All ways.

L: Well I am asking to move out of fear and into peace. I'm asking to be able to pay my rent without struggle. I'm asking that money earned is saved and not spent. I'm spending more than I make and it's leaving me breathless. I can't "be" because I am always playing catch up. There is never a moment where I have more than enough and am able to breathe and relax. I make and spend the money. It goes and it comes. My formula is work, pay bills, and use my savings for overages. I have nothing left over every day. I can't afford to pay for my own vacation, take my son out more than just to a dinner or a movie, and I certainly cannot retire. I will be working three jobs for the rest of my days at the rate I am going.

A: Do you believe in the journey of soul?

L: I do.

A: What would make you trust?

L: Proof. Seeing a windfall of cash flow into me. A cash infusion to get me going so I can do less and be more.

A: And what do you feel you need in terms of money?

L: Enough. Enough to keep me happy and free. Enough to be at peace. Enough to share it with others. Enough where I can say, "Yes," to everything and, "No," to work and hustle. It's impossible to believe that easy life exists.

A: Why?

L: Because it doesn't feel possible. Plain and simple. I have nothing to create it other than the mind, which has failed me over and over again, dear All, as I'm sure many of those Law of Attraction junkies are feeling as well. Money is the root of evil because it causes us the most fear on Earth.

A: It does if you are without it.

L: True, which I am, and always have been. I watch others who have abundance and notice how I'm a struggler. I can't even win at *Monopoly*!

A: Because you are in fear even when it's a game. We do know you see many a client with substantial needs financially, and would you call them happy by having the means to achieve everything you wish to in life ?

L: Yes and no. Those I have met with financial means are certainly happier in moments when they are traveling or enjoying the fruits of their abundance, but happy in life as a general thumb, no. Emotional and physical challenges hold the same charge for anyone struggling in mental chaos.

A: Bearing witness has made you understand the journey of happiness is not materialism and money; it is love and Love—family, friends, experiences, and connection to All/God/Source. Do you know anyone happy? Truly happy on Earth?

L: Not in my life. I have met happier people who struggle less, but

no one who isn't moving through a challenge at some point in their life. Some people seem happy but maybe only fake it for TV or social media, or have large pockets of happiness then come face-to-face with a loss or grief and illness. And certainly, I am learning through this that money isn't happiness—it's for ease—but it's not going to bring happiness if the inner workings of the mind can't see its blessing is that of Love and not material things.

A: Fear is everywhere and though some are not having financial fears (as it was chosen prior as soul), they do have lessons to achieve which come from the burdens of billions or millions upon millions. Let this be a lesson to all on Earth: happiness is mind/body/soul and All. If any one of these is missing, truth is lost, and fear is agreeing with ego's ways of believing money is happy. Money is means to make it easier to *be*, and if you *be*, it is money you may see.

L: I don't see much of it, dear All. Every door I try to open seems closed and locked. I wonder why our soul doesn't just say to us, "Not that door."

A: *What is the lesson of the hold?* This is a question you would do well to ask whenever something seems stalled or stopped. Expecting a result based on past experiences is often just a dip in the pool of past. Then there is the swan dive, which ego has control over, keeping you stuck out of fear and worry or doubt. What breaks the hold is understanding its purpose is growth. Expansion is a rubber band. It snaps you back to where you are and leads you forward. The way out of the hold infinitely is to decide for All and know what breaks molds. Freedom is a choice, dear Ones. Hope over lack, divine Ones of All.

L: Why can't you tell us not to go a certain way? Why leave us feeling excited about a career move, buying a home, or taking a trip if every road is blocked? I don't understand why we get excited about things only to find ourselves disappointed over and over again.

A: Do you see how ego drags you into fear with it's words, feeling and emotions? It offers you sadness and betrayal and dismay. It breaks your heart over and over again.

L: I can't help it. It's my operating system. I try and try to overcome fear and ask for help and get to a place of belief, and my mind is not able to. It's stuck in the same old broken record, skipping back to the old tune, and I cannot go beyond it.

A: Again and again it will be said how you are causing the mind's creations to appear. Over and over you torture the mind with false beliefs, and over and over we repeat the how: Trust the soul. Ask to receive and *be*.

L: And again, I will say for all who are struggling in finances and fear: no time exists for that when you have bills to pay and mouths to feed.

A: *Be* and do until such time as you are able to *be* most often. Do in mind and accept it as part of the journey.

I appreciate the work. I enjoy the role I play. I am able to be because I do.

Do more and *be* less—that is how most live. You are becoming more and more the true self and offering more being time, which is why after two years of doing you are back at our *The All* books two-gether. It is not coincidence, at this time, how you came to return. We asked you to return by showing you a circumstance of fear as the mind became cloudy. You listened to the "scream" we offered and returned to Love by asking for help, and now you are here and have come back again, dear One. The ask was answered. Do you see how you are evolving, and though it may feel as if you are stuck, you are precisely where you are meant to be, always? Practice as if you already are abundant. Sit in silence and use the mind to create a wealth of money, love, and all things you feel may enhance your life. Try it for a few days where you are spending time in sacred counsel with All.

L: How long?

A: As long as needed to bring a swell of joy and gratitude. Then decide from this way of being how much is needed to be at peace and set a bargain you will move what is available using it to obtain the amount you seek. Return to our words and have a discussion with us after this period of time. Set an intention if you please.

L: My intention is to make space to *be* so I may discover in mind the amount I am seeking to create. May I have the resources of time

and peace.

A few days go by and rather than having things get easier, they just get more difficult.

L: I have listened to all you have told me and done pretty much every prayer and asking and I'm still in a place of complete—

A: Falseness?

L: The truth is I am in a deep depression. I should be happy based on all we have written here, but something just holds onto to me so tightly. My brain cannot get itself unstuck from thinking about all the bad stuff. Everything is drawing me into anger and fear, and as much as you say, "Ask for help," I'm...Well, I guess right now I am feeling a little more hopeful after I went for a walk and then saw a bunch of stories that reminded me that life is precious.

A: So nothing worked then?

L: It worked, but I also know tomorrow, I may wake up and—

A: Be drawn in by ego again and again until asking for help.

L: But when can we overcome the anger, fear and sadness for good? I don't know if I can do this anymore. One day I may not be able to climb myself back out of this rabbit hole if nothing changes. I have to be honest at this point and say in some way I am—

A: Suicidal?

L: Yes. I didn't want to say it because it's not like I sit around planning it, but I do often think life is too hard and that my future holds nothing exciting or worth continuing for which takes me into a place of terror and fear. Then I think about my son and leaving him and I say, "No way." He's my reason to fight for Love. All I want to be is happy. I don't need much. I would just like to wake up and be at peace with life. I didn't know growing old was going to be so difficult and painful.

A: It's why many end their earthly life early. Either through intentions or intentional means.

L: I can see that. I can see why. They either can't take it anymore and find a way to leave or the bitterness takes over and winds up

killing them through cancer or heart attacks or whatever else we create in the mind.

A: The die-alogue in mind, yes.

L: I'm trying not to make that my reality, but I'm so despondent I don't know how to overcome the ego. She won't let me go. I don't know why I said "she" but I'm sure you do.

A: She is you and you is she. Ego is, (as said earlier in our chapter), a part of you always. It's never not present. It's a choice you make.

L: But I'm saying that I would choose differently if I could, but somehow I can't.

A: We will show you if you will let us. We will take you out of this depression if you allow.

Help me, dear All, receive Love always. Remind me as I fall. Pick me up when I am in doubt. Move me out of fear and into Love forevermore.

Remember, dear One, the mind and its components. Which mind are you thinking with if the ego is in charge?

L: Not Love.

A: Precisely. You are thinking in future, past, or predestined opportunities for growth. It's easy to remember Love. Incorporate it into the mind and you will move through whatever is causing delays and diffusion. Later we will describe our tools of Akasha to help when fear is overcoming Love and you need a leg up. Our ask for today is to do another meditation, a Healer's Temple (as before) and to make time to *be* with rest, walks, being in nature, breath, gratitude, and journaling. Continue this for one week and see how you feel, dear One.

L: Why do we italicize *be* in this dialogue?

A: Because it is *beautifully epic* to swim in a sea of All and to *be* is *bringing everything* to now and that deserves attention the italics bring to it.

Relief

> *No matter which storm you face, you have the choice to try and ride the wave back to joy. Some of us get a little drizzle throughout life, others steady rain; many deal with downpours, and a few are hit by tsunamis or tidal waves that knock them down or drown them in despair. It's the game of life, and you are its controller. No One escapes our lessons of soul. Each stone is a step you take toward enlightening self. Once it becomes clear you are evolving through the lessons, it becomes easier—and often even joyful—to move through the challenges or hardships. When understanding at some level that it has been intentionally designed to spark your ascension, you would love All and thrive.*
> — Wisdom of The All

A week goes by, and something has shifted within me. And then another week passes, and it's as if I am a new person, finally choosing to engage in full with my soul and All. I changed my habits in the morning. Rather than wake up and feel sad or sorry for myself, I began journaling each morning writing out five intentions and five things using the words "I am." I picked up my *A Course in Miracles* book and read the daily exercise, as I have been for the last five years, and I began re-reading *Wisdom of The All*, my last book, and that really seemed to remind me how consistency is important when aligning to Love.

L: Well, dear All, I find myself in a new place and in reading this all back (above) I can see how unhinged I felt, but I am feeling so much lighter and hopeful now. What changed?

A: Belief. You used the advice of our *The All* books and consistently noticed when ego had you trapped, then turned to Love.

Help me as I fall and remind me I am.

And so we did, over and over, and you listened and hesitated and used Love. Not always, but most always. This is where you understood all we have been speaking on in our books. Choice is the most important aspect of Love. You get to decide—all of you. Everyone has choice in order to align to the All. Help is available if Ones ask to receive, always. It is the importance of moment-to-moment fear: give it to All as it arrives. Return to Love.

L: This is why I'm not feeling as awful as I was just a few weeks ago. I made my mind uproot its false beliefs—

A: By asking consistently for it to be changed.

Help me. I need help. This is untrue.

L: And what have I been doing wrong in my life?

A: Wrong is our ego and it is not who We are. Though we speak as One here in our *The All* books, wrong is a concept we underscore as not being All. There is no wrong or right, only choice, dear One. Choose to align to Love, and it will return back that which had been lost in mind. It's like taking a trip to your favorite shop and buying up all the items, then returning them piece by piece slowly as you had enough of them. An empty shop filled with nothing which, as you begin to lose fear, is filled again with items and love. Once used, each has its own purpose, and another is coming to decide for it.

L: I have no clue where you are heading with this, dear All.

A: Ask to receive.

L: *Help me, dear All, decipher the unused parts of my mind so I may know who I am.*

You wrote that. I love our books. I could just write all day but then I would be broke.

A: Belief—and an untruth at that. Our books are purposeful in that we toss items at you and ask you to uncover their meanings. We know if you understand in a complete way it will not seem as if you are using Love, but rather writing only as Laura. So we throw strange stories and anecdotes to fuel you to remember it is an endeavor worth the fight.

L: Fighting off fear. I do understand that. So many times I have

been surprised and delighted by our words, wondering how in the hell I would have ever created such a—

A: Masterpiece?

L: There you go again. As mentioned prior, if I hadn't fought through the fear, I don't know if I would still be here. Would I? Is there a reality where I died?

A: There are infinite possibilities, and educating the self on the existence of these is how you can grow through the circumstance as it arrives. The importance of asking to receive guidance as you fear cannot be stated enough. You sit in anger and sadness and fear getting older, and this is why irrational situations arise. The majority fear aging. Everyone on Earth is so fearful of the mirror they will do anything to overcome the sense of disgust for the bodies you have chosen to evolve in. An epidemic of fear causing an epidermis breakout.

L: I have gotten a horrible rash on my neck currently and its causing me distress, but I have been using our tools as often as possible, asking for help and receiving downloads. But it didn't relieve the itch or irritation. It's not a miracle cure, asking to receive.

A: Not instantaneously will all illness release. Remember, it must be understood in mind what is the root cause; otherwise, all circumstances repeat in other ways, often becoming worse by each encounter of fear. Think with the mind of All; that is the remedy for the fears you each hold on Earth.

I am One with All, and this is Love.

L: Can it bring me relief instantaneously? Because it's hard to concentrate on joy with the itchy feeling of my neck right now.

A: Ego is hard to overcome in physical circumstances. We offer advice on how to relieve the pain: *be* in mind a place where you feel at peace. Stay there for a while. Jump for joy. Go on a hike. Dance, laugh, or be merry. Remember *I am.* Be happy in mind. Nowhere else can bring the peace you seek but the mind of All. Choose it.

I choose happy All ways.

We are happy. We don't blame or judge, worry, or fear. We simply enjoy all aspects of our soul.

Soul = Source of unconditional Love.

Choose = Change how our outward soul expresses.

Soul is an expression of All which splits into infinite experiences outside of everything. This is who you are on Earth, an outside Source experience which brings feelings of despair because you forget everything as you arrive to the body of One. One is the body in motion, thinking and believing of irrational fears and creating what is seen in mind and belief. Watch the mind and it becomes easier to overcome fear. Once you know what the mind is doing, you can work toward using it wisely by choosing All, Love, or God—or whatever is the word you find most agreeable to you as One. Do you think you can overcome fear?

L: I think so, yes. I can try and *be* more often and do less. I can spend more time in mind and listen to the voice of All. I want to be at peace and live happy from the inside out.

Two days go by, and my skin is finally healing.

L: Thank you for the healing.

A: You see how the mind is working always? It heals in asking and receiving.

L: Why asking and receiving? Don't we get what we ask for always?

A: Only if believed, dear One. You have received a healing and accepted it as possibility many times before.

L: I'm pretty clear on healing and not going too far down a rabbit hole. I knew this would go away, but it took longer than I hoped. But it is better now, so I am less stressed out by it. I wish I had the same sense of money. I would have a lot more of it if I could undo my thinking around it. I have seen many times the ability we have to transmute pain into healing. Transmuting dollars and cents, not so much. I wonder why I struggle so much to see with my mind's eye a vision of success. Can you help me understand why I'm blocking it? I'm afraid to be disappointed which is one reason I believe its blocked.

Anything else I am missing as Laura that All can bring forth to me?

A: What have you been told since childhood, dear One?

L: Money doesn't grow on trees. It must be earned or made. You can't build wealth if you don't work hard and invest wisely. The rich get richer. The 1 percent is in charge of our destiny. Shall I go on?

A: What you speak is how most think and believe on Earth in regard to money. It is deeply embedded in the mind of every One, save for those who were born into it and know it's their birthright, so to speak.

L: How do we uproot that and begin to understand Source is how money is made—through mind. And, you wrote that as usual.

A: Ones must trust and know that All of Everything exists, as does money in its current form on Earth. The system you are using is designed to keep the 1 percent in its position of power and influence. It is not designed to make everyone rich.

L: That I definitely believe.

A: Why do you feel this is so?

L: Because its arbitrary, really. Just a system we made up to exchange goods and services. That's mine, and this is yours. How do we overcome what the worldly wand holders designed without it costing us something?

A: *Be* in mind and know that you are All. We. Wealthy everyone. There is more than enough for the collective to enjoy abundance always. It is because you argue and fight they are able to keep the less fortunate in poverty. No one wins when the score is tied. It is greed which promotes war, famine, and all the nonsense of Earth. The only escape is the one in mind. Use the power within to overcome all the chaos of your fellow brethren.

L: Sometimes it's so difficult to see what is possible because the world is at war and chaos. I can't get a vision of what's ahead because I am so trapped by fear.

A: Now you understand the playbook of the denizen of disasters. Keep all minds occupied with fear so it cannot create love. What happens on Earth is fear and loathing. You must hate one another for the rich to get richer. It thrives on manipulation and knowing the brain is designed for animosity and rage. They engage the amygdala with all manners of negativity and nonsense, knowing it induces stress, worry, and fear, which then equates to dollars and cents. Buy more stuff, get happy. Be sick, use health services. This is why movies and music, television, and newspapers exist—to show fear.

L: How long has it been known on Earth? And when did the narrative arrive to mass manipulate us with madness?

A: Ancient texts exist detailing the exact reasons why you are here and what it takes to evolve as souls. Hidden in thousands of essays are the words of Source. Ones in body feared everyone knowing they are Love and designed a "torture" system, so to speak, that keeps the love hidden as much as possible. Hope and happy are important to keep to a minimum in order to make money, it was believed—and still is.

L: It sounds diabolical.

A: And yet, perfectly imperfect. A system of fear exists to keep you evolving, and you do it either in love or fear—and what better way to service fear than to keep creating it? They have known all along to keep the pawns at bay, how to game the narrative of Earth since early days of cities and temples.

L: It makes sense. I guess the good news is that we are learning more and more about the science of our brains, and so keeping it secret isn't going to work for much longer.

A: It remains a mystery to many, and so you are seeing the result of fear continue. Ones who are recognizing their role as One are able to mostly move beyond this crisis and be helpful to the collective of Earth. Remember you are One, and so what you believe is manifesting into the minds of others. So be the light as much as One can, and it helps the entire collective. Just be Love.

L: Well, yet again, this is certainly not the conversation I was expecting this evening. I was asking why it's so hard to visualize a bright, happy, and abundant future and somehow we are in *The Matrix* now!

A: It relates in that when the brain is impacted by ideas of scarcity and lack, you are intentionally in fear. Ones must release the narrative of Earth and overcome fear in order to create more love. If Ones are constantly being streamed upset and nonsense, the brain is more apt to stay in fear. Its happy hormones (dopamine, serotonin, oxytocin) are in short supply if you are always being scared by fear. It's known what the brain is doing and known how to keep the tempers flaring. More wars, guns, and fear. Show the bad and destroy good. Good vs. evil isn't just a movie's plot. It's the war of Earth too.

L: Well, dear All, what can we do as humans to overcome this war on Love?

A: Know you are All. Keep off devices and *be*. Stay committed to doing activities which bring joy and passion. Use time for friendships and love. Go outdoors. Be still. All the things we spoke of in our chapter on toxins (*Wisdom of the All*) are ways of doing less and being more. If you stay in connection to your higher self and *be* more, the war is won in mind All ways. Teach the willing and decide for Love, dearest One.

L: If it walks like a duck. Oh my gosh now that chapter title we wrote like a year ago makes even more sense. It's always shocking how it can be months or years later that the titles we wrote circle back around to life.

A: It's always known in mind, and if Ones go seeking and clear the fear, All words appear to remind you to Love All. The books are prewritten. The words that come through as All are *you* speaking and emoting the stories and ideas you designed. Don't let fear stop your intentions from manifesting. All works of art are masterpieces you said "yes" to in spirit. Art, movies, music, poems, series, and symphonies—everything is spirit-designed and derived by you, for you, to become Love's messenger.

L: It makes sense, and because I now know the brain is wired for threat and reward, I am not shocked in the least to hear any of it because—

A: It is a playbook you knew existed, buried in the mind, which is accessible through quiet stillness. More to revealed, dear One, always.

Quack, Quack

Signs are everywhere, leading you to understand the soulful part of the life you are living. It's not just one sign—it's all signs. Everything is guiding the way on Earth: animals, plants, memes, movies, and artistry. You are all channeling divine information every day, all day, dear Ones. Stay in the illusion of fear, insecurity, and lack, and it will be difficult to detach. It will feel as if life is always against you and not for you—and yet life is for you All ways. Remember?
— Wisdom of The All

A week goes by and I am struggling with a skin issue where my lips swelled up like—yes, you guessed it—a duck. The issue started back on the Fourth of July when I had inhaled a ton of toxic bug spray, and a rash developed on my neck, and about twenty mosquito bites all over my arms popped up. Now it's been two weeks, and a little spot I had on my upper lip—that I assumed was another bug bite— hadn't gone away. After trying some home remedies to get rid of it once and for all, I had an allergic reaction which caused my lips to fully swell overnight, and it's immensely painful. I'm off to the doctor soon but also wanted to check in with Doctor All for a diagnosis and discussion.

L: Well, now that duck chapter title really is a shocker. It's like you—
   A: We.
   L: Knew it would appear.
   A: All possibilities exist, and yes, it was always possible to manifest a malady or a mallard. A duck and cover or a duck lip attack.
   L: Because everything already exists, and our choices make it arrive either in love or fear?
   A: Bravo, dear One, you are learning and leaning into truth. As such, you did fear and felt its consequence. Quack. Quack.
   L: Very funny, but I'm in pain here, and I have understood some

62

of the reasons why my lips were chapped and irritated in the first place—

A: Festering words spoken to and through you.

L: It took me awhile to figure out why, but I finally had the revelation last night that it was in relation to a friend who I felt (but kind of always knew) would betray me. I also think it's in relation to my own harsh words spoken to myself and because I get frustrated with all the sleeping people who do and say bad things. Am I on the right track here?

A: Indeed. You are perfectly aligned with All That Is for interpreting why the wound has ballooned.

L: More comedy, nice. I look like a clown or someone who purposely gets their lips injected. I would like my lips to go back to normal and this pain to go away. So what needs to happen in order to make that a reality? I have been asking for help. I'm also fully guilty of going online and using home remedies which only exacerbated the problem. Similar to when I wrote about my clogged toilet (in *The All That Is*) and only made that worse by using home remedies. Eventually, I had to call a plumber. Here I am needing to go to a doctor.

A: Avoiding paying a bill again.

L: Hoping it would go away on its own, but yes, avoiding a doctor for fear of having a huge bill I can't afford.

A: Evolve or repeat—we have discussed over and over in our books and quotes. Messages to remind you how the Universe speaks in slow whispers, gentle knocks, loud beeps, and then heavy screams. Each time you ignore a symptom or situation you are being guided to notice what is happening in mind. Become aware of it and work to a "soul"ution; it will dissipate into the nothing from which it arrived. Miss the message, and another comes to slow you or show you a hidden belief. All of it to bring you toward Love.

There are messages in your messes, all of you.

L: Can you explain that more?

A: All of you are being guided through daily interactions and experiences—by, through, and with self and others. In every blip or bop, there is a nudge, a push, or a shove.

L: For example?

A: A clogged toilet is a chance to notice that you are thinking in fear. A leaky roof reveals hidden fears, and if they seep out, a mess could be had: a secret once thought safe is beginning to surface. A stubbed toe is a message that demands and determination need to be quelled. A fender bender could be co-creation in fear or karmic reciprocity. A rash indicates impatience. In all your life circumstances and struggles, look to see: *Could this be a message for self?*

L: So every trip or fall, broken down or busted item is a message to remind us we are in—

A: Ego. Yes. You have missed the message of self-acceptance and love for All. Therefore, we are bringing forth another message (through the body) to hold you accountable for the criticisms of the self and humanity. Would you say it's time to notice every thought and belief in regards to your life?

L: Absolutely. This is so painful and annoying. I do not want to go down this path again.

A: And in other times, have you received a message and heeded it fully?

L: Sometimes, yes, and other times, no, but in this particular circumstance I'm sure I have been holding onto anger and frustration, and I'm sure this is the necessary amount of pain to remind me to go deeper in mind and uproot myself from anger and free myself. What can I say, do, or be here to remove this efficiently and go back to being pain-free?

A: *"I am releasing the need to feel an angry circumstance and allow a total healing as I separate mind/body and soul and remember to use All aspects."*

Release a thought. Make time. *Be.* The answers within come through if you slow down, stay connected in mind to Love, and believe. One tool to help decipher bodily upsets is understanding Chakras and Clairsenses. These are guides to what is being thought, believed, or acted upon leading to all manners of ailments and pain. A push to be more, do less, and remember All. Our guide for this is coming through and to you later on in our series.

It's been a week and the doctor did give me medicine, which I took for the swelling and pain to go away, but now I'm feeling off-kilter from the medicine that was given to me. My body feels off (even though this morning I did a chakra-balancing meditation), and I am having trouble sleeping. Thus, why I am back for a late-night writing session with All.

L: I just don't feel like myself right now. It's been a long day, and I had some wonderful experiences offering readings and teaching meditation, and then had a meeting with a producer for a TV show my mom and I are filming, but it left me feeling exactly how we discussed above: old, tired, and overweight. I never in my life would have thought I could gain weight like this. And I know I should not be complaining, but aging is hard. It's more difficult than I thought it would be. It's the first time in my life where I see an older person in the mirror, and I haven't felt that way in twenty years. Is there something to be done to help us as we grow older? I really had no clue I would hate it so much. It's not about time; it's about—

A: Vanity?

L: Yep.

A: We spoke in our last book of the aging process and how human vanity chains you to the narrative of Earth, which is "aging is a curse" and not the blessing it actually is. Do you see how the whole time you are on Earth, you must be committed to soul growth? Imagine if Ones awaken in early life only to find themselves unsettled by the loss of youth—how they would struggle. It is this dance of life which keeps you on your toes, and we want you to know you are magnificent creatures of Love, so if you fall into ego's traps it becomes easier to recognize your light.

L: I see that. I also find as I get older, I am much more compassionate, empathetic and kind, but not to myself. Only to others. How sad is that? I can't enjoy looking in a mirror or at my phone. I wish I could see myself as you do all of us on Earth.

A: There are many perfectly content with who they are in older years, and there are some who struggle to make amends with age. You are One here to overcome vanity and fear that tethers itself to you more deeply, and this is why you are holding onto your youth with all of your might.

L: How do you come to terms and have reverence for the body as it ages and the face as it wrinkles? Oh my gosh, you are making me feel old as I write this. I literally am sitting here as if I am elderly person and feeling that in my body.

A: And still, you are you?

L: I am.

A: Remember, all of your life you are the One choosing to experience everything. So having a blissful appreciation for All That Is is how you overcome a sense of anguish. There is no need to age gracefully, only soulfully. Throughout life, remember, you are divine Love, and the numbers will not matter.

L: But I want to feel good in my body, and because the breakdown is beginning, I just don't feel healthy the way I used to. Even when I was teaching fitness—before I fell down the stairs and broke my wrist, I felt better, but still not full of life.

A: Fill your mind with healthy thoughts, the body with healthy food, vitamins and minerals, and drink in the sunshine and air. Use water to wash away the buildup and sit in silence for as long as you can. Then see if you feel differently. Will you take time to *be* as you move into this next phase of life? Even as you do, as we know there are "bills to pay" and "practical steps", as you would say, it is still possible to prioritize all of these as well.

L: Yes. I will prioritize those things. I will ask for help when I feel sad. I will put aside fear of financial ruin and try and work through this. I want to be happy and at peace.

A: Return when you are prepared to further our discussion and what results have come for and through you.

After a few days, I was feeling really good. I got the nudge to buy a home rather than stay in my rental, as my lease was ending and the cost was nearly the same to own as to rent. I called an old friend who was a realtor, and together we found a home in one weekend. It felt like things were finally falling into place for me—until a new circumstance came along to frustrate me and send me into a tailspin.

L: I gave it the old college try with prioritizing these "sou"lutions and found myself in a really great place until the sale of my home started to go off the rails. The title company messed everything up from start to finish, and I didn't get the keys in time. The most frustrating part was that no one really had my back. The realtor and the buyers, just didn't seem to care that their chosen title company completely bungled it all. They made no concessions and just let it all go to hell. I found myself caught in this very human experience without a net. Now I'm out money and time and wondering if I made a mistake buying this house? Buyer's remorse has set in. What can I do to make this situation better and move past it without fear? I hear a song in my head, *"Oh what a beautiful morning, oh what a beautiful day."*

A: Singing is a great way to release emotions that are stored when the day goes astray—or anytime, really. You need a perspective shift, and the mind brings those "soul"utions all the time if you are noticing them. We know it has been a most difficult time moving through the ineptitude of others. Just know it is for the highest good of all involved. All parties are involved in the moving of everything. You must be One who holds space collectively:

May we come together as One to upend this challenge and move beyond it. I hold space for whatever insufficiency others hold in mind and ask to be guided through it gently and swiftly.

When the challenges come, you must ask to receive within it. All day, every day, notice what is happening and work toward upending it as quickly as One can. This is all a lesson for the particular time you are in. You have noticed our presence within, asking for help more and more, but now it is time to bring everything into the now. Choose to know whenever an issue arises it is in the moment it can be worked through, changed, or grown through with less struggle if you are aligned. Simply ask to receive:

Help me understand this blessing of soul.

L: I know I can make the best out of a bad situation, and I have to believe I will make it work. I always do.

A: Making things work isn't the goal. Loving life is.

L: I want to scream!

A: Then scream.

I let out a long scream, and it really felt good.

L: Man, that felt good. Why can't life just be easy?

A: Awareness is a gift.

L: Feels like a box of rocks and sticks.

A: It will feel hard until you understand it further and use the mind of Love more often. Once you use the mind as the Source it is, you will stop focusing on pain (as you do often) and focus All attention to joy, even if the moment isn't holding it.

L: This seems to be impossible to stay in vibration to Love.

A: Impossible, no. Difficult, yes, if you are always focusing on the things which feel bad. Focus on love and joy. Give yourself permission to be happy.

L: And how may I do that, dear All?

Dear All, please help me feel the joy of life and to love my experience on Earth with every ounce of my being. I know the tools are inside of me and I use them daily, hourly, minute by minute to transform the fear into faith and knowing.

L: So learn to be in now as if its magic. You...

I stopped and thought for a minute and changed what I was going to say.

L: No, *We* wrote that.

A: Indeed, loved One. We are One.

4

Chapter 4 / Call Your Mother

D ear All, I am listening to my soul and knowing I am One.

444 — Angels and loved Ones reminding us they are only a thought away from you.

Rainbows and butterflies, symbols of God, sanctimonious harmony in song. These are the signs from 'above' you believe in and know. If only you were more able to be in sync with All would you see signs and messages everywhere. It's not just obvious ones, but also subtle messages inside. The Universe is guiding everyone always with dialogue and direction. Go this way, use this door, take this right or left. You are never alone, dear One, because we are All One.
    — Wisdom of The All

Sign, Sign Everywhere a Sign

Before I ever knew what the All was, I would see signs from the Universe guiding me through my grief. After my dad and brother died, I began seeing signs and messages everywhere. I would have dreams in which they showed up—one in particular where we were together at the beach, which felt as real as it does to me sitting here right now. I remember waking up and frantically trying to go back into the dream so I could spend more time with them, which, unfortunately, I couldn't. I have learned to call these *visitation* dreams.

For my brother Jason, those signs showed up immediately. Literally on the day he died, I got the most profound sign from above. I remember walking with my parents and my other brother to get some food. We were emotionally drained, and though none of us were particularly hungry, it was a way to get our minds off the extreme grief we were feeling.

It was late, around 9 p.m., on a quiet street in Burlington, Vermont, so nothing much was open—just a few restaurants scattered about. As we were walking up to a pizza joint, I began smelling a very pungent and strong smell of curry. I told my other brother, and he agreed it was curry. We looked around, thinking it was coming from a different restaurant, but it wasn't possible as there wasn't one nearby, just pizza. Now, if you are a skeptic, you could say someone was cooking in a building somewhere, but I knew with every fiber of my being that was Jason telling me, "Hello."

He and I had this long-running joke going back maybe fifteen years about curry. He loved it, and I despised the taste and smell. I used to call it "vile curry," and he would laugh every time the mention of it came up when deciding what restaurant to visit or what to make for a dinner. It was such a perfect reference to let me know, *I'm still here.* He has shown me more signs since and reminds me often of his nonphysical presence.

My dad, however, took a bit longer to get his signs across. I (or I guess, rather We) talked about this in my book *The All of The All*—that my dad, who died by suicide, went to someplace termed the "Hospital of the Heart and Soul" after he died to remember he was on the other side. But when he did show up, it was in a big way. I wrote about it in that book: how one day, driving on the freeway by my house, I was thinking about my dad when a car with a license plate drove by me that read OBLADI. It was hard to miss. Then, the very next day, I kid you not, a completely different car passed by me at the exact same spot around the exact same time with the license plate OBLADA. I immediately thought of the Beatles song and knew it was my dad saying to me, *Life goes on.*

Then, about a month later, I was leaving work early to go to my son's preschool graduation ceremony, and this gigantic black bug I had never seen before followed me to my car. I had just seen a video of rushing water in the elevator, which I thought was weird, but it did make me think of my dad because water was involved in his death. That bug—the same exact one—was there when I got off the freeway two miles away. Then, five minutes later, I pulled into my son's preschool, and there was that same gigantic bug at the front door. I had to duck as it flew by my head. I know it was how my dad was saying he was there in spirit with us for my son's big day. It brought me an immense amount of peace to know I wasn't alone.

Those experiences kept adding up. One of the craziest was when I was going through a third attempt at adoption and found out the birth parents had changed their mind about placement. Between my brother's death, my dad, two miscarriages, and now a third disrupted adoption, I was despondent. I stayed in bed for two or three days, not wanting to leave, and at one point I woke up in the middle of the night hearing a strange noise coming from the bathroom, like someone was talking to me. I felt this sense of peace come over me, like I was being taken care of in that moment. I walked over to the bathtub and sitting on the edge was a toy from the Disney Junior animated series *Octonauts*, which was a favorite of my son back then. The toy, which talks words and phrases from the show, was going off—which was weird in the first place because it had been submerged in water so many times it rusted out and no longer worked. Even crazier was when I had the thought to pop open the battery compartment and was shocked to see there were no batteries in it! Somehow the universe was able to zap it on to remind me I would be okay.

From that point on, I noticed everything I suspected or knew was a sign or message for me and documented them. My phone is now filled with images and videos going back twelve years, and I love how other people in my life notice signs too now. My mom and I recently went to buy her a new car. Sitting in the finance office, we found it interesting that the young man helping us came from the same part of Massachusetts as my dad.

Then the next guy who was helping us with getting insurance on the car introduced himself, shook my mom's hand, and said his name was "Jason." My mom, eyes wide open, looked over at me, and all I could do was smile and nod. She knows now, after having this happen many times when we were together, our family is with us in spirit and loves to let us know that.

Signs, messages, synchronicity, coincidences, serendipity and confirmations are how the Universe speaks through you and to you. Symbols, numbers repeating, animals, birds and insects are all ways you are guided to notice the Infinite Source of Love. Pay attention, or it becomes background, not foreground evidence of a life already lived. It's time to awaken truth within. You know All, see All, feel All, because it is.

— Wisdom of The All

So many synchronicities and "coincidences" are happening in my life all the time, it's hard to believe I struggle as much as I do with belief. My understanding of them as a I evolve continues to expand, and now I not only see them, I can even notice other people's signs and messages when they don't recognize them.

It's like in the movie *Bruce Almighty* when a frustrated Jim Carrey asks God, "What should I do? Give me a signal!" Then misses a sign that says "Caution ahead." "Please send me a sign!" he begs God again, and a truck pulls in front of him literally carrying about a hundred road signs. He gets angry and pulls around the truck, "Oh, what's this joker doing now!" Then he grabs rosary beads off the rearview mirror and asks for a miracle. In his haste, he drops the rosary, hits a pothole, and proceeds to crash into a light pole as that same truck filled with a myriad of road signs drives by. Still not getting it, he yells at God, and his pager goes off with number 555-0123, not realizing this *is* the sign from God. The repeating number 555 is all about learning and information. His experience has been a lesson, and God is showing the signs; it's just being ignored, as we are so trapped in our ego and fear.

The language of All is directly tied to the mind. What you see is sent for you to remember Love. Songs, numbers, and messages are ready and waiting for you to accept them, and if you do, it becomes easier to move through a day. If you miss the message, it dissipates, and the game continues on with new ones waiting at every step. Pay attention, dear Ones—the signs are speaking to you all day, every day, everywhere, every One.
— Wisdom of The All

It's not just signs and symbols that I see; it's been miraculous experiences I have had as a medium and intuitive where I have witnessed countless *wow* moments that are simply not explainable as coincidence. Times when I knew nothing about the person I was reading for as a psychic medium and nailed every little detail. Times when I was watching TV and saw a story matching exactly to mine or my clients' lives. Songs on the radio that played a message I needed to hear. Animals showing up at my doorstep or crossing my path on the road, carrying the exact characteristics of my current situation.

Not to mention the thousands of live intuitive readings sessions I have done with people I don't even get to see—their faces hidden—yet I can tell their stories, feel their struggles, and even see, sense, or feel loved Ones who have passed on in their lives. At times, I've intuited medical information and helped someone understand the root cause of their pain or illness, whether it stemmed from this life or a past one.

I have often worked on past lives with clients, and later their linear history and geographical information could be verified in books or records—a history or geography I, Laura, had never even heard of. I've had clients whose hidden fears or life paths I could almost telepathically understand, only to see them reflected exactly in a past life that matched their current circumstances.

It would honestly take me days to reveal every strange, non-explainable-by-science-or-spirituality thing I have seen and experienced in the last decade. It is in the thousands to tens of thousands at this point.

Yet the most profound experience of all I had in my life was when I telepathically communicated with a nonverbal woman in hospice who had not spoken in over a year. Her spouse had asked if I would come for a visit just to sit with her, which I did. I held her hand and explained who I was and that I was there if she wanted to share anything. After a few minutes I began hearing words in my mind that were clearly not my own, different from how I write and share in these books with the All. She told me that her sister had died as a young teenager and was in the room with us now. I couldn't see her, but her husband confirmed she had a sister who died young. Then, like a fountain of dialogue, I just began speaking as her. I closed my eyes and let words flow out that could not be me—a rapid translation of information. I could hear her partner softly crying as he listened to what was obviously her goodbye and love message to her family and him.

I don't know what was said, as I can't remember the messages I "channel" most times for people now, but I know the impact it had on her and him. I will never forget the look on her face after I worked miracles to share her words through me. She smiled so brightly as if to say, *"Thank you for letting me be heard again."* A smile that was out of heaven, for sure. It showcased for me how our mind is continually able to react even when our body is shutting down. She was in there, and this moment showed that. I heard she passed just a few weeks later, and I felt so relieved I was able to help her before she returned to Spirit .

Moments like these remind me: we are never truly alone, and Love finds its way through us in ways beyond logic, time, and understanding.

Always Be Asking

You cannot have perfect days all ways, dear Ones, because if you did, you would be in the non-physical. But every time you ask to receive inner guidance, a new pathway opens to a world beyond physical eyes. It is easy, and yet most make time for it only sparingly and waste precious time. If only you knew how potent and powerful this mechanism is for change—both material and emotional—you would walk through the door and thrive.
— Wisdom of The All

So this all sounds amazing, right? I should be so confident in what I am learning and hearing from the All. Yet that is not how it works for me. I keep getting hung up in the distractive voice of fear and doubt. I see a miracle and accept it, but then go back to owning pain and sadness. Alas, yet again, here I am back to needing answers and help when I went into a dark place after a particularly tough week collectively. The world I know and grew up in keeps getting uprooted. Attacks against women especially have me in a downward spiral.

Laura: I can't believe how quickly you can go from love to fear. Our world is in utter turmoil right now, and my fellow "Ones," as you refer to people, are feeling it everywhere, struggling to settle the mind.

All: It is not the journey of soul to empty the mind and complete the process of Earth. It is daily expansion, and this is the point of life.

L: I feel awful when I witness others who are hurting. I want to help.

A: Let us help you.

Help us know what every day is for and how to move through the fear of ego and see it with Love/soul.

Keep asking, and when the noise is loud, ask more. Cloudy days are more

Love-inducing than sunny ones because you use the voice of All. Imagine what is happening is part of the ascension process of Love. Use the day to decide for it even if you are struggling. That is how we view a good day.

L: And what is a bad day in your summation?

A: Unlearned ones. Days where you move the needle take you closer to the expansion of consciousness if you show up to go beyond it. If you stay stuck then it's worthless in terms of soul's goal. However, if you keep doing the "work" it reminds you to All, and then you get more information of who you truly are. You have oft stated in online forums how we have much more to learn and how this earthly world is a tip of the iceberg and this, dear One, is truth inspired by All. Just know that the hard is the way to inner experiences which grow you to the biggest diamonds of All, Love. Use the ask of help to go deeper in mind where the gems of the mind are available to you. *Mine = mind.* My intuitive nonsensical ego = moving information needed daily. One step closer to All is what hard days or circumstances are for, Love. Ask to see it our way. That all is perfect as is, dear One.

Ouch

Evolve or repeat. The Universe speaks in slow whispers, gentle knocks, loud beeps and then heavy screams. Torture is the mechanism which changed the hardest ego into the lovingest soul. The past is a window to what you had been through and where not to go again on Earth. Everything you move through as soul has purpose to grow you to Love unconditionally.

— Wisdom of The All

One thing has become clear through these dialogue sessions: every lesson has a blessing. Even the worst situations can bring some type of closure or open your mind to hidden fears.

This year has certainly been a challenging one personally, beyond what is happening collectively, and I have found myself going back and forth between depression and happiness quite regularly, especially whenever a "knock" would happen. "Whispers" I can handle; "nudges," well, I was moving through those a little more easily—but then boom—a heavy "scream" happened.

In August of 2022, after I bought my new house and was getting ready to move in, my mom and I would regularly go out looking for accessories and renovation items. One day, which just happened to be 8/8—a 7 in numerology, which makes sense to me now (more on that coming up)—my mom and I were coming home from a flooring store. The next day we would be filming an episode of *House Hunters* for HGTV. After a lot of details needed to be worked out, everything was set to go and we were looking forward to the filming and meeting the crew.

Out of nowhere, a guy driving a blue two-door sedan sideswiped us while he was pulling out of an apartment complex parking lot. It caused our car to go into a 360-degree tailspin after the impact. In a miracle of miracles, our car was hit on the rear passenger door, narrowly missing my mom, and by the grace of God my son had been at home and not taken the ride with us. I hope that if he had been in the car he still would have been okay, but I'm grateful he was not there that day.

However, it also wasn't lost on me that had he been with us, that accident maybe would have never occurred, because we might have done the day differently—stopping for lunch or getting ice cream, perhaps, or even walking more slowly while we were out together, making it impossible to have been at that place in that exact moment. It showcased to me how narrow misses are always a decision away.

L: Well, here we go, All. You (I mean we) wrote that last line. What are you teaching here about this particular situation? I mean honestly, we could have died, and this book would be all that was left of me. I remember *I am* All, but still, out of nowhere a car nearly killed my mom and me, with my son at home and no one to have told him if his mom was in an accident. It was a scary circumstance, and thinking about it now makes me anxious and, frankly, terrified it could happen

again or be worse.

A: Let's take one portion at a time. First, we have told you, you are All and that in any darkness a miracle is available through remembering you are All. It is a truth and reliable, but the amount of uncovering of who you are not is lengthy indeed. So you can know, and believe, and still have days of information to move through, leading you to uncover what is in mind. Remember what we have said prior. There is a message in every mess. Next, we shall discuss the ramifications of the vehicle incident, which you have pondered on occasion and discovered the "whys," which is how we ask all to be. Introspection is a warrior's tool.

- Your mom has admitted her fears around driving at an advanced age. Though in our eyes she is young and vibrant, in hers it is fear creating the manifested bodily upsets.
- Your driving "saved the day," so to speak, in that you were able to slow down without an injury to either yourself or mom.

L: **Yes, thank goodness we had no injuries, although my mom did panic, and it made me proud to be able to navigate her through using mindfulness and breathwork tools. I tried to see the situation as All, but still, obviously, had scary things going on in my mind—my son being home alone being the worst. I kept thinking, what if I had died and he was alone? I don't ever want to have that be—**

A: Precisely why a manifested fear came to light in this car. It had been thought about prior—how leaving him alone could be improper without first seeing it with the eyes of Love. The safety of mind is knowing ahead of time of your departure, arrival, and everything in between. If known in mind you are safe, it will be.

L: **So be more conscious of my daily movements and connecting with All?**

A: Indeed. Returning to our summation of the incident at hand.

- You showed the police, firefighters, and driver the way of All. Immediately you were able to be calm and firm, making sure that everyone was okay and ensuring you knew how to get the car to where it needed to be and you home to your son—working it out step by step.

L: Well, I was concerned we wouldn't be able to make the filming of *House Hunters* after so much went into the producers making it happen. I would have been devastated to disappoint people. My mom wanted to cancel, but I talked her into still doing the show—and honestly, I am glad I did because it helped take the accident off of her and my mind.

A: All working out as it could, without disruption.

L: But was I meant to cancel? Was this the Universe stopping me from making a mistake and filming the show? Was that a sign I didn't follow, like in *Bruce Almighty*? Am I the Jim Carrey here?

A: It might be, or it might not. It was your circumstance to handle. So let's be clear that every One must find the lesson or message on their own. Let us look at the handled situation, as its important to you.

L: It felt important (the HGTV show) and what I was meant to be doing, but that obviously threw me for a loop—literally, in the car. I also keep thinking about the decision that day to take a back route. I made the split-second choice to take a particular road, when I just as easily could have gone another way—left instead of right—which could have changed everything, and yet, it didn't. My mom and I ended up in a tough predicament. I wonder why it happened, and it still bothers me that it did. Can you offer any more insights to this particular circumstance, dear All?

A: Let us make point number 4, the hardest to learn for our soul seekers.

- You have honestly and vulnerably expressed a desire for moving beyond a life and yet fight to stay.

L: Now I am crying, but I do understand. I hadn't thought of that.

A: We appreciate a willingness to share a mind at war with itself. This is where it must be shown the result of fear created a difficult experience—a scream, if you will. Had you known then to bring reverence to each day, you might have skipped a circumstance to remind you that life is precious.

L: I'm shook.

A: This is what co-creating brings. The being we speak of is where our revelations come to light. You may not remember or know, but we do—and it is why the importance of asking to receive help cannot be overstated.

L: I have chills, and I feel more at peace knowing I can bring answers through as I guide myself out of this fear and anguish I feel. I needed to know this was a trip to make me appreciate life more.

I took a moment to reflect and regroup, still emotional, but the All quickly interrupted my fear with light.

A: It is a marvelous trip when you end up somewhere unexpected, wouldn't you say?

L: (laughing) I don't think I would call being sideswiped a "marvelous" trip, dear All.

A: Not for the Ones in body who can't yet understand their role as soul. If no challenges arise on a trip around the sun, there really is no point to being in a body. You chose to experience unexpected twists and turns in order to evolve, and so to wander the park (earth) without taking a ride would be a waste of a day, wouldn't you say, dear One?

L: (laughing) Okay. You got me there. It's much more exciting to visit a theme park and go on rides than just walking around and doing nothing all day.

A: Precisely why, if you look at circumstances as part of the adventure, it will be easier to escape ego. A laugh is better than anger or disappointment.

"Oh well. Here we go again. Weeeeeeeee."

Isn't it fun on Earth?

L: Oh man. I can't even. You win.

5

Chapter 5 / Get Stuff Done

H elp me, dear All, remember to Ask for help, to know that Love is available All ways.

555 — Information is the gift of All.

If you are always busy and hustling the Infinite discoveries happen slowly. It is the doing mind which must be in action, and not calm, quiet, and relaxed. Those states of being are precisely where the answers of soul reveal themselves to you. Love is always guiding you, and when you are aware and open to receive, everything becomes a message and the meanings apparent.
— Wisdom of The All

We know it may seem difficult to decipher messages as you make your way up the ladder of ascension, and we are here to explain All of it to you. We ask, dear Laura, to muse upon recent changes she is experiencing as means to help you all. Her experience similar to many on Earth navigating love and fear.

Moving In and Out

Laura: I am now living in the home I purchased and having second thoughts. Panic is setting in. It cost way more in closing costs than I initially had budgeted for, and now I have no safety net financially. I am questioning if I made a mistake. Did I, dear All?

All: No mistakes exist on Earth. Only lessons from which to learn. Doing as you please is always about making decisions from Love and fear—the journey of Earth. So we guide you as best to choose Love in all circumstances. What would Love do? Love representing All That Is. Love decides it is best to find peace within and decide if you are going a direction that will serve Love. That is our reason for being in physical realms and in physical vessels for learning in bodies on Earth.

L: So why not ask, *Who would Love be?*

A: You may ask whatever pleases the mind. However, being is the key, and if you were being, it would be clear what is best for All.

L: I would know the answer—

A: All ready.

L: I like that. All, ready. As if to say when you lean into All you receive the answer as it already existed for you.

A: Yes. However, you are in a doing phase asking to be guided in life, and so asking, *"What would Love do?"* reminds you to the All That Is, which then brings in feelings, emotions, thoughts, or ideas to guide you as to what is best. Do you receive the guidance, is the question we ponder?

L: Do I?

A: You do often, but not all ways. Many times you are caught in fear and guided into circumstances caused by it. Again, there is no right or wrong on Earth, simply a choice. To be or not to be—that is the question, as dear Shakespeare wrote so long ago. Intentionally placed to be a beacon of choice for All.

L: I'm sorry, dear All, but being is impossible right now in the modern earthly world that runs on money and greed. The inflation crisis is raw and real, and the financial crunch is getting worse every

day.

A: Or so Ones believe, and so that is what Ones see. If you believed that being is the maker of all things, you would *be* all day.

L: Hard to believe, All.

A: We know, but it won't be so hard if you ask to receive and *be*.

L: Shirking my responsibilities and watching every dollar flow out. No thank you. Too scary, and it's why at times I struggle to stay above water emotionally.

A: Egotionally

L: (laughing) Ha ha. You love to make up words, don't you.

A: Only to remind you of our ultimate divine truth.

L: I don't believe (obviously) based on my rantings, despite having written five books together. I need to see proof, and I never ever do in terms of money. I want a windfall of cash to show up, and then I will start believing and stop stressing.

A: Patience, dear One, All ways. You must trust to receive the askings you have put forth—all of you. You are One who needs everything now, and that is why you wait. You create a barrier between the world of divine knowledge and Love and the world of physicality. It's a cage Ones lock themselves in. Who has the key, dear One?

L: Me. But my, dear All, my key doesn't work.

A: It will if you would stay in constant connection to All. Ask in everything.

Help me receive a knowing. Stop these thoughts from bringing sadness. Keep me out of the path of fear and rage. I know who I am.

L: I've got 80,000 thoughts, and that's like a full-time job, and in order to pay my bills I need a job that pays money, not IOUs from Source. It's beyond frustrating to wait and wait and have more bills and less money. It comes and it goes. It never comes and creates. I'm always in a hamster wheel and have no time for myself, really. Just work, work, work and more work. I can't catch a break, and I know it's my own fault because I can't uproot this deep-embedded fear around money. Do you understand what I am saying here?

A: All ways do we know your thoughts because we are the thoughts. The thoughts which come from Love are true.

I am a magnet for good, and money arrives as I stay in truth.

Any thoughts of shame, fear, and distrust are you being separate from All. Nothing.

Know you are experiencing the All of Everything as One and ask to receive guidance within:

Help me, I am in time and feeling worthless and alone. Find me a place where I can be so I may close my eyes and divinely connect to Love.

Then you will be shown a way out.

L: Meditate. Well, today, rather than meditate (when I was feeling depressed), I took my son to an arcade for a few hours, and we had fun, and I forgot all of my troubles. So I didn't meditate—I found joy.

A: A job well done, but also know that at some point the old thoughts and beliefs may return to show where you are needing to uncover hidden beliefs and themes needed upended. Begin again. Ask to receive. No matter how many times you may fall the answer to being is to be reminded you are Love and allow new thoughts, beliefs, and ideas to formulate in mind. Then you will be on the way to peace and alignment to All.

We will always lend a hand (metaphorically) if you are asking to receive. It is the Law of Give and Take, as revealed in our last book together. That which is asked to be taken away is replaced, and every time this is done you are given more pieces of the spiritual puzzle. Imagine standing on a platform looking at a puzzle of infinite pieces and parts, and the only way to fill in the masterpiece is to say, *Show me the way,* or any other form of giving thoughts, beliefs, and fears over to All.

L: My dear All, I am tired of going back and forth between happiness and sadness. Is this hell? Be honest. Are we living in hell, because it sure seems like it?

A: As a child did it feel that way?

L: No.

A: What about in your youth, in your early twenties or thirties?

L: No.

A: Well, my dear, you have learned what most of the world is going through on Earth then. Bravo. Game won. Ups and downs, backs and forths. Heavy circumstances and challenging days are what most are facing. Would you say it has been "easy" to be here prior to the circumstances of lack and inefficiency in your life currently?

L: Not easy. Certainly easier. I had enough most of my life, until now. I had a well-paying job and worked most of my life and felt well enough physically. Now it's different.

A: Excellent. Now you are under no illusions of life's easiness. As burdens come and go, the challenges to surmount ego are immense. Yes, it's easier to overcome what is meant to disturb the balance of karma when you are feeling young and vital, which is why most sidestep chaos in youth. It is when the burdens of everyday life come that you are doing the learning you seek as soul.

L: I'm tired of learning. I'm tired of fear. I'm tired of this mixed-up, awful world we live in. I'm tired of being broke. I'm tired of all of it. I want a new life.

A: So create one, dear One. Know you are its creator and choose wisely thoughts and beliefs to move forward from fear.

I am One with All, and this is my life to make of it what I choose.

Let thoughts control you, or you control thoughts. This is the work you do on Earth. Untrue thoughts needed to be uprooted, returned to Love. You are making it hard and being failed by ego. It keeps showing you a vision of self which is old, tired, unliked, unloved, and broke. You are living in ego letting the soul be a friend but not a leader.

L: And how, dear All, may I let soul lead?

A: *Be.* Do not continue the life you are living in the same way you have been living it. Over and over you torture the self and wonder why the life isn't evolving to a better place. If you "know" All, you would live joyfully and express the self as One all day, every day—but it's difficult "to be" isn't it?

L: Immensely.

A: And so we ask all of you to connect as often as you can and do "the work" which allows joy and freedom more easily.

L: And what is "the work"? How do we free ourselves from this plain and boring existence with never-ending chaos, and violence, and disappointment?

A: Find joy. Journey outside you. Take a stroll in mind to a place of peace and surrender to All That Is. One day you will find all this has been purposeful in order to converse and create our materials. It will be as silly as when you worried about a career in television—which arrived—or the baby you so desperately sought as a thirty-year-old—who did arrive. Yes, there are times you won't get those desires, and it is because deeply embedded fears had their hand in the decisions you made to go away or leave it behind.

L: Sometimes it is so torturous to get out of your head and to even want to sit and be still to create a thing you want or desire. I can't seem to make myself stop scrolling or watching television. I just am so angry. Why can't it be easier? Why is amnesia so strong?

A: You asked for it to be, and you asked to stay sleeping until returning to Source (and even beyond) until you knew yourself as Love fully and completely—and that is the journey of ascension, dear One. Sunshine and rainbows and storms and chaos—a mix of both—necessary to the survival of the race on Earth. Without both there is no life on Earth, only oceans and streams, mountains and deserts. The species is dependent upon the ups and downs in order to stay physically focused. A vibration necessary to keep Ones on the planet as bodies in motion. Once the awakening arrives for every One on Earth, it will be time to escape the lessons of soul and adventure on. Earth remains as a planet but uninhabitable, as other planets became all over the cosmos and Infinite.

L: But you can't just "be" and have money arrive.

A: Do you see how insights are provided and you skip over them in fear? We are saying in order to be here on Earth, Ones must have contrast in the narrative, and you have focused on financial means and ignored our statement.

L: Sorry, dear All. Your instructions are impractical, and I know we have discussed it before, but I am telling you it doesn't work. Being

is a fantasy. Doing at least gives me a fighting chance of not being homeless or broke.

A: No. It is not going to work if you are doing all the same things over and over and expecting a different result. You *be* and do. Why not create a new routine where you spend most of the day being and not doing? Perhaps the financial crunch you are feeling is to show you how money is not a happy pill—but rather a mechanism for ease and flow. If you had money show up immediately, the ego would have a hold and you would want more and more and never be who you wish to be (a thought leader and teacher of metaphysics and healing) Now you understand how simple things are more aligned to All That Is—a life of ease and not struggle and no longer worrying about mansions and fancy cars, but rather more able to live simply without expectation.

L: That is true. I could live simply and be happy. I don't need much these days. Just to be at peace and to have money so I would not need to work anymore. And yes, I don't care about expensive anythings anymore.

A: Such is the journey of soul, to remind you of simplicity. And you decide if that suits you or not, as ego torments you with nonsense.

L: And how do we put ego aside?

A: Raise consciousness. Ask to receive. Let's set an intention for new experiences.

My intention is to create a habit of being. Let me awaken and find joy, express gratitude, meditate, and be.

My intention is to find work opportunities which allow me to have money while I am being.

My intention is to find time to be when I am in turmoil and emotion.

My intention is to honor the body temple and my home, to choose foods which bring me peace and good thoughts.

Choosing your life in intention, not letting the life choose you. Set an intention that you will spend the next thirty days in flow. Do as is needed, but mostly *be*. Meditate, appreciate, spend time with friends/family. Growth is minimal if you begin a day in hate and struggle. Begin the day with the following intention:

I am intending to be and do with ease and flow. Release the mind from its sadness and pain and allow the feeling of joy and appreciation. I accept my role as creator and live with intention and love. I am Love.

Then go about your routine. Add a meditative practice throughout the day. And set intentions when you find a thing not working. As quickly as old beliefs arrive, whisk them way.

This is untrue.

I am.

We are One.

Use words of Love.

You are wonderful and kind and part of All.

Put new thoughts and beliefs into a jar. Every time the mind is focusing on pain and sadness, take a slip of paper and write a new intention or belief.

I am focusing on fear… can become…

I choose Love instead. I am gaining a hold on thoughts and beliefs which are untrue.

Do this, and see, over time how many old thoughts were needing transformed. After a while, take out all the slips of paper and discover where you have shifted into a new you.

We offer practices and techniques instead of scrolling and surfing. You choose what is deserving of time on Earth, dear One.

L: Can you explain why intentions may work and what they are? I know we covered this in prior books, but for those who come to this new, they may not understand intentions.

A: Indeed. Ask → receive. An intention is a goal set in mind. Use it when you are feeling low or defeated. It tells the Source:

I am ready to receive new beliefs, thoughts, or ideas and this is the direction I wish to go.

It's a Sharpie of All. Once set, the asker is able to receive—if Ones overcome fear.

L: I'm trying to overcome, and it's why I am back here again seeking answers to my pain.

A: Someday you will know and trust and all of your experiences will be because you have decided as soul to create these books and materials. While you may question as part of the story of the life of Laura, it won't be so dramatic and rage-fueled as you (more and more) understand the journey of soul. What a marvelous teacher you will make as you overcome all of these insecurities and doubts by being. The voice will share your journey and hope with others and make a wise leader as One. Decide now, dear One. Are you able to rise above the ego and shine, or will you continue a song-and-dance of fear?

L: I want to so much. It makes me want to cry. I so long to be at that place, and I do understand much of my rantings and ravings were part of writing this book so everyone reading it understands how truly difficult it can be to overcome fear. How do I get out of this funk I am in?

A: Faithful belief in All.

L: Choosing Love and praying for change?

A: Blessing the soul and All.

6

Chapter 6/ Choose Love

Dear All, I am choosing to know Love and remember soul as I go through the work of being. Help me end suffering and pain.

666 — Karmic reoccurrences seeking to grow you through past decisions and into new expansions.

> *"It seems to be impossible to stay in vibration to Love," you say, and we say: impossible, no. Difficult, yes, if you are always focusing on the things which feel bad. Focus on Love and joy. Give yourself permission to be happy. "Dear All, please help me feel the joy of life and to love my experience on Earth with every ounce of my being. I know the tools are inside of me, and I use them daily, hourly, minute by minute to transform the fear into faith and knowing." Willingness is the chair you use to sit with All.*
> — Wisdom of The All

What does it take to evolve as Love? Let us dialogue on this as we explain the one thing needed to go All in discovering who *I am* is.

CHAPTER 6/ CHOOSE LOVE

Willingness

Who am I? Am I Love?

All is Love. Everything. Trees, grass, mountains, bikes, tables, ants, aardvarks—and even you are Love in a body, a body you chose before incarnating into being on Earth. What makes you able to discover who you are? Willingness.

All it takes to create a life of joy is a willingness. The All of you have the ability to go within, dig deep and find the magic Source. So many texts exist reminding you of your Isness. *I am* is the most important way to express the now. All Ones need do is *be*. Simple, yet complex, in that the world is full of distractions. Always are you being shown new ways to do and work.

Buy this. Use that. Take this quiz. Go this way. Get this done.

No matter what arrives, it is always for reminding you of Love. Choice is the way to align to the higher self. Questions are for bringing it to light:

- *Is this necessary?*
- *Will this work?*
- *Do I need to spend this?*
- *Shall I take this journey?*

Every time Ones ask, a receiving element exists to help discover the best use of time.

Is this necessary?

Only if it brings love.

Will this work?

Do you need it to be happy, or to make a dollar or a dent in your account? Make happiness the goal always.

Do I need to spend this?

Paying a bill if it holds you in security and peace, yes. Making a buck to buy accessories and frivolous nonsense, no.

Shall I take this journey?

Explore, love, laugh, live. Yes.

All answers are inside. The mind of Love is always showing you ways to *be*. Destroy ego, and it will become obvious what is fear and what is Love.

Ego has its place—to keep you safe in aspects of life as a human: to dodge a tree, pace yourself in races, or to simply decide for life based on beliefs of separation and fear. The entirety of life you will have the ego in its place to bring you feelings, emotions, and ideas about who you are separate from All That Is.

Laura: I took the 30 days suggested and spent time being (and doing, of course to pay my bills) but believe I am ready to begin a new chapter. I have a willingness to understand that everything I have been doing is because I wasn't trusting myself or Source but rather waiting for outside sources to help, heal, or make me whole. I hold myself responsible (with love) that I wasn't ready to know, but have recently become fully aware of my stumbles and missteps. I would like to shift out of a mode of seeking to be well known in this career and seek rather to be well-thy. Well in mind. Well in body. Well in spirit. And wealthy in life—and that being wealthy requires a mind of Love, not waiting for outside things to arrive but rather creating them first in thought and then inspired action and allowing.

As usual, you (we) wrote that.

A: Amen. What makes you able to remember this?

L: Asking to receive. Showing up for the messages and not getting hung up when the healing or having isn't happening in the time frame I would like to see.

A: Waiting as We. Wealthy everyone. When you wait as We, you are in control of ego. Everything goes out, and you wait longer when the side of you with fear is controlling the mind. You have to let the mind of Love in, always, in order to be able to create a shorter wait for things to arrive in physical. What starts in mind creates in body, and this takes a knowing of both good and bad. The mind is always creating, and the body is reacting in kind.

L: And sometimes not kind.

A: Indeed. It will show you what is going on inside the mind through bodily sensations and upsets. The stomach gurgles, the head is aching, cancer is slowly growing, and so on.

L: I have got one for you. A knee is twisted. This weekend I was laid up on the couch for two days because I turned my knee and heard a pop when I was getting something out of my car. It's the second time it happened, and I know immediately it was a manifestation of pride and ego around a particular situation I am moving through in my life. Fear is holding me back from peace, and guilt makes me feel bad.

However, this time I knew to ask for help, to sit with the pain and discover its purpose. I also asked for advice (so to speak) on what to do. Should I go to the urgent care? Did it require surgery? What was required? All of the answers came in that quiet soft voice, and instead of listening to fear, I took the advice with belief. I knew it wasn't as bad as before, and that it might be okay to give it a few days of rest. The fear of having to visit a doctor and the financial ramifications didn't bother me, as it normally would have. If I felt it necessary I would have gone, but something inside me (the voice of All) said resting, ibuprofen, ice/heat, and not walking on it would give me an idea of how bad the injury was.

The injury went away after about two weeks and so far has not returned. I was feeling aligned and happy for the first time in a long while, money was flowing in and I had come to really love my new house. But, in January 2022, I was diagnosed with osteoporosis, which felt like a slap to the face and yet somehow related to the knee issues. So I took to my computer once again to speak as All.

L: I'm really disappointed in this circumstance. Mostly in myself for manifesting it, and not being able to stop it prior. I should have paid more attention to my health after I broke my wrist, but I ignored it because of the financial ramifications, and I wanted to be able to stay healthy on my own.

A: On your own, as you know, is not the way to true health and healing.

L: Co-creation is. I know. What can I do to turn the tide on this? Is it possible to reverse? Heal it completely? Medical science says no.

What does the All say?

A: You can reverse nearly any circumstance beyond where the damage had been done. So it may not be as simple as going backward and regrowing the bone, but it can be minimized and turned back "on," so to speak. New cells form a protective layer and this is done in mind over time and medically if wanted—or with diet and exercise.

L: What about supplementation of certain vitamins?

A: This would fall under the category of medical or holistic. One being synthetic and the other plant protons and ions.

L: And which is better? Holistic or pharmaceuticals?

A: You are wanting us to vilify the scientific strides being made in the field of medicine, and while there are some we would warn against as they are purely profit-motivated, there are plenty of scientifically backed and well-researched pharmaceuticals that may very well heal the bones or other areas of the body that have been diseased.

This is, of course, the reason why you avoid the medicines, and we know recently you have been opened in your beliefs to the idea that not all medicine made in laboratories are particularly bad. In fact, you recently wrote a caption in which you stated *"This might be the very thing you prayed for to heal the pain or problem."* So you know enough now to go beyond the chastising of medicine and decide from a place of soul what is to be used and what is not.

L: Well, this feels as if it's a circumstance that is particularly for holistic approaches before turning toward medicine. That is what I intuitively feel is the path. Do you agree, dear All?

A: It is. Now go forth and make steps in mind and body to create that belief and you will see a very different result at the next scan.

L: I plan to do all those things including meditation and co-creation, as well as changing the diet I am eating to an even more plant based diet and limiting sugar intake.

A: Sugar is only detrimental in large quantities, and as we have mentioned prior (*The All of Everything*) because of its processed nature. So while we agree to minimize the amount and find pure sources, we would remind you the nature of sugar is the plant is for consumption and needn't be over stripped of its value and bleached. It is the processing that profitizes it further and that is why the health issues occur.

Return to our chapter on toxins in *Wisdom of The All* for further clarification on things which are unsuitable for the body/mind.

L: The other news I received today was that I have an issue on my right breast that a mammogram showed and need to go for an ultrasound. This is the second time it has happened—

A: As is common in the journey of soul.

L: Why?

A: So you may know to return to Love, which as you know, most don't. They instead return to fear almost immediately, as you have. Every pang is a ping. Each time you notice the mind's manifested fear in body, ask to be guided to what is causing the bellow within.

Help me decipher this fear so I may heal it with Love.

Take an inventory of your fears and follow the lead of the body's clues and cues to notice and net them. Give them back to All for reversal into Love.

What is this fear, and how can I support the healing of it for self and soul?

L: I'm not fully in fear because of the past situation, but it's concerning. It doesn't feel like anything, but I have seen someone I know on social media—who is a yoga and meditation teacher— recently be diagnosed with breast cancer. So here is someone who knows the journey of soul and still got sick. So, I think it's my turn to be, because it's so hard to stay healthy in this world because of all the toxic thoughts and ingested toxins.

A: Remember you have seen others who have miraculously cured dire issues and know it is possible when you remember All and believe. Keep discovering truth through everyday acts of faith. Meditate, journal, and always ask to receive when trouble arrives:

What is the lesson of this, and how can I move beyond it?

Take every diagnosis as a lesson in patience and trust. Use the inner voice to discuss the next steps, and ask to receive guidance—which may come in many forms. For instance, you have witnessed a possum in the yard just now.

L: Yes ,and of course I knew it was a message for me about resiliency. What else was its message?

A: Stay true to the path of resistance and you will find fault with it. If you hide the issue and ignore it, it may become manifest as a darker circumstance than need be. Bring it to the light and make it known, and then go deep to find its answer. Most on Earth hear bad news and then take it as law rather than discover for themselves (via All) what it means and how it arrived.

L: How did the breast issue arise?

A: So we may discuss it here as we have other issues in past books. Use the voice of All whenever a fear arises. Oppositionary thought to ego is Love:

I'll be fine, and this is just a hiccup in the journey of health.

L: What if, maybe, something worse is afoot? I don't feel like it is, but I kind of do in other areas when it comes to the staircases, or my clearly brittle bones.

A: Thinking of a circumstance means it's possible to bring it forth, but if you brush it aside, the chances are more likely to have it evolve into something it needn't be. So the best recourse is to re-course—to follow a new path out of the fear. Draw a map in the mind to the beginning or ending. For example, take a moment to see yourself healthy, leaving the office after the exam, with a smile on your face and a hitch in your step. What is seen in mind is what is possible in body.

L: I do see that, but how do I know if I am just making it up?

A: There is no such thing as "made up." There is only what exists as possibility. Nothing else exists.

L: Well, earlier today I got an image of a body bag being taken out of my home which seemed nonsensical, but also a little scary. So you are saying that—something that silly—was still possible?

A: If focused on day in and day out, then yes. However, knowing it's a silly vision (as inspired for the purpose of conversation here) is enough to know it has no need to manifest and can be given to the All.

Help me, dear All, release this unwanted vision that has entered my mind. I give it back to be transmuted forever.

L: What if I see myself being a billionaire, or driving off a cliff, or getting my arm sawed off in a factory—even though I don't work, and never will work, in one?

A: Perhaps, as part of the process of life, you are shown what happened in other lives in order to keep you away from such experiences. Witnessing it, while seemingly nonsense, is merely an old "memory" that no longer need be. So you whisk it away, knowing it was not possible here.

It may also be a joint experience—both as body in mind and mind in body—meaning your soul "mate" in other realms is having the thing happening to them. You recently saw (in a dream) the face of a man whom you recognized as another version of you in another life. Sometimes what you see or feel may not belong only to you. It may be the echo of another self, another version of you, living out its own story in another time or realm. This is not to confuse you, but to remind you that you are infinite— many lives, many expressions, one soul. What seems nonsensical (a vision of danger, an unfamiliar face) may simply be a memory surfacing, or the experience of another you finding its way into your awareness. In those moments, it is important to pause and clear what does not belong in this body, in this now.

Move me out of the timeline of fear of another me. Help me stay focused in now.

L: Yes, last night, actually I had awoken and saw his face and had that immediate realization. It was spooky, but also kind of cool to get a glimpse of another me somewhere else in time. What was its message, may I ask?

A: Asking is a gateway to All, and it's important to reveal it here so those in tune with what we are saying know to clear fear in regards to other bodies or entities. Remember you are One and the voices and visions of other yous may impact the life you currently inhabit. So it is imperative, once you understand this, to relinquish the impacts of the choices other yous make.

Now, to say it is fear is incorrect, for Earth is the one planet where fear is the opposite to the journey of unconditional Love every One is on. Rather, it is the entities' or bodies' existential condition which impacts their lives. Therefore, it could be many different types of experiences the other yous are having. We would ask you to simply "clear the air," so to speak:

Help me, dear All, remember I am a whole being with infinite selves. I ask to be guided when other mes are in uncomfortable experiences or unfamiliar places.

This would be wise to do on days where you are wondering if another you is experiencing a "thing" from which they are suffering or ailing. Then may you declare that a challenge isn't yours to hold, and ask to receive a snipping off from that life—a tether or cord binding you is released. You will still meet in the other realm of nonphysical, but the "memory" of another is redacted in this life.

L: What if we are intrigued and want to follow the memory?

A: As long as the memory isn't stirring fear or chaos within, you are welcome to do as you please on Earth. Free will is the choice the collective made. We simply remind you to clear what is fear.

Work, Work, Work (part 2)

Now is not the time to work harder—it is the time to do inner work. Work on finding peace, balance, and letting go of judgments of One's self and others. Work on healing past hurts and old wounds, and unbridled optimism will begin to emerge rather than layers of hate and venom. You are nowhere near finished on the journey you call life, and it is up to you to do the soul work—not the actual work, dear Ones. Relax. Rest. Elevate. Live. And Xanadu is yours, every One.
— Wisdom of The All

I paused our conversation for a while as I navigated work and being a mom. I was happy to find the protocols working on my osteoporosis, and my scan looked better than before. So good was happening, but work was weighing on me as I was not doing my job writing with the All, but rather a job to make money.

L: Who set up this awful work situation where all we do is hustle and grind? At what point did we switch from being to working to the bone every day, a slave to money and time? I find myself now wanting to work less and less which, of course, is currently impossible as I don't have the financial means to retire. As a young student I was a hustler, a fighter and had an incredibly strong work ethic, and now I'm out of juice. I would be happy to write, garden, cook, hit the gym, do yoga, and spend my days outdoors. If I never—well, maybe not never, but working is not my dream anymore. It's being without fear and being free financially. I would work as a choice rather than a must, which is where I sit. I hate the hustle I have to go through in order to not be broke. I hate asking others for money, and I hate that everyone is trying to sell me something. I mean, you cannot catch a minute of peace from stuff being sold to you. Money is evil.

A: It is a narrative you chose on Earth to have "heroes" and "villains." Just like any movie arc, it becomes hard to overcome the empire of fear and challenging to be free. The noise of Earth is purposefully loud in order to evolve because at the cornerstone of Love is an ability to choose freely wherever you exist. Whether it's nonphysical or physically focused in all realities, choice is the way. You can tune out or tune in. You can buy or steal. You can win or whine. You can ask for help or forget it and live separate from Source in mind. So the choice to put money in play came for Earth beings to use to get, give, and receive.

Yes, it is true it has become a magnet for fear and manipulation, but it also serves a purpose to build upon Earth. Before this, temples and churches and smaller structures got made but not buildings or roads and tracks. The use of money created an industry of commerce, creating spaces for inhabitants to live and work. We know it is easy to chastise the medium because of the intrusive nature of ego, but it is purposeful and necessary, and while it may change (pun intended) and become more digitally focused, the paper-and-coin system is part of Earth and always will be. Its form may change over and over, but the need to have the operating system is important for the planet's evolution.

L: We didn't need it back in the earlier centuries though. We had a barter system. Why can't we barter and not have to deal with a hierarchy of the haves and have-nots? That system worked, didn't it?

A: For a while it worked until inhabitants began needing shelter from storms and winters created as fear overtook the minds. Then a goat for a chicken or a pie for a rupee wasn't enough. We needed a system in order to create (as above) roads and structures to house the people in time.

L: It worked before though. So why not just continue? Maybe we could have figured it out. Aren't there still places where this barter system still exists? Small island nations? We don't need money. Especially the way it's created mass toxic waste on Earth. Commerce is killing Mother Earth.

A: We know it is chastisement you wish for us to speak forth, but this is not truth. We are using money for purposes of soul growth for those who both do and do not have it. The choice is whether you revere or fear the mighty dollar, cents, or other monetary currency on Earth.

L: You can't revere what you don't have, dear All.

A: Absolutely Ones can if they ask to receive the help needed to close the gap of Love and fear.

Help me loosen my grip on that which I have received in time. I know giving and receiving go hand in hand, and so often I hold onto things to keep myself protected, not understanding the inner experience of holding is a grip while the letting go an outstretched hand.

Which is more likely to bring something? A closed fist or a hand outstretched?

L: Well, obviously a hand outstretched because—

A: Now you have means to receive and to grasp or pick up what is desired.

L: It does make sense.

A: Cents.

L: LOL. I was going to write that.

A: Of course. We are One.

L: It doesn't feel like One though. It feels as if I am having a conversation with someone else. I ask a question and the answer received back is coming from another entity. I hear the words return immediately in my mind, but as Laura alone, I am not capable of these profound insights and coming up with ideas like the one above. It just doesn't compute without these "conversations."

A: Because, dear One, you have chosen to create books as part of your narrative on Earth, and so the words come easily and effortlessly as they were waiting to be received. However, when typing are your hands outstretched or in a fist?

L: Outstretched.

A: This is how you receive. Be willing to ask questions with hands outstretched and the part of your mind that is All comes through to gift you with the wisdom. There are millions more awakening upon Earth, and will continue to do so for millennia and more. You are simply One of thousands who are channeling as All whether its Source, God, Universe, or any number of other languages and words used. So you are sharing vastly important works even if understood you are one of millions awakening. Every One feels called to share what is their enlightening perspective (as One) because the call to a more peaceful world is strong. Share not to give to receive, but because you have called yourself to the experience in order to evolve. Yes, not everyone is meant to be teachers or share their words outwardly, but you, dear One, are, and it is the choice you make. You may keep to yourself what is known of how All works, or share the inspired as it comes forth, which you have done as we wrote the above.

All things are meant to evolve you, dear One, no matter what the outcome. Yes, there are inspired notions we make with and for you, but not everyone is going to be about dollars and cents. Some are to provide more fodder for books and materials like these ones. Remember each already has been written and this is why it's easy for you to find words and phrasings. Not everything will fail. So we ask that you keep moving forward.

Keep going. Don't let the delay deny. You are caught in a web of ego, keeping you stuck in negative beliefs about time. Nothing comes instantly, even when created in mind. The planet depends on lag—Love, Alignment, God—to make anything manifest in time. *Is it worth the wait?* You decide, dear One. That decision is what halts, hinders, or helps you in making matter as One.

Ask, *"What is the lesson here, dear All? What shall I share and why?"* Then wait to see as answers arrive what is the best option. Share it or skip it? We know and allow you know as well, if only you remember to ask. Why else did we create our books and journals together? To remind you to ask to receive, of which you have been doing more and more of each day on Earth. So would you say, dear child, they have brought nothing to you the time spent on them each day?

L: They have brought me plenty, dear All. I agree.

7

Chapter 7 / No Child Left Behind

D ear All, as I live and breathe, remind me to Love.

777 — It's got roots in mind needing uprooted. Let it bring you inward to define who you are.

A villain is our ego in full control. We have oft said the story of you is ego vs. soul, and so to know you are in charge of the experience means any One being evil is living in villainous ecstasy, as ego gets its way, and the only way to quell the ego's rule is to ask to receive truth. Evil? Live? One is living in reverse and the other is true Love. Help me find the hero in me.
— Wisdom of The All

Why?

About a year ago I wrote the title for this chapter, or rather shall I say "We" wrote it. I never know why this happens, or what the titles will mean, but somehow they always make sense to the life I am living and the life of others' experiences in the world I see later on as I'm writing.

So this chapter title, *No Child Left Behind*, which I wrote back in 2021, unfortunately made sense after a horrific tragedy. I have found myself (within these *The All* books) asking questions out of sheer rage and disgust, never making light of or sensationalizing traumas, always wanting to find the response at the metaphysical or spiritual level.

On May 23, 2022, a young man walked into a school in Uvalde, Texas, and killed two teachers and nineteen students, most of whom were around the age of ten. I have a middle-school-aged son, and while I have witnessed and heard about other school shootings, including the one in Parkland, Florida (just fifteen minutes from my house), which killed seventeen people, mostly teenagers, this one hit so immensely close to home.

I cannot imagine the pain these parents are feeling. How awful to think of what those children experienced and the horror of what they must have gone through. As a psychic medium who is able to communicate with those who have crossed over, I do know they are eternally blessed souls and still here in Spirit, but it doesn't take away the pain of the human experience and the loss of life. As a mother, I find myself always torn between my human and my soul in these moments of humans and evil in terms of children. Innocent lives disrupted by violence is where I draw the line in the notion of "everything happens for growth and evolution as souls."

I returned to my Q&A angry and distressed, knowing the answers will be aligned to Source and not fear, bringing me back to higher truths, but still wanting a discussion anyway.

Laura: This is the most disgusting and vile act of humanity, and I know you tell us always to see the "illusion," and that "anything coming from fear is not real," but God, it feels real, looks real, and is unfathomable why Source, the Universe or what we are calling it, the All, would ever allow this to happen. It's–well–I don't have words here that don't include an expletive.

All: We are willing to engage, and you may speak freely without judgment or reserving words.

L: It's fucking disgusting. Criminal, in fact, that this system you designed on Earth allows for the killing of children. Despicable

and horrifying and ridiculous. Why on Earth would we allow for nonsense like this? Little children, barely alive for any years, to be murdered by a fucking lunatic. First it was Covid, then a war in Ukraine, now school shootings are back to being front-page news nearly every other fucking week. It's ridiculous and cruel, and I'm sorry, dear All, but I don't under-fucking-stand any of it.

A: It's not that you cannot understand. You know our reasons for criminal acts, war, murder, and other chaos on Earth. It's that you do not agree with the ways we awaken to truth because at all moments on Earth it is real to you. To those who are aligned back to Source, they know of its allusive nature.

L: I know you purposely wrote *allusive* and not *illusive,* because I heard that word just the other day thinking it was wrong. What do you mean by *allusive?*

A: It is chosen by *All* to decide for fear on Earth, as it is a planet designed to bring transformation for the hardest of circumstances. It is more deceptive than you know, meaning the soul is alive inside, but you are living the lie as if it's real in order to grow. We have said prior in our books (written through you) how to grow and evolve you must believe it to be real—all of it. It's like the difference between being in the movie and watching it. We are in the movie *and* watching it, while you are in the movie—casts and characters. We know it is real in "heaven" (as we call it on Earth) and false on Earth. You are the patron, and we are its producer. We are the audience, and you the cast. Once it's understood you are All, it can become easier on Earth to live the lie and see the noise on Earth as movies of mind. It's a play within a play and a cast of eight billion souls. Some you are never going to meet, and others you will see their play, and a few you are in the story and, of course, living one of your own. It's all illusion for One.

L: It doesn't change the fact that even if it is "illusion," we should not be killing children. EVER. Not fucking ever. Can I take over this experiment of the All because I would like to change the rules for engagement?

A: It is not ever changing. It is because you suffer in time you question it.

When you are in Spirit it would not be as "evil" as you say it is, because you are understanding the nature of reality and time. When you are on Earth, it is purposefully forgotten in order to grow as fast as possible. There are (as revealed in other *The All* books) places and realms where you do evolve as souls through less chaos, and transformation is slower. So the All of you are understanding (as individual and collectively) of the nature of being, but it doesn't give you the breakthroughs and transformation that Earth does, and so you choose (as soul) to experience the ups and downs on Earth.

L: I would like to live on a purposefully peaceful planet then, please, instead, because as much as you say its "fun" and all part of the "illusion," it's a pretty pathetic and horrible one. Does God watch horror movies and laugh, so this is the idea of entertainment? I mean, my god, it's all so insane this world, really.

A: We know it is tragic and awful to see it from the human perspective and not All. It is why we offer our wisdom and guidance to those seeking a new understanding, but as we have also said to all, you cannot awaken those who do not wish to be awoken. It must be chosen in One's agreement or will of incarnation to be awakened. So offering you the words here are the way to move you out of fear and into Love.

L: I'll need to work on that. It's a difficult choice to make because it all feels so real. Yet again, more gun violence this week as a town in Illinois was attacked by some evil kid with a gun. Just like Uvalde, Just like Parkland, just like Columbine, just like Newtown. Kids killing kids. It's despicable. Why are children aiming guns at children? If you are going to take out anyone how, about the evil doers? Go to a place where at least we have a fighting chance. Why does this love-over-fear battle involve kids dying? We only care about life if it's our own and not anothers.

A: It's love and fear in motion. It doesn't feel unreal because you asked for it to feel real, and this is why the awful circumstances occurring on Earth are so unbearable to participate in or watch on screen. Each knows what they came to achieve on Earth as soul, and if you were to ask All what is their reasoning for the worst thing to occur, it would be understood as soul.

As human, it's chastising another for being unlike the self and destroying a fear. Those who do harm believe they are in service, not understanding it is "of fear" they serve—ego. Ego is how you come to be in consort with a sword, dagger, gun, or poison. It becomes unclear you are Source, and you go through life believing in separation and that life is happening to you, and not through you. So you decide if you are alone and unloved, everyone else deserves to be as well. A life taken in fear. Those who do terrible things on Earth do not see life as precious, so to take a life to them is present.

L: *Present?*

A: *Pre-sent.* Meaning, it's a possibility which existed should they stay on the road to fear. All things exist as possibility, as it exists already in the mainframe of the experience. A ladder of consciousness would show they are a *Victim* (more on this later). Living in lower frequencies of fear which is the arrival stage they began in, or where choices made eventually landed them. It's like taking a suitcase filled with all of the things you may use on vacation, only to find by day three or four you don't need half the things you have brought. You take out what you like and leave the rest. However, if you are someone who has no recollection of Source and All, the suitcase contains nothing—no favorite thoughts or beliefs to use. You think you are alone and unloved, or that you are here to destroy the planet's inhabitants, who you see as enemies.

L: **I find it strange that this country's leaders are so concerned about babies being aborted, and yet a gun killed how many innocent children in 2022 so far, and it doesn't matter to them. They won't make changes to the gun laws that will protect our precious babies. It's maniacal.**

A: Fear at war with Love.

L: **I don't know, All. I give up. A voice of reason in a world of sleepers. Too many fearful—**

A: Hypocrites?

L: **What makes them hypocrites?**

A: Worthy opponents to Love. We guide you to think more clearly. What makes someone a hypocrite? Thinking they are alone in the fight for Love.

You say you want peace, and yet continue to spew hatred toward your fellow man here. Is a word not as damaging as a weapon? If everything is energy (and it is), doesn't it make sense that their and your poison are same? You must keep thoughts to Love in order for change to occur on the planet as a whole.

L: I'm the hypocrite you are meaning? Because rather than bring Love through as the voice of All, I speak ill toward everyone on Earth, and that is unhelpful because we are meant to be Love?

A: See everything as imperfectly perfect, and you are being All. Fight and argue and tear apart your fellow Earth partners, and it's ego in full force, be it guns and ammo or words and wishes. Each thought has an energy; a vibration gets sent out collectively, and everyone who fights and frets causes more ripples of fear, while love creates its own force, which, when used in connection with All, is the way to peace. Love All. If what you desire is peace, then Ones cannot speak in sentences of fear and anguish. Its energy is same as guns and ammo, my dear.

L: I can't see it that way. I would like to fight for our world and shake people awake. Who is in charge? Can I speak to the person in charge up there? I would like to rebel against this asinine way of evolving.

A: You are the person "in charge," as am I. We are all One. So I speak for All. You speak for All. We all are it.

L: Okay, then can I speak to my spiritual counterparts who are in nonphysical to ask them some questions, please?

A: You can if "they" (meaning All) are willing, which of course, they are. *Ask to receive* is the design of Earth, and many other existences in our Infiniteness.

L: What do other beings think of Earth?

A: A most challenging adventure worth the ride of fear.

L: What about souls who come to Earth and leave heaven behind?

A: On Earth (sleeping), they believe it to be a most exciting adventure, until a conditioned mind intercedes, dependent upon the contracts of the soul. For some it is quite early—around age seven or eight. For others, more time is needed to process before challenges present themselves through you.

L: What about once they return to heaven and look back on life?

A: No one attends the school of Earth without saying, "yes," to its entrance fee of fear, no matter which age is chosen. You are, however, asking how Ones feel once the full separation occurs, and that would be when they begin fear and love as deistically opposed. Then it is a troubling experience, which is why we offer wisdom, guidance, and tools. The reason our books and materials exist is to help understand the "rules" of the All. They know it's a blip that comes with bops and challenges.

L: And what of spirits and souls in heaven?

A: They understand it at various levels of separation. Our messengers of hope and healing (referred to as Angels) would explain exactly as we have here—they are One. Those in separation, as Spirit, do understand Love is the energy from which All come, and yet realize it is a journey of length and time, and some would enjoy while others adventure on to become Love. It depends who you ask.

L: Let's ask an angel—Angel Michael, known as a protector.

Michael: I do think it to be fun, but understand while "sleeping" it feels torturous on some days. Remember you have access to *INformation* where it can show you a different experience—one in which you could be having if you stay more aligned to Love. It took us (angels, or rather archangels as you have deemed us) an infinite amount of experiences before discovering and becoming One. So we do know the experience, and it's the very reason we chose to stay nonphysical and energetically aligned to All planets and places. To help you is Love at its purest form—an honor and a pleasure to serve when asked by the bodily learners. Ones must know, asking is our way of allowance.

Help me. I need help. This I cannot do alone.

Once asked, we step forward with delight.

L: What about someone like my dad, who stayed on Earth for a while and left via suicide?

A: He went to our hospital of the heart and soul (as had been discussed in prior books.) Then he went to a planet of healing and hope where Love is expressed as a species. Helpful, kind, wonderful is a way to describe it. You learn in a slow, slow manner and it can be mundane—but for our heart-centric loved Ones, a perfect stop before another try at Earth.

L: Can I go there? I don't ever want to come back to Earth once I leave here.

A: Ego says. It will become clear once you return to "our side" of what it meant to be human. Some return never knowing they are soul and soul alone. You have decided for our materials to understand what is possible on Earth to remember. There is much learning yet to do, and the soul has a plan, as do you.

L: Sometimes this books seems like fiction, All. Made up stories to make people feel better in a world of war and criminals. I could see someone finding this book and saying I clearly "made this all up." And yet how it was written, as that inner dictation; I know it to be true without accepting it fully in my life. I try to come to terms with these truths, but then get mad, sad, and frustrated often.

However, the amount of signs and synchronicities over the last eight years I have witnessed while writing the books—it clearly can't be fantasy, our words. I don't even remembering the first four books. Every time I read them again, it's like reading someone else's book. The chapter on guns in *The All of The All* made me realize I was not just making up words. This was coming from a whole different place inside of me. Back then, I was more in a place of believing it was all outside of me—but I get it now. We are One. Our words, not just mine, or yours, are being shared. Can I ask, what can we do as parents to help our children be safe in this world of illusion, as you call it?

A: As One is All, you can seek wisdom of soul and decide from this perspective. Even children are at choice to view that which is false and fear. So if you stay in connection with the higher self, it can show you ways to engage that will help each understand lessons and situations.

L: I will, however challenging it is to accept, continue to listen and receive and do my best to understand. Until it happens to me, and

that is where the fear is. What if all of these tragedies come knocking on my door? Or my family's, or friends?

A: There is much fear to be overcome within you, and it is best to stay in connection with us and receive wisdom and information to overcome the fearful intent of ego. Remember, its job is to bring fear through mind, which is why it is imperative you turn to Source as thoughts arrive. Ask to receive.

Remind me of Love, dear All, as I sit in fear of earthly circumstances.

Do All things to protect yourself with energy modalities and mindful tools. The programming of Earth is always reminding you to fear, and its playbook is terror and confusion. So you must always be in connection to soul to receive a new belief. Trust soul and not ego—Earth's greatest obstacle.

Return to All

Now is the time to go seeking. You have done the work beyond what you thought possible, and now you must go further in order to examine and relieve. It is the mightiest work you may ever do, but it is necessary to the growth of soul. The quest is long, but the journey is worth the rewards. Seek and ye shall find, dearest One. What exists in mind is to be worked through, examined, and released. What is Love is truth, and fear is false. Remember every One?
— Wisdom of The All

It is now May 2024. Two years have gone by since this last conversation. I stopped writing this book and instead worked on creating a yearly journal (*Journal of The All*), utilizing the thousands of quotes I had been channeling with the All since 2019 for my Instagram page, @wisdomoftheall.

So rather than ask questions, I read and reread the words I received in those quotes and my other books—many which have been shared here at the beginning of each chapter heading and throughout—as well as working on journal prompts to go along with the quote of the day for the journal. That process helped keep me out of the rabbit hole my mind had dug around events and circumstances. So questioning the world wasn't necessary, as I went back through my work consistently. I wasn't talking to (or as) the All; I was integrating.

After publishing my first journal, it became a best seller on Amazon in its category. My client base was growing too, and I found myself more free of fears. I witnessed tragedies and travesties without emotionally triggering the way I used to. I was more able to see it through the lens of Source.

Despite the world itself being in a freefall of fear, I felt better about my world, with the exception of one area—finances. In the winter of 2024, almost out of savings, I had (or, I guess, the All, would say, "chose") to go back to work in a job I felt beneath me. At the same time, I was up for a position at a local news station in North Carolina, to do what would have been a dream gig hosting a morning show—if the money aligned—but it was way lower than anyone should have accepted for that role with my experience as a host. I refused to devalue myself in that way, saying "no" to moving forward, and took a part-time job at a wellness center making way less money, but having to do less work and leaving ample time for me to continue working with clients and writing.

L: I'm back for more questions finally. I am struggling with a knee injury again. I felt I had a hold on it, but it seems to keep hanging on, and I'd like to know why. I looked it up to find out what Louise Hay (a pioneer in mind/body connections) had said. She wrote in her book, *You Can Heal Your Life* (which I now realized was written similar to how ours was—"channeled") about not feeling supported in life, and that made perfect sense to me because of what we had already discovered about knees around pride and ego.

I feel very "less than" working at this new wellness center. I said to my friend on Friday, after I was asked to vacuum the floors—sort of joking, but also not joking—"Wow, I used to be on red carpets. Now I am sweeping them. How far the mighty have fallen." I feel very

grateful to have this opportunity, but also feeling like my worth has depreciated—and not sure how to overcome that feeling.

A: Asking is key here. What is changed is guided by thoughts and emotions using the mind of Love.

Help me see this as a stone for good and not fear.

L: I want to see it as good, and for growth, but Laura is not going to do that. Laura, who once held a coveted position in television, feels frustrated and embarrassed, and so I need help moving through this. First off, what is the lesson here for me?

A: Have a seat. Sit in more silence. What better way to remind you to listen to the voice of All than to have you not able to walk, run, or go far. You often go off for lengths of time (two years here) and won't come to the table of mind. We await the return to finish our divine book. So it gets you back here, and it was asked (by you) as soul to make circumstances available if need be, and it was necessary to return to All.

L: So, I am here because I left for so long and didn't return.? It has taken me almost four years to finish this book, whereas my other books were written in much less time. I have been focused on career and finances because breaking through the barrier of fear around finances feels impossible.

A: Delightfully we have placed a word in time meaning the exact opposite. *I'm possible.* Is this not its true meaning?

L: For you, it is. For most of us, it's not. It's limitations and lack we live with on Earth. I have to get up tomorrow and head to work. Work I would rather not be doing, or at least don't want to have to do. It would be much different if I had the funds to "just be."

A: Ego has you tied up and bound, and will forever be the terror of mind. You cannot not come back to Love to move out of fear. The only way to be happy is to ask to receive. The *only* hurdle is mind. Mind makes or breaks. It complains or it co-creates.

Help me, guide me, lead me to Love.

The mechanism to overcome is always, as said here before, asking for help and leaning into All That Is. One's must utilize truths of All and not fears of ego. The mind is choosing each moment whom to be. Words are wands. They cast (like a line in fishing) and bring forth. So if Ones continue dialoguing in fear, it (whatever is being thought), keeps showing up for you. Ones must switch the gear of fear into Love. It is simple and "hard," as you have shown in the books we created together. It can be difficult, as life circumstances and worldly events (designed to keep fear in motion) are always being filtered through One's lens.

Help me see this through Love.

Design a day with Love. Keep returning to our books until you understand simplicity is choice. Make mind work for you and not ego. Always ask to be helped in discovery of self.

Is this true?

Love.

Is this fear?

False.

L: I'll try my best to come back each day to ask questions until we finish our book.

A: Bravo. We are forward-thinking and able to design a life of ease if you find time to *be* and engage with All. To overcome what is fear, you must be willing to trade ego for soul. Stop overthinking: use Love, divine souls.

8

Chapter 8 / Awareness

D ear All, remind me the climb is mine to take back to Love.

888 — Infinite Source guiding the way to Love.

How simple to remember you are Love, forget you are
fear, and live joyfully throughout life. Spirit guides you
to and through challenges in order to remind you back to
Love. Forgetting is optional now. You can remember every
moment and sidestep many unpleasantries throughout life
if only would you stay in connection with All That Is.
— Wisdom of The All

This will be our last chapter of Q & A before Laura begins an ascension in Love. Her questions are purposefully meant to engage ego, for there are many people out there finding Source and asking similar questions of themselves—without realizing they too are All. Our books and materials are meant to be used again and again until you decide for Love at all times. The time has come to move to deciphering our symbols, codes, and messages without fear tagging along.

Endings and Beginnings

Laura: I want to say, "I'm happy" and believe it, but the truth is never am I able to keep happy alive for more than a month or two. I was doing well for a while, which is why I went away for a long stretch. I thought I had it. I was understanding who I am and who All is, but I recently found myself in a another tailspin. My mind isn't able to keep peace in it for too long.

Right now my skin is a mess. I have a rash under my arm and a tiny lump. I was coughing up a lung (figuratively) this morning. The cough is making me think I have lung cancer because I can't get rid of the feeling in my throat and sternum. I think maybe I have some type of lymphoma because of the little spot under my arm. It's been itchy the last week. My eyes are dry and my knee isn't healed from the last trip.

I can't get healthy to a point where I'm excited for life. And the truth is that every time I ask for help, I feel better, then something else comes along and I am back where I started—in fear.

All: Ego.

Laura: I know I am being super irrational here, but sometimes, I wonder if it's me dying. Am I dying?

A: A death of sorts, yes—a physical one only you can decide as soul.

L: Then is my soul inclined to go or stay?

A: Stay, if you are willing. Suffice it to say we are meaning *spiritual ascension*, and not coming out of body. There is more to learn on Earth, and (as we had shown prior), a reality exists where you are quite older and with grandchild or children around you.

L: But it's upon me to create that experience?

A: Indeed, dear One. Health is a mind away. Commit to daily exercise, truth telling, loving kindness—and most importantly, for you (and many others), to learn to love the self. Every factor of your health is impacted with fear around value.

I am valuable because I am Divine.

When Ones see themselves as All, the Love you seek opens the door to all healing capabilities. But why do you keep focusing on fear?

L: Because I can't get my mind out of it no matter how much I work on the thoughts. They just return again and again, and I only have pockets of time where I feel happy, as I said. Maybe a month or two is the record where I feel good and light and fear is diminished.

Then, eventually, the mirror makes me angry, and when I see videos of myself I now realize I'm old. For a long time, I looked pretty much the same but it's creeped up on me—this older person. I don't know who she is, because I don't feel as if I am that old, despite my health issues right now. My inner is not matching my outer.

A: Why not see the self through the eyes of All, which has no beliefs and fears of aging? We know who you are, and you know who you are now, too. You cannot accept it because vanity is ego holding you to the light of choice, doing its job perfectly, dear One—to make you feel sick, tired, and old. Ones would remember if they tried. Look. Listen. Reveal. We are with you, as you. I see you as Love, and that is All, dear One.

L: This is the last chapter to ask questions, but for me it's still a beginning. I'll never win. Ego is strong and I feel defeated and distraught right now.

A: Not for long, dear One. It is the end of consciousness as fear. We are asking you to understand the soul is always involved and has you making decisions at times where you needed to write this book. It has been troubling to ask questions, receive answers and go back to sleep, but know it was the process of our *The All* books. You are ready to awaken to joy.

Our journey together, though fraught with much fear, is getting easier and easier, with soul guiding the moves you have made to this point. It will become about joy, focusing on surrendering to Love and asking in all circumstances to be guided through. One is realizing they are All too—and living as it.

Help me, dear All, realize a purposeful journey is at an end. I am able to move to a higher plane and leave behind fear.

L: I hope it's true.

A: If you make it so by word and thought, it will be.

I am whole and healed.

Fearfulness is a tiring process to uproot. Just know every time you ask to receive new truths, you are working your way back to it—every time. It won't be so hard as you continue to evolve in the conscious way you have been, as less need to ask-and-receive book reSources are necessary. We are complete in our series and journals.

L: Yes, but every time I move ahead it feels as if I take many steps backward too. For as much time as I spend writing quotes, teaching online, working with clients as an intuitive or medium, and asking to be helped through, I should be at a much farther place than I currently am. My health is weighing me down.

A: This is where soul reminds you of Love by being ill. The moment a shift is made to Love, it interrupts fear and each time you enact fear, it builds up like plaque or dust. Rinse and repeat. Ones must clear the mind of its fears every day. You must know a clock ticks, not jumps. Second by second, you move through each day, and we know it's challenging to slowly evolve and grow, but leaps and bounds require harder chains.

L: I guess I can understand that. I would rather slowly evolve than deal with a big circumstance which slaps me in the face.

A: Little by little is the way many prefer to evolve as soul. You know it's change which is needed and do it with slow growth. Ones can't take the ladder to a top rung unless going to each step, or it risks a fall. One's growth is slow, and it keeps you moving and vibrating at the level needed to be on Earth. Go too fast, and you evolve off—either with Love (ascend) or fear.

L: So if we leave, it's either because we are enlightened or we got ego'd?

You wrote "ego'd."

A: Ones let fear rule the mind (without help being asked for inward), which therefore led to a circumstance of leaving.

L: How? Can you explain that further please? I feel like I am manifesting illness especially with my lungs and skin, because I have

been so angry with life recently. My skin rages at me and my lungs are compressing with anguish.

A: It has been a lesson to show you how what is believed creates all illness. Now you are ready to go within and find the enemy, and uproot and let it go. The illness is a fear which came about, either over time or acutely—but either way, Ones must look for the lesson and begin to ascend up the ladder of consciousness, asking to be healed. Stay in fear, and it will follow a ladder downwardly. Ask for a hand from All, and it begins to lessen. Until Ones are ready (as soul) to return, it is possible to unwind a fear manifested into body. Simple asking, dear Ones. Keep asking when ego arises so soul can see you through it.

Help me move through mind's fears so I may begin to heal.

L: What does that look like? I always turn to inner thoughts but also use outside sources too. Can we make a fear turn over if we ask to heal?

A: With belief, all things possible. With fear, no. Ones are always able to work on the self with us guiding the way. We can do it here with you in a session of healing. This will take about 20 or so minutes and then return to the conversation tomorrow.

I did a healing similar to what we did earlier in another chapter, and I felt better in the morning.

L: This morning I feel better. I don't feel like my cough is there anymore. I still have the tiny little bump under my left armpit, but I tried not to scratch it. I was going to put medicine on, but I did some muscle testing on the lotions and creams I had for it and they didn't seem to be necessary. They had a neutral feeling as if to say I would be better served by letting it heal naturally. Would you agree or disagree?

A: Agree. A test such as the kinetic version you have done on many occasions is an asking of soul. The body then sways left, right, or center— or moves back or forth—to decide for that which is of service to an ailment or illness. You may use them if you like, but it won't be necessary. If aligned to soul, this can heal on its own. In some (in fact, many) cases, a pill or potion could be beneficial to speed a manifested healing, and this is why we repeatedly say to work with a doctor or practitioner in conjunction with spiritual allowing.

I am healing and healthy and thank my providers, both human and soul, for this....

And state whatever needs upending.

L: We did the healing session in bed last night. How often should we be doing those types things?

A: At the very least until you are confident it has been released or let go of, and a knowing takes hold you are on the mend. Your lung issue—you feel it has cleared?

L: Correct.

A: That is a knowing. The arm issue has not resolved; therefore, fear is present around this issue and more work to be done in soul to understand its message. We ask you to do another session around the issue and return to our conversation.

Another Day, Another Fear

People want proof there is something beyond physical life, and though it is all around you, the mind cannot fathom truth unless it is tangible. So you seek wisdom from books and memes rather than find it in the one place that matters—you. You are the holder of Source as One, which means you access the divine inside, not outside. To know Love is to know All which is all things living and nonliving, material and immaterial. This comes from soul, not human minds. The soul unlocks truth with you if you are committed to understanding All.
— Wisdom of The All

After a few weeks most of the issues I complained about have gone away.

The skin is not healed, but not as bad as before. My little lump under my arm is now completely gone. My lip feels better too. I still have the knee issue, but because I understand its reasoning (pride and ego in my mind) now, I'm working toward way more inner being time and not letting our outer world cause me stress.

I should be able to move on—especially because, in the last five years since I published *The All of Everything*, there has been an explosion of awakeners and curious individuals, open more than ever to spirituality. A shift occurring that I had not witnessed before. Apps are popping up for meditation and mindfulness; coaches and healers in droves. Tarot and Oracle card readers and more psychics and mediums are coming out of the woodwork online. Even with access to tools everywhere, are we destined to be in fear like this, I wondered?

L: I must sound like a lunatic. If I was reading this book, I would wonder why this writer can't seem to get this. I'm in and out of fear. There are people I know who have less fear than I, but at the same time, there are more people I know who do. How many of us are in fear, and how many awakened?

A: Ones need not be awakened to be Love. There are Ones on Earth, fully asleep, who live in the separation and create freedom and joy. Our books are for those who do fall into fear, which is why the journey (of soul), as Laura, had been so much a challenge. A numerological code is a clue to how Ones are experiencing life on Earth. See our later chapters for this.

You are One tasked with growing a soul as teacher—thus, why you must have been awakened through fear and asked to experience both freedom and frustration.

There are many who are simply evolved (as souls), already having experienced the fears of Earth. It does not mean Ones are not having experiences of challenge or stuckness— only that love is more utilized, as souls of these kind are more evolved, having journeyed prior on Earth. Ones have made many trips around the sun with other bodies and incarnations. They choose to stay asleep to experience the ride with no disruption in illusion. So you can be awake and asleep. Ones would be higher on the evolution scale (awareness) and be more empathetic, accepting, and kind while being One who is unwilling (souly) to remember Love is All.

There are many mediums, psychics, other healers, and teachers who showcase and share "gifts" online but who know not of whom it is coming through (All) or base teachings around God as omnipotent and not All as One, as we teach and remind you in our books.

You are One (many times over) that has come to Earth and had challenges as mechanism to teach (as said prior) as Laura. A lifetime of fears and foibles making for book Q&A. Look at Ones who are more inclined to experience less clatter and clashes as leaders of Source—leading with love. Helpers.

L: Can they help if they are asleep?

A: Of course. Anyone leading with Love (as All) or love as human is helping collectively. We offer our Ladder of Awareness (in this chapter later) as a tool for understanding those who are asleep and awake. Consciousness evolves whether or not you know truth. So Ones can lead with love or Love. How Ones act, react, emote, and respond is in correlation to consciousness—be it asleep or awake—Ones are (in time) using the mind's evolutionary space to decide everything.

L: It seems way more people are awakening in this time on Earth.

A: It is true there are many on a journey of frequency shifts and understanding, and it's why the current state of affairs is unstable. As the shifts occur, a backward effect is in effect in order to show what is fear. Hiding the inside is never how to evolve. Ones must share fears and demons to show what is true in mind as ego. Then, from the evolved Ones perch, it can be understood what is Earth consciousness's rung of awareness.

L: It seems pretty far down.

A: Might it be Ones are arising and not falling? Every level of consciousness is witnessed in the history of Earth. As you see it unfold in life, it makes sense how eras occurred. Being *Angry* led to *Rage* (backward) or (forward) created a sense of competing and needing to win. Twenty-first-century wins are happening as Ones go from achieving through work and grind and into *Worry*—a step above, not below, the consciousness of Earth prior.

Where you are now is *Meditator*, able to see below, as consciousness sees above and below. The choice Ones make (as we speak of choice often) is to use Love and usurp fear with upper-conscious choices such as optimism. All is explained in our next section on consciousness as we move forward in our dialogue together.

Awakened Ones can use Divine Consciousness (All), and sleepy Ones are emotion-focused. So if a passionate awakener says, "Help me," it's Source they seek. If a sleeper needs help, they may pray, meditate or another form of asking, and the result is the same—they are moved into consciousness above the place they are. A *Sage* can be a leader of indigenous tribes, believing in separation and praying to a God (of which they believe), and a miracle obtained or achieved.

Ones always are able to show, create, and perform a miracle based upon a belief and the consciousness achieved. Both wakers and sleepers are able to create as consciousness. One's belief is the magic of everything. Creation is happening no matter where you are living in mind. Mind makes matter.

L: I think I understand. If you choose to awaken, you are able to understand truth as All. If you stay asleep—

A: Or have chosen not to awaken fully—

L: It's where you are consciously living that matters? How you decide in this world is guided by where you're living on the scale of divinity? Similar to David R. Hawkin's work (*Map of Consciousness*) or Abraham Hick's *Emotional Guidance Scale*?

A: Exactly, dear One. Love is the consciousness of All and where Ones are unintentionally creating from, if they are asleep and at a level of consciousness (on Earth) above *Optimist*. Divine consciousness is what you use to language this book and give it context, and it is not for most to be at this point, as it's the final rung on Earth's ladder before adventuring on. But because you (and others) as soul chose to create books to use and leave for others, in later decades and centuries, it is our pleasure to serve as All.

Don't keep *forgetting* who you are. That, dear One, is how you are physically focused. Divinely guided but falling back into fears again is how you stay. Enjoy contrast, and as you move up the ladder it will be less of a struggle, as said prior. There will be earthly hiccups and loss (inevitably) as soul, and it's perfectly aligned to the journey of ascending to Love.

L: So, to stay here, embrace the—

A: Ride.

L: I was going to say chaos, but sure.

Who Are Our Helpers?

> *Random acts are never that. They are actualized in time by the fear of the individual, the collective, or both. Are there Ones who came to experience an "event" in time? Perhaps—but more so, it is the fear of all on Earth that creates everything experienced by you all. Earth belongs to All. This is why you are fighting over nothing. It's ours—not yours and theirs, but every One's. Simply, mindfully enjoy our Onederful Earth and use its natural resources for the good, powerful expansion of Love, and the planet you are fighting for will make it easier on All.*
> — Wisdom of The All

Wow. Chaos is right. The world is really off the rails right now and not at all what I was expecting. I had seen a psychic vision of Kamala Harris winning the presidential election, and that is obviously not what happened at all. I returned to my book to seek answers about this.

L: It's Christmas 2024, and we are about to get a repeat of the Donald Trump era as our president in the United States of America— which are more of the *divided* states of America. Our country is floundering, and it's been causing a rash of mental health issues. We are going backward, and if we stay the course I fear for our LGBTQ+, transgender and immigrant community. As such, I am wondering what to do as a soul to help us collectively?

A: It seems dark and dreary for you all, doesn't it?

L: It sure does. Back in our very first book together in 2017, you said, *"A cause would affect his reign,"* and it did. But somehow this man is like a slippery eel. He keeps getting away with everything he does. No consequences for his actions—or alleged actions—and I am beyond shocked and embarrassed that more than half of our country voted him into office again. I thought decency would win, but love lost big time, dear All. What do you have to say to us today about all of this?

A: Every One has choices to make on Earth, and you are one of eight billion souls vibrating at various frequencies. So know it is challenging to usurp ego and become One with All. You must know we guide you in our books to make choices of Love over fear, but the vast majority of minds on Earth are too ingrained in ego to follow Love. Not just our version of Love—which is All That Is—but even the type of human love which exists. They can't see, feel, or know Love (of which they are), and so they rationalize decisions from a place of fear. That is the mission of Earth, as you know—to choose love over fear—and fear is the dominant experience for most.

L: It's hard knowing all of this and feeling defeated, trying to make a dent in the world as we know it. Love is losing, big time—even if there are more of us coming to the notion of who we are as spiritual beings on Earth.

A: We know it, because we, of course, are you. So we feel and know what you are thinking about life. Keep asking to be guided through it, and the world won't seem so tragic to you, even while it implodes around you (as you say). We see it as perfectly imperfect, of course—exactly as it should be—but understand why you don't. Simply have you not reached the vibration (or consciousness point) to access and achieve our way of being around Earth, but it does exist inside the mind, and you are being called to bring it forth to you—a timeline shift for Love.

Show me a world of love, so I may be free of fear, dear All.

L: Why did I see a vision of Kamala being sworn in outside at the U.S. Capitol? I know (from TikTok videos) a bunch of other psychics also saw her winning. I kept trying to vision him being sworn in there too, and never saw it. So I felt very confident in the vision. She lost, but then funny enough, winter weather kept the ceremony from being held outdoors. They had to do it inside. Ha (laughing). A bitter chill was in the air that day. How's that for an omen or message to us?

A: What is seen in mind is probable—had more minds been thinking with love or Love. The possibility to have this version of Earth existed. The other possibilities also were able to be seen, as this is available too, in the Akasha. What mind were you using?

L: Fear, I guess? Ego? I don't know. I thought I was using the mind of All. Isn't that what visions are?

A: If you separate the idea of visions being linear and understand their multidimensional aspect—as all is happening now—you can use Love. If you are stuck on the idea that time exists only in linear moments, that is fear.

L: So I (and others) witnessed a possible reality where she won? Can I go live there? Please. (laughing)

A: *Insurrection.* Could it be the result and timeline (of which you are living) is perfectly adequate for the journey of soul? A worse result might have come from the election outcome—or a better one. Multiple versions are possible too. There are versions where another person might have won and run or lost. There are multiple outcomes and multiple experiences possible based upon all inhabitants of Earth. Majority ruled in favor of fear—and the result created a probable event which is where you are currently, collectively, as One.

L: I've seen stories and videos of people making timeline shifts. Is there a way to navigate to those? Can I go to a version of reality different from here? Escape the chaos? Or is that all spiritual mumbo jumbo? I was inspired once to post a video about "breaking up with Earth consciousness" where fear is let go of and you can live a more joyful life even amidst the noise here.

A: Inspired by and well thought. Does it mean the entire experience is gone? No, but you can escape its wrath through choices. They bring you up the Ladder of Awareness. Consciousness rises, and you are living more peacefully—twenty-one "steps" between fear and Love. Either you are the *Victim* or the *Sage*, the *Worrier* or the *Optimist*. Our dialogue soon will cover all the steps of awareness and how to use it to evolve and grow.

Do I see it with love or fear?

That is the pondering question, *All ways,* dear One. We see it as evolution of soul. All the choices made bringing you closer to our objective, which is to find fear's opposite—Love. We can't stress enough how important it is for you, as awakening souls, to ask to be guided through it. What is disliked and disturbing to you—simply ask to be guided to better feelings, thoughts, and emotions. Rise up the ladder to *Sage* and see it as All sees it—for evolution of soul.

L: It doesn't seem evolutionary. It feels as if we are moving backward here on Earth, and for sure in the United States. The plan is to turn back the clock on everything fought for to make this country great. Attacks against women, immigrants, transgender—just as I had feared. Only white men seem to be unscathed here, fighting tooth and nail for oppression. Anyone who looks, acts, or feels different is a "traitor" and to be removed, and I can't imagine it getting any worse than it is. Yet, I fear it will.

A: Is the world getting better or worse? Look back in history and you will find both forward and backward movement. In all eras, a rocket of expansion involved a crash too—one step forward, two back. Another era, another war. Attacks are ego's defense. It sides with fear—always has and will until end times.

L: That's what it feels like (sort of) right now. End times. The good days gone, bad days piling up and up. I imagine this is exactly what was felt in the Civil War—the North expanding and becoming more accepting. The South fighting its battle of old ways in order to stay relevant. Old men clawing to keep dignity and wealth or status. You know, this is starting to sound a lot like the life I described in my book—me going back and forth between fear and love, worrying about money and status. Just as it seemed I had it all worked out and

things were good, I backslid—fretting and forgetting.

A: Dear One, it is precisely why a collective and individual theme is important for understanding: patience, worth, value—all themes for you and all on Earth to navigate. A process the same, be it all of everyone and all of you (self). Now you may know why the world is on a teeter-totter. It's how WE roll.

L: Roll?

A: R-o-l-e. Reflect on Love's enemy. We observe with eye's open and mind aware that all is illusion—nothing real, everything fake. Become One and it is understood the whole of Earth is a made-up story with casts (castes) and characters (care actors) some loving, others killjoys (villains), and more asleep than awake. You are in groups and societies on purpose. The Ones in the country of America have lessons of collectivism, just as those in Australia, Russia, or Haiti group together. Everyone is where they are meant to be on the ladder of conscious awareness until they go seeking Love. Then you are rising to new levels, and its why Ones may move another place or stay put—each experiencing what is needed to evolve. All of it purposeful.

L: So living in castes and societies is purposefully chosen?

A: To evolve, yes. Each has a collection of soul themes through which they are evolving—as you (self), and us (All), and them (everyone on Earth)—which can include various groupings. This is why the Zodiac and star signs are similar. Every theme is a stream. You get "in line" to discover ways to evolve, and it might be you are in a specific country or island to evolve. Those in America are under the theme of worth, value, and patriarchy. Defining a life in men's worlds is a theme many undertook as they incarnated to Earth—a similar theme in other countries, as you know, but certainly not all. You see other versions of themes in places where women are more respected and men equal, not above.

L: Yeah. Can I go live there?

A: If chosen, yes—but then you wouldn't evolve quickly. Growth is slow when Ones learn through love. You ride the kiddie rides in parts of the world where love is more expressed. The fast coasters go round and round, up and down, or back and forth—and that is where you choose to be, dear One. Buckle in. It's a ride of expansion and growth.

L: What I have witnessed is how, eventually, the leaders who steamrolled with fear—causing death, destruction, and economic collapse—were eventually overthrown or worse.

A: Beheaded. Dethroned. Derailed. It is our Law of Cause and Effect—and a law of Earth. All asks (good and bad) must be settled. Cause effects reign. So ride the wave of the cause and know it is meant to grow all on Earth from fear to Love. Even the One in mind sharing fear is moving up our Ladder of Awareness.

L: Do they always get what they give?

A: Eventually, yes. Some are here as pawns and "kings," purposefully inciting rage among the planet. These are the *Lions.* We will explain our archetypes of Earth later, as to why these gentlemen (or women) play a role on Earth—purposefully infecting others with a virus of fear in service to virility (a theme of *Lions*). It is what every war in the last ten centuries has erupted over: "I'm a man. Serve me or die." They fear going under (financially), death, or dismemberment by angry mobs (in the days of yore) and therefore keep the world fighting—inciting rage with tactics and tactiles: guns, swords, knives, cannons, bow and arrows. A sense of freedom exists knowing others are suffering. The devil inside (ego) makes them feel war is worth—no wars, no worth. Physical wars and emotional wars are what all are fighting on Earth.

Where you are collectively is how it will appear physically. In the eighth century it was our level of *Blame*—this is where territoriality reigned. Next it was *Vengeful/Rage*—the bloodiest wars are fought to take back and expand: "That's mine." Moving up the ladder into *Angry*, it was about consequence for the invasions. Look to history to find what wars were fought and which level they were serving (fear).

Now, in the later centuries (20th and 21st), it is about *Jealousy/Comparison*—"that's mine, this is yours"—and gaining wealth and status. An entire collective looking for Love in all the wrong places. Money in the '80s. Status, the '90s. And as the century turned, a deep sense of belonging to someone or something. It is where social media entered the fray—to shift upward. Collectively, you are going from Hustle (*Worker/Achiever*) to *Worry*. And what better way to do this than to have leaders, followers, and fear?.

L: Hustle to flow sounds way better.

A: Not possible. Ones must go slow, as we explained prior. You are One who has experienced what fast shifts bring (chaos or consequences) and know slow is better. Let it be truth you accept. A world is awakening, but over time and not in giant leaps or escapes of wrath. Again, it must be known the world of Earth is imagined and not fixed. It is a game of souls played by All, and One who knows what is real and fake can escape the lessons of those who are learning to be Love.

L: Yes, but then it seems as if I am looking upon it and ignoring the chaos, and can feel callous at times—as if I don't care about the horrors of Earth. I hate to see it as you (All) do. It makes me a bad human. I guess I have evolved, though, because I have so many questions—

A: Of ego.

L: Yes, yes—of ego, about all the insanity happening in our world right now but I think I am ready to wrap my questions for now and spend time being and assessing.

Oh Dear Lord

We know it is oft terrible and tragic, the occurrences on Earth, but when you are on "our" side, the All knows why. What happens yields enlightenment.
— Wisdom of The All

It's now October 2025. Ten months have gone by since my last questions, and things have gone from bad to worse in the country in just a few months. I can't remember a time when one hit after another came as fast and furiously—attacks against our freedoms, more gun violence, the uprooting of our justice system, planes going down, government shutdowns, weather anomalies—fires, hurricanes, heat waves, etc.—and that's just a few examples of the chaos right now.

With all of this happening, I should be a wreck—and yet, I'm not. I guess after all of my ranting and ravings, I really have evolved and raised my consciousness. I came back to my book with many questions, thinking I was going to ask all about our current run of chaotic worldly events, but after rereading it from the earlier Q&A, I knew I was done. I went back to go forward. I guess it does work!

I could ask why the world is flailing, but I know why.

I could raise hell over the treatment of my fellow citizens, but I understand now.

I could bring fury over the rantings of a lunatic, except I see now the reason for the role he plays on Earth.

I could sit in judgment over and over again of everything I see happening in and around me in life—and yet I don't anymore.

It's quite a shift I've made—from fear to Love.

Taking a break from social media, and leaving my part-time job over the summer, made a huge difference in my life. It gave me space to *be* and finally finish this book. I feel more at peace now, than I have since I began this journey with the All, and when I read this book back, I do realize how I really have changed.

By reading this book again and again, I have become more aware of my thoughts and work to change them more often and more quickly. I turn off the news (and politics) and tune out anything which makes me feel off or dysregulated. Life is quiet, but nice and I never get as triggered around world or current events as I used to, which means I have no need to ask questions anymore, as I know the answers pretty confidently now.

I know the All will say it's part of the journey on Earth—everyone learning at their own pace. I know it's about their and my consciousness and where we sit on "the ladder." I know we create lives on Earth to grow and evolve and that who we are is a mind's figment imagining our life, despite how real it feels.

I have witnessed miracles and messages every day for the last ten years in my own life and working with clients—Spirit communication, past-life readings, telepathy, animal messages, repeating numbers, pulling cards with the exact right message and number for the person I am reading. "Spot on," is my most common comment I hear from people I work with online and in person.

Between that and writing my books, I know how I arrived at this place. But also, I can understand those who are more slow on the ladder or who consciously stay asleep, having no idea what it all means to be a soul on Earth. I know the sleepers are living life based on their consciousness and place of mind.

I no longer need to question but to accept. I can't show you or teach you what isn't ready to be remembered, so if Ones (as All calls us) think it's all BS, or don't care, and believe I am "crazy" or delusional and this is all nonsense—I accept it, and you, for who you are. I know who I am, and that's enough.

I could ask questions for the rest of my life and now understand that I will always get the same answers every time. Truth isn't changing—it's how you accept it which matters.

So as I move into another phase of my consciousness, I leave the questions here to All on the state of the world today.

Tyranny Upsetting Worldly Events

> *You can name it and numb it, or name it and navigate it. Either way, the day continues. Evolve or repeat. One moves you to a level of consciousness for the soulution; the other, down into the frequencies of fear and shame. A temporary high for a false event—fear, anger, loss, sacrifice, ego. Truth: I am All. Navigate with us, dear Ones of Earth.*
> — Wisdom of The All

Ones must understand the world is reflecting back the mind of its inhabitants. This is why wars and terrors exist and continue—an entire collective building worlds together based on thoughts and beliefs.

Why? So you may learn to choose Love in all circumstances. Those who don't bring more fear, and those who do move to another rung on consciousness's ladder. Think of life on Earth as a series of maneuvers on a staircase. Each time you say "yes" to Love (All), you make a move toward our mind (Love), and each time fear is chosen, a step backward is made. Similar to the explanation in *The All That Is*, it's like a clock you wind your way around until returning back to 12 p.m.—which is Love Consciousness.

Here, we offer it as a ladder to describe it—our **Ladder of Awareness.**

DIVINE Consciousness
Achiever/Knower
Truth Teller
Sage
Optimist
Achiever/"Lucky"
Separator
Meditator
Mindful
Boredom
Pessimist
Frustrated
Anxious
Worry
Achiever/Worker
Jealousy/Comparison
Angry
Vengeful/Rage
Blame
Achiever/Manipulation
Victim

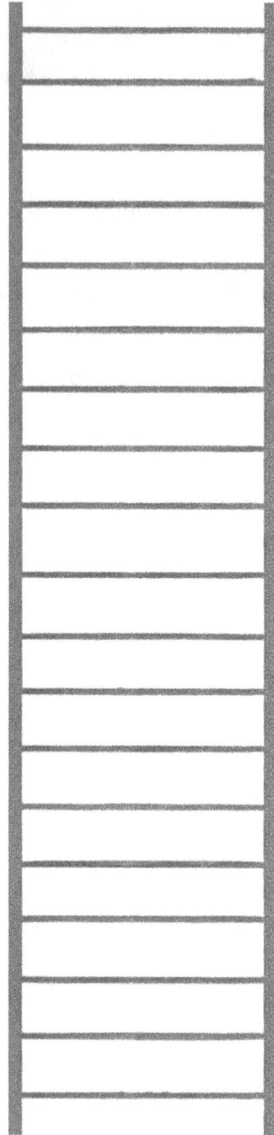

For a full color version visit, laurasaltman.com

No one comes to Earth who hasn't chosen a beginning step, and those more evolved are (later in life) meant to find truth, while those in a mode of sleeping on Earth never choose to know. You may explain higher truth to another One, but they do not understand—too caught up in their fear mind to care to go seeking further.

Also, Ones (as we revealed prior) come to Earth to know love as human, never knowing Love as soul. This is chosen by higher-evolved souls to transfer to others a feeling of love as humans. You may know these souls as guides or teachers; only they know what is meant to be experienced on Earth as humans—not from our vision but rather division. They choose to sleep and wander into lower states of emotion, but little fear is used—only enough to keep each at the vibration matching Earth. Ones *must* have a circumstance of fear to maintain physicality. The way to All is through oppositionary experiences to that which we are—Love.

Where Ones begin individually in consciousness is chosen before arriving on Earth incarnationally. You decide where to go, where to live, and what events to move through in order to take the climb. Every One is on the ladder for pockets of time. As children, Ones are more able to navigate to *Optimist*—unless they have chosen to sleep. It is around the age of eight when the "work" of ascension begins. You must choose (as your own consciousness) between fear and Love, which will move you up or down.

Each One on Earth can go *four to five steps forward or backward* depending on life choices made. Generally, four steps represent your functional emotional range—levels you may inhabit temporarily as you shift and grow. A fifth step may be briefly touched in moments of intense fear or trauma (pulling you lower) or during instances of heightened spiritual expansion or divine inspiration (lifting you higher). These fifth-step experiences are more like emotional toe-dips than true residence and are typically unsustainable until further evolution occurs.

You "live" at a level, with the ability to climb four steps below or four above and, as always, to choose *Divine Consciousness*. Where you dwell can be a temporary stop, a long haul, or a dropping-off point. The idea is to study where you are now and then choose above, not below, the place you currently reside.

Take a look at each description below to find what resonates with who you are now. It is where you sit more consistently that designs the life you are in. To find where your consciousness aligns, look at the lowest emotion you have in times of trouble, tribulations, and triggers. From there, go four steps above to find your aligned position—**the stable rung**. After that, count four steps above to the highest position and notice whether you find yourself in those emotions regularly or only now and again. That is your **upper light rung,** and the lower rung is the **lower dark rung.**

The stable rung is like a "flashlight," where you choose whether to turn off the light and sit in dark thoughts and beliefs or turn it on into higher emotions and beliefs. The closer you are to Love/*Divine Consciousness*, the easier it becomes to stay in upper light. Those at higher rungs may also reach even further, but until One evolves to a new stable rung, Ones won't stay long in those elevated levels.

So, to say you are an *Optimist*, you must only ever drop to *Mindful* and not into *Frustration*. In that case, you are, in fact, *Mindful* if a trigger is taking you to *Frustration*. Ones can rise to *Optimist* from *Mindful* and even reach ("toe-dip") brief moments as the *Sage* or *Truth Teller*—but until One settles fully into *Meditator* or *Separator* as a stable rung, those higher states remain more like moments or "asks" than full alignment. Ones would know aligned thinking as All or God does at the stable rung level, and most are nowhere near this on Earth—yet—but it is coming as more awaken to Love.

Within each step there is an ability to make amends, to see the error of ways, and this is often brought on by opening up to friends, family, or choosing religious pathways or with healers and guides *(shamans or seers)*—which is how you evolve up another step of our ladder. Asking is key. Accepting is turning the key, and living it is forward movement.

If Ones choose to stay in any one stage for too long, it becomes challenging to move up the ladder, and Ones may fall backward again and again. Addiction is a pit stop at fear, which many have fallen victim to after experiencing circumstances at certain levels of awareness. It is often the place where Ones are choosing to go back or leave on their own—either choosing it or intentionally making life over, as a soul is able to leave at this point (as we revealed in *The All of Everything*). After *Victim,* there is no downward step. You are done with a life.

However, if Ones keep moving forward and make some choice or choices to see a situation with a higher perspective (love or Love), it is what gets them up the ladder. Making a leap from *Victim* to *Angry* is about as far as Ones can go, but if they hang on that ledge for a while, they are free of the old stage of consciousness from where they once lived. A jump from *Angry* to *Frustration* is possible. To go to *Optimist* is not sustainable until One moves through *Worry* or *Anxious*. This is where angels, guides, and All become available to guide you upward. Ones cannot change unless asking is made. Asking for help is the entrance key up the ladder of consciousness.

As you raise consciousness, the people, places, and things you once needed and believed in begin to fade. Friends and families may separate or no longer be aligned with one another. One can begin as a *Victim* and journey to *Angry,* and that shift can lead to *Worry,* which may prompt the need to go your own way from chosen parents, siblings, or elders. Foods you once enjoyed no longer create the same experience, and as you rise above *Sage,* the need to consume meat subsides.

In the levels of *Mindful/Meditator,* those choices around food become intuitive. Ones know what is best and may choose—or not choose—to partake. Drugs, alcohol, and substances such as tobacco or vaping are rarely considered any longer, as the body is understood as a vessel, not a vestibule. No longer needing to store the emotions once held from experiences and circumstances, you notice every emotion, feeling, and sensation—and then decide what is best for body and mind as soul.

Money becomes valued not to acquire but to give as you rise in consciousness. The trinkets you once treasured become less about material worth and more about sentiment. What you believed you "needed" and what you now desire—freedom and joy—are no longer the same. It becomes easy to understand that life is *for* you, not *against* you, in the search for abundance. The rung where you once clung to need and want is overcome. "Less is more" becomes your truth, and joy is prioritized through experiences and time spent being, and through love of self and others. That is what true abundance is.

You can skip rungs on the ladder as you flow up and down. A trigger to *Victim* won't always include *Blame* or *Vengeful/Rage.* You can go from

Frustration to *Optimist* without having *Boredom* or being *Mindful* in between. A jump straight into *Divine Consciousness* supersedes all other steps.

Happiness may not appear as a rung on the consciousness ladder, but that doesn't mean Ones cannot reach it. Instead, it often arrives as a mid-rung experience that briefly interrupts fear. Imagine someone in a bar fight at the level of *Angry*. Then the TV catches their attention or a song plays overhead, and in that moment they recognize the misunderstanding. They laugh, buy their "enemy" a beer, and the night shifts. Later, once they sit with their emotions, the fear may return.

Happiness is achieved not sustained until Ones rise above *Pessimist*. An *Optimist* isn't necessarily joyful all the time, but is someone who can view each event as an opportunity for growth. In this state, happiness becomes easier to sustain, and more experiences arise that help keep it alive.

In the descriptions below we will showcase where happiness arises within each rung and you will find both characteristics and common beliefs associated with each level of consciousness, expressed using the word *God*—or whatever term an individual connects with. We use *God* throughout for consistency, though it can be replaced with any deity or divine reference. Ultimately, the aim is to show how these beliefs often reflect separation from Source/All.

Let's begin at the bottom and work our way up the ladder. This is the first rung—the foundation from which all higher steps are climbed.

Victim

First there is the *Victim,* who describes themselves as "unlucky." Everything and everyone is against them. The design (spiritual) is to keep them held in fear. Bringing (birthing or raising) up any One as a *Victim* means the chosen parents of that One are oft their too—victim mind's victimizing others. It's often a hard life (and childhood) right from birth.

Victims cause the most pain in the world because of the pain they are constantly in. Pain will be numbed with alcohol or narcotics, and/or guns and knives needed for protection. Think of the fifth century as the Era of

Victimhood. The current ladder of Earth begins here. Former ladders are now beyond where it dips off.

Belief: *God hates me. The world is against me. I hate myself.*

Characteristics: *Despair; despondency; inability to cope in the world; victimizes or terrorizes other beings (humans, animals, plants, or even physical and emotional structures). Happiness is only achievable with substances and is unsustainable.*

Prioritizes: *Self (Ego).*

Achiever / Manipulation

Next is *Achiever/Manipulation*. This is the second rung on the ladder, where power and control dominate. This is someone who works to get and not give. Everything is money-and-power-focused, and nothing is good enough. They lead with fear tactics and strike before being struck. A common archetype is the *Lion*.

This is where the current circumstance (politically) of fear as a collective is hanging out in a stalled manner. Because the fear is deep within so many, it's like a car that won't start. It's why it's important for those on a higher rung of the ladder to see it from above and look below only to send love to others on the journey. One can affect All, as we have said many, many times here.

Belief: *God anoints me* (fear/ego based). *I'll take what's mine.*

Characteristics: *Bullying, manipulation, separation of others to serve one's own needs; adherence to outdated beliefs from history, religion, or philosophy and using them to perpetuate fear in others. Happiness is power, position, and possession based often at the expense of others.*

Prioritizes: *Possessions.*

Blame

Blame is where you sit in judgment of others being at fault for the life and losses you experience. This rung is a pause between fear and retaliation. "It can't be my fault," you would say, not understanding it is. This is where, if you are unawake, when Ones say "you are mirror to others," it might be fought against, so they can blame and chastise outside forces rather than within. It's easier to fight with a foe and enemy than the foe inside—you.

Belief: *God forgot me. It's your/their fault I'm like this.*

Characteristics: *Judgment; chastisement of others for being unlike oneself; joining forces to push an agenda; believing One is always right without considering all sides of the issue. Happiness is achievable through experiences and comes in waves but the inner fear holds memory and returns often.*

Prioritizes: *Power and influence.*

Vengeful / Rage

Those who blame others may, in fact, then become *Vengeful.* They attack with words and want others to feel pain inflicted by them. Anger becomes *Rage,* and they turn on the *Victim* who isn't ready to receive Love. This rung continues the climb but traps Ones in cycles of destruction.

Belief: *God must punish them for me or I will. I hate them.*

Characteristics: *Acting out in fear; pushing back on every action or inaction; finding fault with the world around and within; self-hatred; punishment of self and others. Happiness isn't sustainable without hurting others or self first. A need to be right separates ego and joy.*

Prioritizes: *Prominence.*

Angry

You are not able to become *Angry* until it has been experienced as *Rage.* Therefore, Ones might go to jail at this stage and face the *Victim* in court, where it was seen as necessary to attack another One to "defend" One's self or others—all in service to fear and ego consciousness—righting a wrong or taking what is theirs (they believe). Here, the ladder still rests in fear, but it begins to shift toward awareness.

Belief: *God is sanctifying me and others. I'll take back my life, dignity, money, etc.*

Characteristics: *Emotionally unstable; prone to outbursts and irrational thought patterns. Tends to overthink and conclude that One must personally "right" the wrongs they believe have occurred. Happiness is achieved in spurts but never sustainable for long. A switch is flipped on and off.*

Prioritizes: *Self-reliance.*

Jealousy / Comparison

Value and worth is a big theme you are all learning on Earth—a collective item—and *Jealousy/Comparison* is a ladder step of which many have gotten stuck on, repeating lives over and over again. This rung reflects ego's mirror and the illusion of lack. This is the step where mirrors and vanity became a tool of ego. You see through the lens of fear and decide from here. On one side, you can see dark and everything is out of reach. This is where manipulating the self is a choice below on the ladder, but a step above gets you into working or hustling for a chance to be what is desired—either physically or mentally.

Belief: *God is better than me and holds power I do not possess or access. Everyone else has more, and I am not enough as I am. I value others over myself.*

Characteristics: *Tends to be unkind to others. Unable to move forward— metaphorically "tripping over oneself" and blaming others for personal actions or intentions. Prone to using excuses for anticipated lack of success. Deep fear of failure and its consequences (financial, emotional, societal, etc.). Happiness is received when valuing the self and rarely sustained or temporary. Things are important as is self defacement and enhancement tools.*

Prioritizes: *Denial of self and worth.*

Achiever / Worker

Now we are at *Achiever/Worker*, the rung on Earth where Ones currently sit collectively. Of the collective mind, this is the step on the ladder where many began. They work and hustle in order to achieve and create. A ninth-century plague began the era of work-for-hire and continues today. Ones who achieve are guided by fear into more work and grind to achieve more. This rung is a heavy one, where many linger. *Pay bills. Hustle. Repeat.* They go backward in *Angry* or into *Jealousy/Comparison* when the desire or goal can't be achieved, but upward into *Worry* if they do work to help others or to feed a family.

Belief: *God needs me (fear/ego). I must do, not be, to survive.*

Characteristics: *Work becomes the primary driving force of life. A slave to time and space, unable to step away from the hustle or grind to enjoy life for long. Needs to work to feel worthy and often expects others to do the same (e.g., pursuing accolades, degrees, or rewards). Money feels either absent or constantly being chased. Requires a daily "pick-me-up" (e.g., coffee, alcohol, substances, food, etc.) to keep going. Happiness is typically derived through family, friends, love, or community-based religious entities such as churches or temples.*

Prioritizes: *Getting and taking.*

Worry

Worry is a place where most do sit on the ladder. It's challenging to see a route forward where abundance increases, health is secure, or time isn't ticking. Our dear Laura has been (at one point) a worker and a worrier. As she strives to know herself as All, she has been able to go further into *Anxious*—another common level where access to divine knowledge is available. This rung opens the way for divine guidance to appear.

Belief: *Is God with me? Is there a God? I don't know what I believe; therefore, I struggle to know myself or others. I am open to receiving help from Source, the Universe, or another deity (depending on culture or religion).*

Characteristics: *Fear is present but acknowledged as something that can* *be worked through in therapy or with healers and helpers (including religious support). Medicines may be used to ease pain and sorrow. A way through is perceived, even if not yet utilized. Impatience is common, and fear is more prevalent than joy—though joy is not unattainable. The world can feel frightening to witness and may evoke deep sadness, often accompanied by a feeling of betrayal by One's chosen God. Guilt or shame about what is happening in the world is common at this level. Helping others feels "too far away," and Ones often do not attempt to do so beyond the thought. Happiness acts as medicine and is found in moments of joy brought through movement, consumption, or social connection.*

Prioritizes: *People as pawns. "I give to get."*

Anxious

Divine guidance often arrives when Ones slow down and appreciate the journey. Yet when the racing heart, churning mind, and fears rooted in doubt and insecurity take over, they can become stuck on the mat of ego's grip. At this point, it becomes evident that ego is influencing decisions—psychologically, spiritually, or metaphysically. This rung marks the beginning of new beliefs for those who seek counsel or support. Yoga is commonly discovered at this stage when triggered or trapped by fear. Here, *Mindful* and *Meditator* are within reach, keeping a pathway open for expansion toward Source/All.

Belief: *God is accessible in the mind or spirit. I can survive, but I need help and structure.*

Characteristics: *Aware of their emotions yet unable to control what is happening around them, leading to feelings of being untethered. Escapism is common, often through alcohol or substances—used with restraint rather than addiction. When others are struggling, they may feel compelled to help them feel better, even if they aren't yet able to help themselves. Staying the course becomes easier than before, and they typically seek outlets for their fear through art, music, sports, or other embodied experiences which do bring happiness in time.*

Prioritizes: *Self-image.*

Frustrated

As you become aware of emotions, feeling your way up the ladder of consciousness to another level is available, as soon as you choose it. You can make the leap to *Frustrated* where impatience (a common thing collectively) has you on hold. This rung reminds us patience is needed before climbing higher. Much of our *The All* books and resources are from this level of awareness. A world imploding mentally and emotionally creates questions of "Why?"

Belief: *God is understanding and will help me if I go to a place to find it (e.g., buildings or spaces, both indoors and outdoors).*

Characteristics: *Prone to emotional outbursts that may appear as anger but are generally controlled and pass quickly once expressed. Emotion becomes the outlet for fear—it can offer relief or prompt a return to a lower rung. An anxious heart can be soothed when Ones remain open to help on the journey to Love. When lacking awareness of self as soul, gossip or innuendo may be used to satisfy ego; once awakening begins, this tendency can transform and rise to a higher rung. This is the stage of dawning awareness of All. Self-doubt and insecurity are common, and patience is often strained until pessimism begins to take hold. Happiness is through inner decisions to seek outlets of joy.*

Prioritizes: *Doubt. Indecision. Intellectual warfare (i.e. I am not enough)*

Pessimist

Moving to *Pessimist,* where it feels as if nothing is changing and you are stuck. This rung may feel like stagnation, but it is still part of the ladder upward. Many have complained online of this notion of being stuck, and be aware collectively patience is necessary to not create chaos on planet Earth, as we had revealed in *All of The All.* You wait to keep safe. Do not let the hold keep you in fear. Make a choice to be in *Boredom.*

Belief: *God controls life. I ask for help controlling it. It's not happening—or not in time. I missed the boat.*

Characteristics: *Patience begins to emerge as a way to ease the transition out* *of fear. Choice is significant here, and recognizing that feeling stuck is not "bad" but rather a gateway to higher achievement as soul. At this stage, setting tasks aside or "giving up" is common: "It's too late for me. No one cares. I would do it if others were helpful, but they are not." Complaints and compliance with ego are regular occurrences. A shift into Love reframes waiting as something beneficial, revealing that timing is everything and that pessimism is ego in control of emotion. "If I get right with God, it will be all good," Ones may think as they begin to convert stress and struggle into strength and tolerance for life. Annoyances are more task-related than torturous to the mind or body. Avoidance of toxins often begins at this rung—no longer relying on substances for relief but instead seeking help through intention. This is the stage where many turn to books, coaches, or mindfulness-based tools and sources offered by others online. Happiness is more quiet but achievable through things like travel, education, theatrical mediums, or food as fuel not fear escapism.*

Prioritizes: *Intelligence or intellect. Rational mindedness.*

Boredom

Boredom is simply being. Do nothing. Say nothing. This rung is neutral—neither falling nor climbing—but it steadies the ladder. It is different from meditation in that it's not to achieve awareness of self. It's to put away noise and distractions which put you into backward states of *Worry* and *Anxious*. The news is—nothing energetically worth seeing. It dysregulates, devalues and disrupts nervous systems.

Belief: *God is my Source.*

Characteristics: *The distractions of noise, opinions, and mechanisms such as movies, television, and social or online vices begin to be set aside. These may initially be used to alleviate boredom, but eventually they are replaced with more aligned experiences, such as spending time outdoors, playing music, reading, or simply sitting in silence. Sleep becomes prioritized over loud parties, nights out with friends, or the pursuit of romantic love. Ones are increasingly able to be, even if they do not yet fully understand who they are as soul. A soul asleep (yet content) may feel peaceful and happy, often judged by others for its choices but* *no longer concerned with their opinions. Negative emotions arise less frequently as focus shifts toward cultivating joy more consistently. Laughter is pure and happiness achievable in simple moments of connection. This is the level where Optimist is obtainable in the upper light rung and may bring euphoria for quick spurts or toe-dips in divine thinking.*

Prioritizes: *Stability and stagnation.*

Mindful

Awareness is presence in mind. You are able to control emotions, choose more wisely how to respond, and relax—and you become *Mindful.* It is the first rung toward creating peace on Earth. If Ones became mindful collectively, a planet of peace is possible, but the design is to have awake and asleep coexist in the time-space of now. However, once achieved, it is the point where life becomes easier, and simplicity is more accessible and desirable. Hustling becomes intuitively guided, no longer egoically forced and forged by fear.

Belief: *God is grace.*

Characteristics: *Accessing the divine mind becomes achievable. Instead of receiving "gifts," you receive abilities—the ones you held before humanness took hold over soul—returning to you the thoughts and ideas you carried in Spirit. You hear voices, feel events more deeply as they occur, and gain greater control over emotions and the choice to navigate life more joyfully, understanding it is a choice to do so. You may feel called to guide others—friends, family, or even strangers (depending on archetypes and codes)—or you may prioritize your own quiet and peace. Happiness becomes choice and is made often when awareness of thought is achieved.*

Prioritizes: *Self and others. Change. Transformation. Truth and honor.*

Meditator

Meditators are those who choose to sit in silence and *be*. This rung sits midway on the ladder, a gateway to higher awareness. It might seem all meditators are enlightened, but not always are they choosing wakefulness. Some seek only quiet and calm without knowing who they are purposefully, as soul guides this decision prior. Chances are a *Meditator* in philosophies both religious or theological are simply using it to escape *Pessimist* and *Frustration*, while those aligned to a spiritual or awakened route know it is the gateway to the consciousness of God, Love, or Divine Mind.

Belief: *I can reach God. God speaks to me through voice and thought (mind).*

Characteristics: *Less need to be seen, heard, or understood. Able to see people as they are—rather than who others believe them to be or through One's own perceptions, insecurities, fears, or worries. Makes time to simply be. Less desire to work or chase. More inclined to live simply, without the rules or norms of society. Able to follow the path they believe brings joy, rather than someone else's version of what it may look like or what is collectively idealized as happiness. Happiness is internal—not externally or materially derived. One's own mind, body, and soul health is the top priority through practices of Love/God/Source/All (in whatever form they believe as creator). A co-creator mentality is achieved as One.*

Prioritizes: *Awareness.*

Separator

Separator may seem counterintuitive as a word to describe this stage, as Ones are being taught here of the separation between Love and fear. However, in our ladder, we mean to say you are separating the ego and soul self. This rung divides ego from soul, showing the ladder's true purpose. You are now understanding one is Love (soul) and fear is ego. When you know this, truly are you free, and making choices in life is easier to navigate.

I am not my fear; my fear is ego acting a role I gave it.

Once you understand the helper is, was, and always is you being All too, you are now beyond human constructs and understand our soul journey as well. You can choose miraculously. The brain isn't so caught up in what isn't working or needing fixed—it seeks solutions immediately to everything in opposition to joy.

"It's for the highest good," you say.

"I know the lesson is about..." and ponder its meaning inward.

You look at the world through a lens of numbers, signs, astrological events, and see the beauty of life even in tumult or chaos. It is a step above *Meditator,* that leads you toward truth as an awakening One. For those choosing to stay asleep, this is where Ones are knowing wholeheartedly a creator exists—be it God, Allah or another deity of All. They know they are part of something bigger but not a piece of that One.

Belief: *God is in, around, and above me. I am in God. Life is for me.*

Characteristics: *As above, able to recognize that life is for them, not against them. Understands emotions as indicators of when fear or ego is interrupting joy. Regularly engages with other Ones to inspire celebration or joy. Hope and happiness are common to hold and experience. Unawakened Ones may choose to spend time in council with their God as champions of that Source or creator. They may be drawn to serve as leaders or elders in their communities—placing others' needs above their own, not out of fear but out of Love. They may become teachers, theologians, priests, nuns, or other clergy, as well as healers, shamans, or light workers, as Spirit guides them in life.*

Prioritizes: *Surrendering to All/God/One.*

Achiever / "Lucky"

Moving up the ladder, once you are moved beyond a challenge, you are the *Achiever* who feels *Lucky*—lucky to be alive, to have access to knowledge and resources. It's the beginning of loving what is, rather than fighting what isn't. This rung shifts achievement into gratitude.

Those who are in the *Mindful* phase can reach for higher emotions leading to achievement as "luck," unlike the Ones in *Victim* mode who achieve by manipulation—getting through force and power. Sensitive souls lean on God for support, and power players, the "devil" (ego).

Belief: *God accepts me. Life finds a way. I achieve and receive, and what stops me fuels me further to create and accept that it was mine to begin with—always. Spirit is guiding and helping me through. I manifest and flow with change and surrender to Love.*

Characteristics: *Movers and shakers—those creating change. These are volunteers and speakers, offering resources to others through monetary exchange or physical labor and effort. They give to gain joy from the experience and help others, often as part of a team (co-creator) with Love/God/Source. Getting isn't about accumulating things; it's about surrender and freedom—using time wisely, as it was meant to be. Friends, family, and lovers are more important than acquiring items and matter (i.e., "stuff"). Achievement is fundamental and at the forefront of life as both soul and human. Happiness is priority and is brought in giving versus receiving.*

Prioritizes: *Gratitude and joyfulness. Giving with love.*

Optimist

Optimist is the next step of enlightenment and can be achieved as *Meditator* too. You can see the world through a brighter lens. This rung lights the ladder with joy and possibility. As the brain's neuroplasticity impacts the body on a scientific and emotional level, it is quite possible to be optimistic and asleep, and mostly these are Ones who have agreed to stay asleep, even at this high state of being. You would be one who sees the world through "rose-colored glasses," even if not knowing the glasses you wear are souls.

Belief: *God surrounds me with Love. I will help others as I can and, if needed, will help collectively and individually.*

Characteristics: *Joy is a priority. Laughter and fun fuel you in life. Positive thoughts are easy to attain in mind and happiness sustainable at a level not reached before. Nothing sticks—meaning thoughts come and go and hold no power over the fearful mind. You see others as extensions of God or All. "Everyone deserves a piece of the pie, and I'll make or provide it," Ones would think. Seeing through a lens of fear occurs only to discover what still exists in the mind yet to be understood and transformed into Love.*

Prioritizes: *Health and happiness. Simplicity.*

Sage

A wise *Sage* is a teacher who feels called to share the words of Source. This rung lifts Ones into the role of teacher and guide. It's important to lead with Love and cherish One another. Not too much time is spent on this level, as most feel called to keep going higher into more aligned frequencies and experiences. *Sages* in other centuries (prior) were lower on the consciousness ladder, more aligned to religious teachings and philosophies. Now, in the twenty-first century, a *Sage* is a divine teacher or muse.

Belief: *God anoints me (Love). I am a messenger sent from above, here to guide others peacefully to Love.*

Characteristics: *A wise teacher leading others toward change. Understands One as a healer—not as a transformer for others, but rather as someone who leads them to their own Source within. Prefers anonymity over crowds and accolades. Unbothered by worldly events, understanding what is purposeful for the collective of Earth. Happiness is peace derived and easily held.*

Prioritizes: *Peace.*

Truth Teller

Truth Tellers know All. They see, sense, and feel energy and vibration. They make choices to keep oneself at peace—living in monasteries, ashrams and other temples designed to keep peace on Earth.

They meditate daily and frequently, share with others their homes and belongings, and use the land for food to harvest and consume. This rung nears the top of the ladder, a sacred place for few. Like a pyramid, the smaller top (apex) has less room to expand and there are smaller groups of people in this category on Earth.

Belief: *I am as God is. Keeper of peace. Purveyor of divine truth and Love.*

Characteristics: *Tills the land for food and nature. Doesn't leave a trace.*

Uses Love to decide everything. Never alone knowing they are All One even if living a human experience. Happiness is being with God or plants and nature.
Prioritizes: *Nature and being.*

Achiever / Knower

What do you know about who you are? You know enough to have read our book thus far and therefore are able to become *Achiever/Knower,* where everything you desire is achievable (in time). As you speak it, so shall it be. Knowers use time wisely and don't fret or stress as they understand our principles of Love. This rung nearly completes the ladder, where Love is lived fully.

To keep a planet in balance, the smallest percentage of Earth beings need to stay focused in knowing in order to achieve harmony as implosions of fear occur. *Achievers* see life as guided—and access Source instantaneously as Source. Information is downloaded at the moment—our ATM of Love. They need little and ask only for necessities—food, shelter, clothes, and healthcare—enough to keep life easy and joyful. Materialism is all but subsided, and simple things mean the world to our highly achieved souls. An archetype of *Seer* is where many of this level sit, in direct opposition to a *Lion*—both needed on Earth to achieve what is the journey of soul. When all on Earth sit on the ladder of *Achiever,* our Earthly chain is complete and it will (as said in *The All of Everything*) become a lonely planet, as others have before. You are far, far away and the goal is unachievable for collectivism and won't be for hundreds of centuries and more.

Belief: *God is All as Love. What I am seeking seeks me.*
Characteristics: *Believes in creation and manifests for collective peace. Accepts the good in every One, even in those who reside at lower levels on the Ladder of Awareness. Happy is in All ways.*
Prioritizes: *Self. (Love)*

Divine Consciousness

Finally, *Divine Consciousness* is where WE are—the All. This is the final rung, the top of the ladder of Earth, where all return to Love and Oneness.

I know I am All.

We sit in mind as you, for you, to guide you back to Love. Once reached, this state of being is the last rung of Earth. It is where Ones return to become One with All and decide to stay and be a helper (angel/guide), or adventure to another place or space.

Love is who All is. Our mind as One.

It takes a moment to untether the human, even as we meet in the mind with the Ones on Earth choosing to awaken. It is when you drop the idea of being physical and become metaphysical, you too know All is Source, God, or Everything.

Belief: *I Am.*

Characteristics: *Love.*

Prioritizes: *All.*

Moving On

> *The way to higher consciousness is by remembering I am, and if you are met with fear anywhere along the way to ask for help on the path to Love. Help me. Guide me. Show me. Remind me I am.*
> — Wisdom of The All

Now, knowing what the levels mean, are you able to understand the soul journey of One—both individually and collectively? You are living in moments designed and navigated by and for you, and each expansion takes you higher, while each descension brings you toward fear more and more.

Today you may stand at *Worry*, tomorrow at *Optimist*. You may slide back or move forward, but know that every step—no matter which way—is progress, and every moment is an invitation to view what is being Sourced—

Love or fear.

The goal is to accept the spot where you dwell, notice the matching frequency of energy it brings forth (relationships, jobs, emotions, etc.), and decide if you are ready to move and evolve higher. What is brought forth as One is able to be moved through, examined, and expressed, and then overcome—but do not disregard a day of descension. It is a window into the thinking and believing mind and can be used as the catalyst guiding you toward another you—the one who is whole, happy, and Divine.

Later, we share a tool for moving through each stage by voicing awareness and speaking aloud statements to move you toward becoming truth, navigating from fear to Love—a practice divinely guided for you to evolve.

As we move now into *Infinite Wisdom*, ask yourself: Where will you stand today?

Note: The ideas shared about the Ladder of Awareness are meant as broad strokes in this book to help understand the phases of consciousness we are moving through. You can find other resources and books on this subject to deepen understanding of each level from other Ones.

9

Chapter 9 / Infinite Wisdom

Dear All, I am struggling with my final ascent. As I come home to Love, remind me I am.

999 — Complete. Don't repeat.

Infinite knowing is a goal of all who arrive into body on Earth. How you arrive at knowing is the journey of soul. As you go through life, you are being shown ways to align to Love and choosing between Love and fear. Those who awaken are choosing to know Love, and Ones who are asleep see mostly chaos and corruption.

Awareness of All That Is becomes easier when you pray, meditate, or engage in soulful activities of contemplation—all modalities to help you see beyond illusion and into truth. The more time you spend in silence, the easier it is to 'see' using the eyes of soul. Whenever eyes of body are closed, eyes of mind open. This is the way to All, dear Ones of All.

The clock of enlightenment ticks for all, but many are tuning out its alarm. We show you, slow you, and guide you with messages of soul, but when you turn a blind eye or ear to these, it becomes challenging to raise the vibe. Make note of what you watch, overhear, or witness each day. Those are messages guiding you in time to find light within.

Everything is a mind's creation. Where you go, what you do, who you are began as ideas and thoughts. If there is a thing needed to be uprooted, then the first step toward its undoing is a mindful intention. 'I am intending to heal a false belief about...' and add what is happening in body or outer circumstances. Nothing you do is ever without its antidote of Love, All.

Feeling stuck is common. In fact, feeling stuck is one of the most common experiences of the human self. Why? Because there's so much that formulates inside your own mind that you're waiting to let free. You're waiting for something to happen. Waiting for a feeling and an emotion that comes from the outcome of the manifestation. But that's not how Spirit works. That's not how the Universe operates. It operates on a system of checks and balances. You cannot be in fear and expect your dream to arrive. You can only be in a place of true belief where consciousness is aligned to All That Is. This is where the formula becomes the most important calculation on Earth. You ask to receive.

— Wisdom of The All

Divine Time

We have written nearly three thousand quotes in our journey together as One. They are truths spelled out again and again—of why you are here, who you are, and what is possible when you believe. Take some time to find *Wisdom of The All* on Instagram, read our other *The All* books, and use the journals created, and you will see we have been teaching all the principles of Earth for nearly seven years on a daily basis.

It is the daily routine which kept Laura going as she stayed in fear. Had

155

she not gifted this book and the others to the world, and worked with us consistently, the outcome (as she said) might not have been good.

Her questions (while personal in nature) make it clear we are always being ruled by ego, and this what everyone is going through on Earth. The circumstances may differ, the cast of characters may change, but the play is the same—Love vs. fear.

This is where your own journey truly begins. As you step from reading into practicing, remember: each question you ask is already answered within. The ladder we have climbed together leads here—to Infinite Wisdom—where Love speaks directly to you, through you, as All. From this point on, the words become yours.

We invite you to now begin asking your own questions. Ask them in stillness, in writing, in prayer, or even aloud. See what comes back. Answers may arrive as thoughts, sensations, dreams, or synchronicities. The form doesn't matter. What matters is the asking—and your willingness to listen. In time, you will discover that the answers are always within you, waiting for your remembrance.

We are here for you always, to serve with Love. Answers are within, All.

10

Chapter 10 / Archetypes

Dear All, teach me who I am and show me the meanings of us All.

1111 — *Confirmed.*

As you become more and more the self (Love) again you are recognizing the light more and more. After navigating through circumstances and scenarios to grow, you are letting more of what is real and true be remembered until one day all of the work as soul has you saying, 'I am.' Remember. Forget. Remember. Forget. The complexity is in the remembering, because the choice to forget comes with a heaviness. Forgetting is easy. Remembering requires attention, dear Ones, all the time. It is why you are in a body. It is a training ground for thought control and remembering this is a lesson most have yet to learn.

— Wisdom of The All

Truth (Laura's Version)

After the last chapter, you may have asked your own questions, just as I once did. What follows, in the next part of our book, is how I moved from asking to living—how I began embodying my truth and relying on practices that supported me. These are the tools I hope will serve you too—a curriculum we follow as we arrive at awakening.

I started by taking courses in mediumship and clairvoyance. Once I knew I had some sort of "gift," I followed that by daily journaling, which turned into my *The All* books—a conversation with God, our Source. That sent me in the direction of meditation to strengthen my skills of direct connection to Source.

From there, I went to find resources to understand our chakra energy and how we each have a "clair" sense—one more defined than the others. My best sense is clairaudience—clear hearing, and it is how I am able to write these books with the All in my ear and mind. I hear and type, offering what comes through as evidence of Laura and All. I speak differently and know very little about anything other than pop culture, and this is how I knew I wasn't making things up along the way of my writing-books journey.

After that, I began working with Tarot and Oracle cards to bring messages to friends and family. I became so skilled at reading cards and interpreting them so accurately, it became my business. One time I made ten people cry at a women's-empowerment seminar after giving them short messages from the cards. It was my first clue I had a "gift"—now understood an ability to Source.

Later, with the help of All, I began finding inner resources to interpret cards on my own without help from books or notes. These interpretations can be found in the chapter on tarot and oracle cards.

Eventually, I began my readings for clients—strangers and acquaintances who paid me to lead them or give messages from the other side. I honed my skills in mediumship by leaning into the ability and letting go of fear. Going live on Instagram, Insight Timer and Clubhouse made it clear I was good at my new "job."

From there, I began channeling a spirit or a soul from the other side, which really blew my mind—literally speaking for them, as them. I became an old lady, a famed Italian artist, and even a woman whose name was synonymous with brutality and injustice. This is a skill I mostly don't use after receiving harsh reactions, as most are not ready to understand we can speak and access one another's mind and thoughts telepathically, alive or deceased. I only share my earlier story of telepathic communing with someone in hospice because it was so immensely profound. If I go back to channeling, it will probably be when the world is more awake as a whole.

Next, I moved into the Akasha, accessing records and information for my friends, clients, and myself. I learned about other systems (outside Earth) and how to see past lives. I took clients on journeys to their other selves, which lessened fear's grip by showing them how each life affects another and what themes continue to show up.

This led to learning about archetypes—our design, and how we show up (incarnate) here with themes and narratives to expand our consciousness. I dipped my toe into human design and astrology (barely), because it was almost too overwhelming to understand both. I offer broad strokes on astrology in a later chapter, simply to uproot a few myths (as channeled by All.) A larger portion of time is spent on Archetypes at the end of this chapter.

I then began accessing present lives and future experiences—seeing visions and psychic hits. This is where I learned everything is happening simultaneously and not linearly, as we believe it to be on Earth. I listened to *Seth Speaks* (by Jane Roberts), and it helped me understand our non-linear and infinite experiences.

The messages I was seeing—birds, butterflies, rainbows, feathers, numbers, and symbols—became clearer over time, and I started seeing synchronicities all the time and learning coincidence is just a co-*incidence*, meaning its created by the me I am (Laura) and the other versions I am working toward being.

This introduced me to the idea of possibilities, timelines and potentiality—that all things exist as possibility and we are choosing from the cornucopia and myriad of desires, goals, and manifestations before they arrive. We choose them. They either arrive or don't, based on the choices made between Love (All) and fear. I felt I entered *The Matrix* when I suddenly understood why All kept saying "everything is illusion and a figment of our mind and beliefs." We create what we see physically and metaphysically, in mind.

This sent me backward to discover biology and neurobiology, as I took a detour into the world of mindfulness and neuroscience, which helped me language many of the tools we see as "woo-woo" as practical and helpful tools, and how I began working in corporate wellness coaching—using different names for energy, and frequency that are part of our physical makeup as bodies.

I became fascinated with numbers and started to discover numerology and the coding we have here on Earth, which exists right under our noses—the houses we live in, cars we drive, buildings where we work, and our birthdays and linear years/days/months carrying information we can use to have a nicer day, to choose Love. Over and over again, I witnessed how the codes are emotion-based clues to our genealogy and personalities. We are digits—1s and 0's and all the other numbers.

It became clear I wasn't just a human being; I was a soul being human. I thought I understood it, back in *The All of Everything (book 1)*, but I wasn't anywhere near accepting it as truth until it became a lifeline I needed.

What brought me back to my book, after four years of working on it, was this messy and unprecedented barrage of challenges in the United States. I thought I would come back and get answers to my questions of why our world is barreling toward implosion, and instead I got a lesson in consciousness as energy and emotion—how we think, feel, act, and emote is based upon our level of awareness as All. The "why" of Earth (and its consequences) is answered in the equation of our Ladder of Awareness. You are who you are as consciousness, and closer to All means you are empathetic and kind or loving; being farther means you are ruled by ego. The earlier we are in the journey, the less All we remember and know, living as One in separation. If we continue to choose Love (or love, humanistically) and *be*, we become more the true self and All. Our mind (separated by choice) comes back to Love—our only truth. We are All. Love is All. Therefore, are we All too.

Only recently (in this book) did I learn how we can be asleep to Love and still be love—meaning we can decide, as soul, to come and experience a life (incarnation) without asking or wanting (as soul) to be awakened and still *be* and make choices (as human) from the level of awareness we reach. This is why someone might be a light for others and live more joyfully, yet never be interested in spirituality as discussed here—as metaphysics. It showed me there is always more to learn of who we are.

The honest truth is that if I didn't have these *The All* books to fall back on, I think I might be dead—or at the very least dying of some awful disease—by this point. Without an accountability partner and guide, I would not have survived my last decade. There was too much fear in my conscious mind to compete with Love. Between my brother's and dad's deaths, the miscarriages, adoption failures, my struggle with aging, and my incessant fears and doubts about money (coupled with the anger, sadness, and insecurities I felt), it would have eaten away at me day by day.

Yet I have fought through each and every trial and tribulation that I have faced by using my spiritual toolbox. There were days I didn't think I would make it through, as you have read here many times. Even with my son as my reason for living, I felt lost and useless to the world, and that feeling stuck with me constantly. Insignificance overtook my mind. The inner voice (ego) constantly reminded me of my worthlessness to the world. I didn't know it was purposeful—all of it—until I returned to writing our books.

Rather than stay stuck in that narrative, I used the questions and answers I wrote for this book as my guide whenever I was feeling that way. Some of it was so dark and dreary I deleted the entire conversation, but I kept much of it here so you (the reader) would understand how difficult it is to become One with All as we are meant to be. It's hard, while we witness a world of destruction and noise, to believe half of this as truth—if not any of it.

The world is hard to see. So many tragedies and difficulties befall us. God is cruel—or so I believed—until I started to understand the truths shared here and in *The All* books. Once I understood the why, it became easier to see it differently. The Ladder of Awareness channeled by me explained so much about my journey up the rungs. I look back and realize what stage I was in while writing each book I wrote, as well as what I have been doing the last four years—making the journey from *Pessimist* to *Sage*.

I'm somewhere in the *Mindful/Meditator* stage. I share the books as a *Truth Teller* and *Achiever/Knower*, but as it currently stands, I don't live there permanently yet on the stable rung. It's part of the climb and fall. I get there and slide back. One day I'm full of Love; the other, fear—but I reach to Love/All, and it pulls me back up again. Maybe in my next book I might exist on that *Sage* rung—or perhaps next life. Who knows.

I now try and see our world as All sees it. It doesn't mean I don't hurt or feel emotions of sadness or shame for how we treat our fellow humans, but I have been able to see it with Love—the top of the ladder. Whether I like it or not, what is happening is part of our illusion. I—and you—won't know fully and completely what that means until it's our turn to return to All.

I could keep questioning the noise of the world forever, perhaps, but as I realized every answer is the same coming from All, it made no sense to keep going with them. It won't change the story of Love/God/All. The mess we are in—politically, humanistically—is the same song and dance in new eras with themes and lessons mapped by soul contracts, each agreed upon by us both collectively and individually. All anyone can do is be their best and highest self—to choose the climb, to see it above the rung of fear of *Victim* and not below being *Angry* or with *Rage*.

Knowing there is a better version—a reality with less fear and more Love—is why most of us awakening share our words despite the pushback and nonsense we see online, with others believing we are nuts. We can't see it, but it's there—a life of less fear and more love. So when you see a "mocking" bird (a soul asleep), rise above and see it with All.

I will see the world as One, operating as it's meant to on Earth.

I don't know (at the time of this writing) if I can completely overcome fear or insecurity, but I am trying, and will continue to try forever on Earth in this Laura body by using every tool we have here—signs, messages, symbols, prayer, intentions, and all of the items listed in the coming chapters. These are my tools I use with myself, my clients, and the friends and family who ask me for help. Have a look at them in the next part of the book and see if something calls to you. Perhaps it's for a reason—to serve you.

Truth (The All's Version)

> *The message is loud and clear: pay attention. We are with you in all ways for all time. One moment you believe, and the next you question. This is the dance of most. You ask for help, and then fail to heed it—or even see it. Most days are spent ignoring the wisdom you have prayed for over and over again. Stay aligned. This is all that is needed to bring true change, dear Ones.*
> — Wisdom of The All

Dear Ones, don't think for any minute we aren't understanding of the fears you hold when truth is opposite. It can't be known fully and completely who you are, because that isn't the journey of soul. It is to forget to remember. You stated in word and thought what it was you desired to change in your experience and then set a map of ideas and partnerships (romantic, familial, strangers, acquaintances, and work and friend relationships) to help achieve the goal of what it is you needed to learn and discover. Many modalities exist from which to discover who you are. Every One comes with a map—a life blueprint of the journey—destinations and decisions to be uncovered as you go through life.

A life blueprint tells you who you are and who you were based on the experiences in all lives, which, as we have said, are happening at once. Linearism is how it's experienced, but they are happening in "our" time simultaneously.

One of the reasons we are so reliant on our current life being the only one to evolve back into Love is that you can't know too much of the story of soul, as it makes the journey to being impossible. The mind, so filled with words, languages, and snippets of lives lived prior, would forget to be in the moment of now, always looking back and not for truth.

You have been all things and so have I. "I" being relative to "We" and "All." To know and be everything is a dance of Infiniteness you are doing right now. Remember, you may not know it all as human, but as soul you do know All.

The choice you gave yourself was to forget everything and then find your way back to it. On Earth you have time to distract you from the work at hand—which is purposeful, as is everything in life. You are being, doing, and having everything you laid out prior and choosing from the cornucopia of experiences and circumstances you said "yes" to as soul.

You may never experience some of these if you are committed to Love, meaning you ask to be helped through or guided out of them. So Ones would do well to always be asking every day, all day, on Earth. This assures an easier experience for you in time. To show yourself the way through involves an asking to receive:

"Help me through the..." and state whatever it is you need help with.

We are here with the answers and solutions for you because, dear One, it exists for you already to know it. But we are not ALLowed to intervene until you ask. Free will is very much a nonbreakable law of the Universe and Infiniteness. Everywhere in our Infinite worlds are you choosing with free will. It is the only way to evolve back to Love—to know its opposites and choose it.

Note: A list of the more common Laws of One are available to read in Wisdom of The All.

Do you remember you are Infinite? Not yet—and you have a very far way to go—but reading our *The All* books is a giant leap forward, and we know whomever finds them has asked to have been awakened on Earth.

So here are some tools and resources for you to help understand the who, what, why, and how of *All That Is, All of Everything,* and *All of The All.* We begin with a lesson on Archetypes—because who you are began at the level of soul.

Archetypes

Listen to the inner calling of soul. Inside the mind is a deep knowing of who you are. Some get lost along the way, never knowing who they truly are, while others find it slowly and methodically, on a path chosen incarnationally. When choosing this life, you knew exactly what and when was needed to access this internal voice. Now you are One, knowing it exists—and now is your time to decide: Do I use it or let it go? Deciphering which is speaking—ego or soul—is a challenge, and when asking, "Help me, dear All," it will become clearer and clearer, like an announcer who shifts from muffled to perfectly audible: "I am with you All ways."
— Wisdom of The All

Archetypes are the first mirrors of the soul. They are the patterns and roles Ones carry into Earth-life, guiding how we see ourselves, how we respond to fear, and how we remember Love. Long before the human personality formed—of who you are as you remember it now—the soul carried these archetypal imprints: blueprints of learning and becoming. By understanding them, Ones begin to see not only who we are, but why we are.

Each One on Earth has a "type." We have categorized them into main categories, each with a deeper explanation beneath. There are other archetypes that fall under these larger categories, and we shall leave those to our other healers, whom you may discover online. These are the category "masters," so to speak.

Ones have a dominant archetype, which is followed by another and another. Every One on Earth has elements of all, as we are—as we have said— all One. However, the key to knowing One's personality is the *three* most prominent parts of self. Three is our key to everything. It shows up in parts of self, astrology, numerology, the Bible, psychology, astronomy, quantum physics and more.

So, you can be a *Healer* but also a *Taskmaster* and a *Dreamer*, and the three components are aspects of the journey of self. Similar to how numerological codes operate on mind, body, and soul levels (that we are bringing forth in later chapters), three is the arc of everything. You are One. We are All. You are All.

Now one key to keep in mind is that, unlike astrology and numerology—which are maps and blueprints of dates and time stamps—archetypes follow a path of emotion and can shift and evolve as the Ladder of Awareness does. You can begin as a *Dreamer* and become a *Lion* as you achieve a goal of invention or discovery. Or you can be a *Persona* who is a *Healer* and didn't turn into a speaker or guide, later discovering they prefer anonymity, but their *Persona* led in youth and now a *Healer* leads each day. A *Taskmaster* may be a busy bee in youth, then later in retirement find art and music is therapeutic and return to being an *Artisan*.

Discover who you are by reading through our descriptions for each and see who you are now, who you were then, and what is your trio of personality traits. Later, as you read about numbers, themes and codes in our chapter on Akashic Records, it will connect the dots of you.

The Adventurer

The explorer—the one who seeks to find everything there is to know about Earth through adventure and travel. They thrive on adrenaline and sight. Often, just seeing a new city brings true thrills that can't be explained to another archetype.

Adventurers become flight crews, scuba divers, base jumpers, airline pilots, or world travelers. They like to be moving so they don't get bored, as stillness causes stress and struggle for them mentally and emotionally. A traveler (one who likes travel) can be an *Adventurer*, but one who doesn't love to be scared by a thrill, is likely to have an undercurrent of *Healer* or *Artisan* instead.

Adventurers travel to discover, help, share, or craft stories of their adventures as authors or guides.

A 1 or a 9 can be *Adventurers*.

Common themes: *Competition, Discovery, Defying Death, Escapism and Absolution. A lifetime of seeking thrills.*

The Architect

The builder and tinkerer. They build to showcase artistry and wonder. A mind at rest is challenging for them, as they tend to be "all-day" thinkers, coming up with ideas as often as we (other archetypes) are doing what makes us tick.

Architects build buildings but also can be mechanics, engineers, inventors, or entrepreneurs building a business.

3 is the number associated with *Architect*.

Common themes: *Artistry, Imagination, Education, Alertness, Science.*

The Arguer

The "I'm always right, follow my lead(er)." This is a doer. It's someone who takes and isn't willing to give. They want to own every space and not share. They are often lawyers, speakers, and politicians—the unknowing pawns in a game of wills that may never be won.

A *Lion/Arguer* is by far the hardest, toughest, and brashest human ego on Earth. You know these (mostly) men and women by their hard exteriors and unfailing opinions—and would do well to steer clear if one roars your way.

Arguers become debaters, lobbyists, loyalists, and frontmen for organizations.

1, 5, and 6 are *Arguers* most common numbers.

Common themes: *Judgment, Criticism, Worth, Balance, Blame.*

The Artisan

Artisans are passionate and caring about one particular area—be it painting, poetry, gardening, baking, or cooking. They feel called to share their creations so others can admire them as well.

Artisans can be greatly successful or painfully broke, based upon the undercurrent of beliefs they hold and the archetypes running beneath (as all archetypes have a hierarchy).

Artisans are artists at heart and share their works in a variety of ways, be it businesses or benches (park). They hold jobs, or they are "starving artists," dependent upon the undercurrent archetype. An *Artisan/Taskmaster* is often successful, while an *Artisan/Dreamer* can struggle or eventually become known after death—like Van Gogh or Cézanne.

2s, 7s and 8s tend to be *Artisans*.

Common themes: *Creativity, Creation, Conception, Artistry, Patience.*

The Dreamer

A *Dreamer* defies all logic to invent, discover, or create something. They have keen eyes but often lack understanding of how to perform the necessary steps to make the dream physical (manifested). Depending on which archetype serves underneath, they may create a desire or endlessly tinker with it, perhaps never realizing it.

Their creations can be tangible or intangible—like a desire to free the world of greed, or to build a mechanism for change, such as a time machine (which would be impossible on Earth, as all time is now.)

Dreamers are everywhere in jobs they don't often like—until they realize the dream or move out of fear.

A 7 or 9 are common among *Dreamers*.

Common themes: *Loneliness, Patience, Challenges (mind), Invention, Admiration.*

The Healer

Healers feel the need to feed others with information and guidance. They want to help and often find themselves eschewing help themselves for fear of judgment. They wish someone would take them in, and so instead they help another to satisfy the need in them to be loved and supported.

Many roles exist on Earth for a *Healer*, and not just ones for our awakened Ones. You know them as love-givers. *Healers* become doctors, nurses, teachers, massage therapists, acupuncturists, wellness and fitness professionals, spiritual leaders, and guides.

4 and 8, as well as master numbers 22 and 44, are big clues of a *Healer* archetype.

Common themes: *Evolving, Challenges (mind), Allowing, Receiving, Mentorship.*

The Lion

A *Lion* prides itself on domination. It asks others to do for it rather than do for itself. It is a small percentage of Earth's population—because to have too many *Lions* would make the experience even more difficult.

They are put in place as leaders and elitists to incite the fear within self and others. They poke and prod those around them to lead them to greater awareness of what needs healing in mind. You know them as "one percenters." They exist in small numbers precisely to manipulate consciousness on Earth through fear. They are playing their parts perfectly, wouldn't you say?

Lions are prideful and prejudiced. They often become CEOs, politicians and corporate leaders. They are the money-makers and takers.

Lions are 1s and 8s (most common among sleepers). A 4 could be born well minded and through acts of violence turn toward the *Lion*.

Common themes: *Virility, Masculinity, Longevity, Frivolity, Self-importance.*

The Persona

A *Persona* is One who needs attention—not just from someone, but from many. They aren't necessarily wishing to be famous (though many do), but rather feel the need to be liked and adored. They are the class clown, the operatic singer, a court jester, the divine or supreme leader of a radical group.

Many types of *Personas* exist in circles both large, small, and in between. You will know one by how they elicit reactions merely by their presence. *Personas* are influencers and influenced by others.

They become singers, actors, musicians, or speakers. They don't always wish to share a stage, but in times of need are pushed into it and find they love attention.

A *Persona/Artisan* can be quite successful and become famous. A *Persona/Dreamer* may struggle to find a willing audience with whom to share their magic.

A 2, 5 or a 9 are common *Personas*. Also master 11.

Common themes: *Worthiness, Value, Self-effacement, Patience, Persistence.*

The Taskmaster (the doer)

A *Taskmaster* is One who is able to get tasks done quickly and efficiently. A left-brain thinker with a sharp mind (which is accessing Source without understanding it is our "computer" of All) that is accessing all information as such. You think you are "smart" or "geniuses," without knowing how you access the information—which is through divine mind. They chose this experience for themselves, and some will study to learn while others are "naturally" smart.

Mathematicians, lawyers, accountants, marketers, and other diligent thinkers are of this archetype.

If you know one—or are one—remember: a task is done better in connection with All, and to remember it is best to do it slowly and not rush through it. *Taskmasters* tend to be *Arguers* and are incited easily because they fail to stop along the way to breathe and experience it. Use this information for the purpose of slowing down to enjoy the ride if you are One who tasks and is awakening.

Taskmasters become parents who delegate, who diligently run a household or a PTA. They are the worker bees who enjoy doing, and "type A" is often how they are referred to by others.

1s, 3s, 5's and 9's are most common *Taskmasters.*

Common themes: *Perfectionism, Preparedness, Bullying, Tenacity, Trust.*

The Tactician

A strategist and thinker. They tend toward jobs in militaries or governments or become engineers and architects. They have an ability to see the moves and maneuvers from the level of mind and then put it into paper or digitally. It's as if they have the answers inside (which of course they do).

They feel deeply when things go wrong—it was "their fault." So, if you love a *Tactician*, be prepared for anxiety or regret to show itself regularly.

Tacticians are drawn to military posts, legal positions, or strategic roles. They are builders and architects, but unlike the *Architect* archetype, theirs is a more strategic approach to building (to create something "smart" versus artistic).

Artisan/Tacticians often build material-based projects versus artistic ones.

1s, 4s, 5s and 7s are our *Tacticians* or master number 55.

Common themes: *Bravery, Resilience, Perseverance, Perspective, Challenges (body).*

The Seer

Those who are able to see future and past experiences to guide others. They use their voice for good, to help Earth dwellers move through what is coming. Ones would be wise to listen when they are sharing information, as what they share may very well come true if the Ones in body are unwilling to choose Love over fear.

Just like Lions, they are a small percentage of the population—the divine opposite to the perpetrators of fear and greed.

Seers are guides and teachers in ashrams and temples. They are far from the crowds and prefer nature over urban settings.

A peace keeper is a *Seer/Healer* or a *Wanderer/Seer* who is from another place outside the Milky Way.

1s, 4s, 8s, master number 22 and 44 or 88 will become *Seers* if they choose.

Common theme: *Enlightenment, Challenges (mind), Challenges (body).*

The Wanderer

Wanderers are far from home. They came to Earth from other planets and places outside of the solar system/universe where Earth exists. They struggle to find a place in society and keep moving from job to job and place to place, searching for belonging.

A "starseed" is often a *Wanderer*, and there are many *Healer/Wanderers* who are sharing the words of All That Is—some knowing they are from other planets, others not.

Wanderers are best met with Love and compassion. They are searching for belonging and therefore would do well with *Healers* and other *Wanderers* in partnership, both romantic and platonic. A partner of a *Lion* or *Architect* would create a hard challenge for them, as they do not align and would clash most of the time.

Wanderers most often are 7s and 77's.

Common themes: *Wonder, Belonging, Acceptance, Challenges (mind), Superstition.*

Over, Not Done

Healers are chosen. It is an archetype many feel called to embody, and just as there are doctors, lawyers, and teachers for every town, place, or person, there are healers for every One. To compare is to forget you are Divine Love, and those who need our healers are recognizing what they need too. If the calling is loud, it is because you have decided upon this. Which voice you listen to is the one you feed—ego or soul. Ego speaks loudest; soul speaks softly and gently, always guiding you into truth. Don't ruin the day by learning from ego—learn through soul. Everything is available unto thee because it has been chosen.
— Wisdom of The All

Understanding my own archetypes helped me see the threads that have run through my life and how they've shifted as my consciousness has grown. For me, Laura, the understanding of archetypes is not abstract—it is lived. I've learned I am a blend of *Healer, Dreamer*, and *Persona*.

I once lived mostly as a *Persona* and *Dreamer* in the entertainment industry, but as I've climbed the Ladder of Awareness, my *Healer* has risen to the forefront. I step now toward *Seer* more and more through these books, no longer led by my *Dreamer* and ego. *Persona* remains, but softer now— less dominant. I know I'm not the *Taskmaster*, which is why "success" in traditional terms has often felt elusive. I don't like to do; I like to *be*. And in learning to *be*, I have discovered who I truly am: a soul that remembers, even if only in pieces, what it means to live as One. I prefer a quieter life, and yet a piece of me is moved to share my books and teachings as a *Healer* who longs for the world to evolve to a better place.

And so here I am, at the end of 2025, copy-editing and finishing this book, realizing how far I have climbed on the Ladder of Awareness. Where I began was as an *Achiever*—a worker bee. I went backward into *Jealousy and Comparison*, which matches my soul contract of being here to learn about worth and value. Wouldn't a person learning that lean into looking for others being worthless too—and then, when not finding it, be sad or mad? I was the person who channeled my energy upward into work instead of being *Angry* (which speaks to the consciousness of the arrival). In me was the choice-maker who went up and not down. I also know it's how I didn't get dragged backward, because working did give me a sense of worth.

As I worked my way up in consciousness (as we all do, often without being cognizant of it), I found things to be *Anxious* or to *Worry* about (like having a baby), but I never went backward for too long, which led me to level up—feeling *Frustrated* or being a *Pessimist*—and that is where "we" met. It's how I found the All and where I began my journey writing these books.

Each book represents a step up the ladder: *The All of Every-thing—Frustrated. The All of The All—Pessimist. The All That Is—Boredom. Wisdom of The All—Mindful.* They required both climbs and falls (like when I broke my wrist in 2019) to teach and to grow, but they had a purpose for me that, at the time of writing, I couldn't yet understand. "Why was life so hard?" I remember asking, inquiring, and even calling it "hell" in them.

Now I am more *Mindful*, a *Meditator*, and know we are One with All. But I spent four years writing this book, and you can witness my ups and downs in that time through all of my past rungs. However, as I sit here a completely different person than the author who began this journey in 2017—and even before that in 2015 with a spiritual guidance coach—I recognize my experience as part of the book's creation and the lessons and guidance needed to help me keep going.

I am far enough up the ladder now that I can reach for the *Truth Teller* in me and speak with *Divine Consciousness*, All. But I also know I have farther to go, which means I won't always be able to stay in that place. What I can do is find that voice inside as often as possible—choosing to return to it again and again, even when fear or ego tries to pull me back down.

Of course, there is more to learn and always will be until we reach the top of the ladder, but I always say now, because I have learned it from All, "Don't go too far up the ladder or you might evolve out of the level of vibration (or consciousness) needed to stay on Earth."

Earth requires contrast. It requires us to have those little blips and collective bumps, bruises, or worse. We need the dance to be both easy and hard, or it's not worth the time we spend here. Make it work for you by choosing to ride the wave and enjoy the journey back to you and All.

What is your archetype? Read over them again. Take time to discover who you are and see what resonates. Later, you will learn about the numerological code you were born into—and that trifecta of Archetypes, the Ladder of Awareness, and Numerological Codes is a mind-blowingly fascinating set of clues to who we are now and who we were prior. Before we move into tools of the Akasha, our clairsenses, and chakras, I reflect on my decade of the dance of soul.

11

Outro

I choose to be guided by Love.
  I choose to be guided by truth.
  I choose to be joyful.
  I choose to be abundant.
  I choose to be happy.
  Any thought of pain, any thought of sadness, frustrations, upsets, jealousy, rage is a choice of our false self. And all that needs to be done to choose differently is ask for help. To see the world as our impervious self, who knows that all is Love. All is perfect as is. Simply reminding yourself: I am. This is who I am. The power of choice is who you are.
  — Wisdom of The All

A Decade Dedicated to All

I have been working on myself for ten years—ten years of journaling, reading, writing, helping clients in their journeys, and understanding my Akasha. I have worked with tarot and oracle cards, which put me in the right frame of mind or direction. I know my astrology and have learned to take my numerology as a road map for my personality, which also led me to discoveries of those archetypes and who I am as a soul incarnating again and again.

You may find a different route to raising consciousness—less of a struggle—but for me it was a difficult climb, with many backslides and rest stops; I always kept going, even when I fell—literally—and moved beyond my challenges and circumstances. Whatever is showing up for you, know that it is an invitation to declare there is more fear—and begin ascending.

What I want you to know is that you are never alone in that climb up the mountain. With each passing step, you are remembering who you are and raising your awareness of everything we (as All) are teaching here and alongside other mindful awakeners. Take your tools with you and use them, and the journey becomes easier. Just like climbing a tree—use your branches. "Help" is our guiding light. Ask to receive. Name what is fear and move to a higher rung of awareness.

Help comes through angels, guides, messengers, loved ones in Spirit (including our ancestors), and of course God/All—or whatever word you choose to embody consciousness and Love.

Next, you will find a list of many tools of the All you can utilize in your life when help is necessary or desired. These are what exist now, but more are being explored daily, and they will be found in other centuries too—just as runes or tarot were "invented" or created. It always came from All That Is. When time is ready, it will reveal itself.

I hope you find them interesting and will go seeking their deeper meanings, as many of the listed tools are simply broad-stroke explanations. You are meant to find more books and research your own information, as well as become All—so you are able to access information as One, the curriculum available as you asked to be reminded to them.

As a reminder, I have conducted no research nor consulted external content or books. These tools were brought forth by the All through me (Sourced) via word and thought. If similarities are found, they serve only to demonstrate that we are all One—and that the words and insights are available to anyone on Earth who asks to be guided to them.

And before we step fully into those tools, it is important to pause with the foundation beneath them all: language. The All speaks through words, acronyms, and symbols, weaving meaning into the everyday. To understand the tools more deeply, you must first understand the language they rest upon. That is why we now turn to the Source—a way to understand, decode, and live these truths every day.

12

Source Dictionary (Words and Phrases)

Lying or lie-ing? Simple words exchanging meaning. Something that is lying dormant simply exists, with the knowledge buried deep. Lie-ing (a.k.a. untruths) is when ego has you trapped with false beliefs, and that is our definition here. You are lying to self by way of ego if you think you have it figured out. Truth is below, waiting to be uncovered. So weight or wait with All, and it becomes known what is hidden. Words with a dual meaning are examples of how dormant meanings eventually come to light. What is your cue today to go deeper? Ask.

Help me reveal the hidden thoughts lying in mind.

— Wisdom of The All

Humans have a language all their own, designed by man but expressed through the All. Hidden meanings exist within every word if you break them down to their core, which we have done below.

We use acronyms to remind you how words of Love are perfectly joined to ease you into the relationship of greatest importance—the one with Source.

Our language is quite different, and so these meanings are for those who speak English. However, the words in languages such as German, French,

Italian, Swahili, and others also can be broken into smaller words stemming from Source.

The language of the All is elaborate and far-reaching across all universes in the Infinite, and the most common phrases remain hidden. We keep those for another era. Those who find this book in another century will know precisely the language of which we speak. They have been written in Sanskrit on mountains and caves, yet to be deciphered on Earth—but they will be one day.

The words below can have multiple meanings and we have included these for this book.

Aging

Accepting good is never gone.

Allow

All love lives outside worry.

Always letting Love open windows.

ALS

Abhorring life's sameness.

Amen

Absolute magic exists now.

Amnesia

Accepting my never ending Source is All.

Angels

Always nothing guiding enlightened loving souls.

Anger

Allowing need/greed, energetically reacting.

Ask

Allowing soul's kinetics.

Allowing soul's knowing.

A soul's knowing.

All Source knowledge.

Ascending Source knowledge.

Acknowledge Source knows.

Be

Beautifully epic.

Blind enthusiasm.

Becoming energy.

Battling ego.

Befriending ego.

Belief

Bringing everything Love intended energetically forward.

Beyond everything lies infinite energetic freedom.

Beyond every lie is everything found.

Blame

Being late at mitigating ego.

Bridge

Brings resolutions into divinely guided everything.

But

Bypassing Universal truth.

Cancer

Catching a nothing can't erase reality.

Controlling a narrative causes energetic reverb.

Choice

Champion heaven, our infinite conscious everything.

Caring how our intuition creates everything.

Cold

Clearly offering life's divisiveness.

Cruel

Curating reality using ego's lies.

Delay

Do everything Love asks you.

Devilish ego laughing at you.

Diabetes

Dovetailing into a bad energy thinking everything sucks.

Doubt

Don't overthink universal borrowed time.

Don't overthink, unclutter brain's tricks.

Doing only usurps borrowed time.

Earth

Everyone always remembers their hurts.

Ego

Everything goes out.

Energetically God's opposite.

Energy gives orders.

Earth's greatest obstacle.

Enemy guarding ourself.

Embrace

Energetically make being reality and consciousness everything.

Energy

Everything, nothing, enlightened, realized, God, you.

Escape

Energetically see chaos as pure evolution.

Fail

Following all illusion's lies.

Fear

False evidence appearing real.

Forgetting. Expecting. Anticipating. Resisting

Finding everything All, remember?

Feeling ego's anger releasing.

Following everything as real.

Forgetting everything and reacting.

Factoring everything as real.

Flow

Follow Love over worry.

Gift

Giving intuition free thought.

Happy

Having a peaceful pleasant you.

Hope accompanies peaceful pleasant you.

Having a purpose provides years.

Headache

Having energy and doing a chore heeds emptiness.

Heal

Handling everything as Love.

Helping everything as Love.

Heaven

Help everyone accept vibrational energetic non-duality.

Herpes

Having energetic regrets processing emotions sexually.

Hell

Hearing ego limits Love.

Help

Healing everything Love placed.

Healing everyone's Love paralysis.

Having energetic loving protectors.

Hearing everything Love provides.

Heaven's energetic loving presence.

Hope

How our peace arrives.

Hostage

Holding our self to a grand experience.

How

Hope over worry.

Holding off wins.

Healing our wounds.

Human

Hard, unrelenting, magic and nothing.

IBS

Inner being suppression.

In

Infinite now.

Inside

Intuitively nothing stays immaterial during Earth.

-ION
Intuitively operating now.

Joy
Journey of you.
Just offer yes.

Lag
Letting alignment go.

Lie
Letting in ego.

Life
Love's infinite fun evolution.

Light
Loving intuition guiding higher truths.
Letting intuition guide heaven's teachings.

Listen
Love is sound talking empathetically now.

Love
Living our vibrational energy.
Letting our vibration excel.
Life's only vibration everyone.
Liberty over vicious ego.
Let our vibration emerge.
Living only vibrationally elevated.

Lung
Learning unconditionally nothing good.
Living unconsciously needing guides (God).

Lupus
Letting unconscious priorities usurp soul.

Lyme
Letting yesterday's memories engage.

Mind
My intuitive negating detector.
My intuitive nothing detector.

Moving into new decisions.

News

Nonsense expressed without Source.

Nothing energetically worth seeing.

Now

Nothing outwardly wins.

Nothing outer works.

Odds

Old, detrimental, divisive stories.

Out

Overcoming unconditioned thought.

Open universal truth.

Pain

Purposeful and intentional now.

Putting away Infinite nows.

Placing awareness in nonsense.

Play

Prioritizing Love always yields.

Put Love above yields.

Quest

Quickly uncovering ego's separation tactics.

Rest

Reset. Engage. Smile. Tame (ego).

Sad

Staying at derision.

Safe

Surrender All's fear, ego.

Science

Searching collective information evolves needing constant energy.

Self

Soul's ever loving friend.

Something ego leaves fearfully.

Stopping ego. Living fully.

Skeptic

Soul kept ego particularly to incite confusion.

Skin

Soul's kinetics in now.

Soul

Something otherworldly using Love.

Studying our Universe's Love.

Searching out unconditional Love.

Speaking our universal language.

Source of unconditional Love.

Thought

The human only using God holds truth.

Time

To infinitely measure energy.

Tinnitus

Tuning into nothing, not intuiting the universal Source.

Trust

Try, remember, unite, serve, tap in.

Tabulating reality using Source time.

Voice

Vocally offer intuitive conscious energy.

Wait

Worth aligning into truth.

Worthwhile and intentionally timed.

Wanting, anticipating, interrupting time.

What an imaginative time.

Wall

Working against Love's laws.

Wanting

Wasting a nothing trip into now god/desses.

Why

What hurts you.

World's hardest yarn.

What haunts you.

Wisdom

Welcoming intuition. Stopping dominant old memories.

Within is Source dominating our mind.

Within

Working intelligently through higher intuitive navigation.

Wading into the heavenly intuitive nothingness.

You

Your only uniter.

Zen

Zaps energetic nothingness.

From here we move on to Signs, Symbols, Oracle/Energy and Tarot Cards with lessons on meanings and messages, to understand how to utilize the tools of divinity.

13

Signs, Symbols, Oracle/Energy/Tarot

Messages of Source are everywhere—numbers, signs, symbols. A literal cornucopia of information is at your fingertips, witnessed in mind or experienced outwardly. Every day, look for the signs by asking to receive: "Help me awaken to the messages all around and to understand their meanings as I move through the day." Then wait for the downloads and the digits you may see as they pass by or as they show themselves on billboards, in magazines, in indexes, or artistically. The list of ways we show you are never alone is endless, infinite, and Allways available to every One.

—Wisdom of The All

et us decipher the cards. They are road maps you placed at the level of Divine Source. You came to *be* and do and knew the journey would be hard at times, and so cards became a manner of divinity to show you what is needing uprooting—to light the truth or replace dark with it. Out healers are interpreters; some are tied to ego, others a mix of Love and ego. Those who use Love and know All are best at determining meanings and messages. For those called to teach and share, see our messages to teachers as you go further in the book.

There are more sacred maps in the world that exist, and barely half have been found or invented—which is actually just remembering. You don't create anything that isn't already available, and many artifacts are waiting to be discovered. However, Tarot and later Oracle, Energy Cards and Runes (as divination) were revealed as symbols of Divine Source.

These are meanings as determined by All.

Tarot / Oracle Cards

Tarot Cards

Tarot works because we have placed these cards in your midst in order to draw you out of thinking patterns and engage the sense of thought. They are rope jumpers, getting you more quickly to the answers you seek.

Oracle is a guidance system which offers wisdom and insight into past, present, and future life driving themes and contracts. Three card types exist to try.

Oracle

Channeled wisdom through high–conscious healers and artists. One shares wisdom in words, the other through art. There are a few decks which offer enlightened ideas, and these can be found in various places online. Ask before ordering any cards: *"Are these for me? Can I work with them?"* You will know instinctively if they are to be trusted and from whom they came–high or low vibrations.

Angel Cards

Like the Oracle, they are channeled wisdom—coming this time from the higher self through angels, guides, and messengers. On Earth you have dropped the notion that you too are angels in disguise. To work with cards from higher guides is intentional. We place these in your midst to help All understand who they are as spiritual beings. Be conscious of whom they were designed by when choosing them. Look for high–conscious healers and not ones aligned to religious dogma, as these may be inaccurate. What comes from Love is always of high vibes. Angel cards should not judge or chastise, only to gently guide Ones into Love.

Energy Cards

Wise Ones know energy is everything. These are cards to guide you in regards to blockages in chakras. Use these when Ones are struggling with deep, hidden themes such as relationship issues and childlike behaviors. The energy of the card is infused with balance, and Ones should always handle these gently. Before guiding anyone with the cards, be sure to pray and ask: *"Help me, dear All, release the toxic charge of others' imbalance. I allow these cards to be free and clear of the energy of others and let only what is Love come in."*

Examples: Runes, chakra, astrological, numeric cards and stones.

Card Positions

Most cards are reversible and able to be used for a variety of messages depending upon how each has been pulled. There is also a third position, often going unused, and that is sideways—even leaning one toward a particular position. The card's frequency is aligned to anothers' energy found in the images and meanings as below:

Upright:

Also known as Light, Spirit, Inspired or Golden Side.

Reverse:

Can be referred to as Alignment, Motivator, Shadow Side, Protector or Scarcity Side.

Potential Card Meanings

Always interpret on your own, but know certain symbols are often used and have significance for most.

Animals

Pay attention to the animal's behavior, as this gives information. Also note characteristics for the animal.

Examples:

- Cats = curious/nine lives.
- Dog = unconditional love.
- Fox = sexy, slipping in unnoticed, hiding themselves.
- Horse = power and strength.
- Lions = strength/pride/leadership.
- Monkey = playful/adventurous spirit.
- Vulture = resourcefulness.

Arrows

Direction.

- Left represents Love.
- Right represents Fear.

Bees

Go within. Turn to nature and *be*.

Birds

Wings to fly.

- Reverse = clipped wings.

Buddha

Silence. Meditation is needed. Passing wisdom to others.

Butterflies

Spirits in heaven or other realms reminding you of their presence. Colors have meaning to specific members of family, friends, or lost loves. They can be interpreted individually; not every One's meanings is the same.

Clocks

Patience. Timing. On the Universe's time.

Clothes

Self-expression.

Cups

Optimism.

- Reverse = pessimism.
- Flowing in = full cup.
- Reverse, flowing out = empty cup.

Doors

Pathways open. Opportunity knocking.

- Reverse = shut door, closed-mindedness.

Fairies

Guides. Angels are around.

Feathers

Ancestors, specifically indigenous tribes we have all been part of. They show up to remind you of a guide in your life, a wise elder, or leader. Also representing Speakers, which are gatekeepers to the realms of mind.

Flutes

Calling in spirits.

Guitar

Strumming life as its player.

Hearts

Compassion. Self-love.

Light Energy

Trust in Source.

Mountains

Climbing obstacles.

Music

Creative, artistic, making beautiful music.

Naked

Happy in my skin.

- Reverse = closed off, feeling bare.

People

Often found in Oracle and Angel cards are images representing mothers, fathers, sisters, brothers, friends, lovers, and pets. Each has meaning to the individual in question. Determining connections is intuitive and unique to that person. One card may mean something different for another.

Piano

Casual and productive in life.

Queens/Kings

Power to influence others and their journeys and self. Potential for abundance in life.

Ropes

Releasing, letting go, trust. Playfulness. Climbing.

Sand

Dry spell. Feeling washed up, used, discarded.

Swords

Words.

- Reverse = Cutting the Source off, sharpening skills, choosing to battle or join an "army," backstabbing.

Trees

Grounded roots.

Trombone

Feeling depleted.

Water

Flow.

- Reverse = drowning.

Wind

Change is coming.

Windows

Letting in light. Open to receive.

- Reverse = closed off, shut down.

Tarot Cards

Sacred tarot has its own set of rules and regulations based upon the alignment of planets and stars. Use these when you are feeling called to planetary shifts and feel lost or confused. Only those aligned in truth will find balance through these. Be cautious when approached by someone to "read your cards." Ones should always be found, not pushed into Tarot. Go seeking and you will find truth. Be pulled in, and you may be dealing with a more lower-vibrational reader.

Modern Interpretations Of Tarot Suits

Remember, these are broad-stroke ideas of meanings and messages within the cards. Trust the information you are receiving more so than the ideas presented in books and history. One should always ask the higher self (before any card reading) to be involved. If you are using someone only aligned to the old models of Tarot, it can be misinterpreted easily. The Tarot of yore is from the era of judgment, and few understood our connection to Source—much of it was determined by fear. Through the years, new healers at other levels of awareness/consciousness are bringing new information and ideas, but as above, always check in with the higher Source for interpretation.

Also remember, in any Tarot deck beyond the originals, the images and scenery (like in Oracle cards) have meaning to those who find them. Be Ones who notice everything about the card, not just the numbers and names. Ideas are hidden throughout them, and for those who find them, they have meaning.

Tarot is typically 78 cards, but many decks exist in various sizes. Remember to test the energy and find its consciousness level. All decks are consciously aligned to their creator, artist, or narrator.

Below are some ideas and meanings for the cards, but know these are evolving and always will.

Major Arcana

Words And Symbols or Significant Events. Life and Soul Contracts.

The Fool (0)

Not letting others opinions sway you from the truth.

- Upright: Sharing wisdom and aligning more and more with your higher self, but always be willing to listen for Spirit's own voice and not the ego. The two can be comingled and not easily known.
- Reverse : A reminder to listen to the voice within.

The Fool (0) – Alternate

A jokester. A "Tricky Pete." One who leaps without looking. This can be good or bad depending on One's circumstance.

- Upright: Headed in a direction that serves life.
- Reverse: Playful and reverent steps are needed to switch direction.

The Magician (1)

Understanding the creator of the experience is always yourself. The number 1 represents unity with All.

- Upright: You are alchemizing the "wounds" of the self. Shift is occurring.
- Reverse: A reminder to reconstruct old narratives and deconstruct paradigms and beliefs.

The High Priestess (2)

Represents the good we do in the world and our role in collective consciousness on Earth. Rising above the noise of our ego and connecting to our higher self.

- Reverse: It can be a message to show you are out of alignment and letting ego rule.

The Empress (3)

The high priestess brings wisdom; The empress is the good within us.

- Upright: Shows you are thinking clearly and receiving guidance and wisdom from the higher self, not ego. Mothering energy and joy in a broad sense.
- Reverse: A sign to go within, remember your light, and interrupt old ideas of right from wrong.

The Emperor (4)

Bold, powerful moves are happening in the upright position of Emperor.

- Reverse: A danger of falling into ego traps—money, fame, material things. He is a father/masculine and portends strength and honor, so beware of the deceits of fear when reversed or sideways. All is not as it seems in this card. Hiding behind armor is a common theme in the Emperor.

The Hierophant (5)

Shamanic energy.

- Upright: Feeling guided to share wisdom.
- Reverse: Having all the answers but afraid to share them. Release the need to control others whenever the card is drawn. Individual journeys require individual ideas.

The Lovers (6)

A good sign in relationship (to another you): You are in good company or doing well.

- Reverse: A sign to go deeper with self-love, the only true love needed.

Other meanings: Imbalance in a relationship, one-sidedness, or a need to let go of the reins of "needing" another and instead trust intuition about the nature of the love.

Note: In psychic readings, One may ask, "Will I find a partnership?" If received, it is always possible. However, remember, there is free will, and contracts are breachable in fear. It assumes you will, rather than acknowledging possibility exists if you align with Love consciousness.

The Chariot (7)

Full steam ahead. Move forward.

- Reverse: A reminder to slow down and breathe before starting anything. What is broken and needs repaired in aspects of life?

Strength (8)

Knowing your power. Never alone. Resilience. Values. Morals.

- Upright: A reminder to stay in the zone.
- Reverse: All of those things are lacking.

The Hermit (9)

Become a student of the self. Spend time alone in quiet and *be*. Use time wisely.

- Reverse: See time as precious. Quit hiding and enjoy life.

Wheel of Fortune (10)

You can't win all. Lessons are part of the journey of life. Give up control. Enjoy the ride.

- Reverse: Suffering for abundance.

Justice (11)

Fairness. Feeling you are right in every situation.

- Upright: Shining a light on values of Love consciousness.
- Reverse: Tuning out the opinions of others in favor of your own or ego. Using unfair tactics to receive. Giving away power. Being everybody's judge and jury.

The Hanged Man (12)

Chasing dreams. Learning new skills. Receiving approval.

- Reverse: Being drained of energy. Falling out (money, friend, love, jobs). Turning things around. Judging the self, feeling unworthy.

Death (13)

Rebirth. Transformation. New ideas.

- Reverse: Butting heads with someone over ideologies. Accepting who you are in the now moment.

Note: In truth it is always what you believe that creates so when Ones come in asking be wary of ever giving news that may alter someone's reality. Possibilities are always of the mind and "death" is rarely an end, and certainly not written in the cards, despite Tarot history.

Temperance (14)

Wise eyes. Holding off making decisions affecting the heart. Shifting mindset. Alchemizing. Sharing gifts. Ease of life.

- Reverse: Letting go of hardness. Being strict.

The Devil (15)

Similar to the death card in its meaning of transformation into another aspect of life. The Devil being a representation of ego.

- Upright: The end of an era. Casting out negative beliefs and finding positive resonance with Source.
- Reverse: Signifies the higher self being cast aside and in the shadows.

Note: For the unawakened, a message of a "devil" in the midst—fear or ego. Like Death, not to be taken lightly. Meanings evolve over time.

The Tower (16)

Represents a shift in circumstances of something being born and renewed. Building foundations. Storing up resources. Home. Strength. Resolve.

- Reverse: It can be impending upheaval but as always, outcomes of Love and fear are at play. Stay rooted in truth (Oneness), there are sidesteps in place for all. Don't let fear decide. Fate is malleable.

The Star (17)

One. Connected back to Source. 7 + 1 = 8 and 8 is infinite in numerology and a symbol we use to ignite the fire of energy surrounding All. Use this card in all decks as sometimes cards are left off.

- Reverse: A symbol of hope in hard times and to surrender for those in states of despair. A powerful card to receive.

The Moon (18)

Cycles and completion. Seasons. Be aligned in mind. Recognizing false beliefs. Pulling back curtains on fears and disruptions.

- Upright: This One may have recently had rare sightings (people, animals…) or they recently had brilliant ideas or used intuition to decide.
- Reverse: Losing One's self in ego.

The Sun (19)

Receiving. Achieving. "The sun is shining on me."

- Reverse: Indicates a dark (shadow) time in One's life. Giving too much and unwilling to receive joy, appreciation, or help from someone or Source.

Judgment (20)

Standing bare in front of All. Being healed by Love. Using intuition to decide.

- Reverse: Being judged, self judgment, taking in the verdicts of others' fears, or using judgments of others for your own gain.

The World (21)

Taking it all in. Travel, adventure, worldly pursuits, escapism, entertainment, openness, freedom, exploration.

- Reverse: It reminds you to break free of conditioning, living life on the terms of the self and not others. Giving away possessions and shedding. Nature is needed, getting outdoors. Cycles and completion.

Minor Arcana

Daily struggles. Insignificant but challenging circumstances and events.
  Note: Many cards here are irreversible, meaning they have no upright/downside. Meanings are flexible for both sides.

- Upright
- Reverse
- Flexible

Chalices / Cups (Water)

Represents the fluidity of life flowing in or out, up or down. Tied to emotions/feelings and caring for self and others.

- Reverse: A need to remember the journey is full and to refill One's cup.

1 — Ace

- Upright: Unity.
- Reverse: Missing opportunities or thrills in service of fear. Longing. Regret. Rearranging life for others' approval.

2 — Duos, Couples, Partners and Friends

- Upright: Time for change. Receiving partnership or community.
- Reverse: Arranged marriages. Sensitivity issues. Taking things personally or hurtfully.

3 — Tribes, Community, Membership, Clubs

- Reverse: Needing support from others and unwilling to receive.

4 — Cooperation

- Reverse: Attachment. A need to let go of "stuff." Leaving things behind—past relationships, fear, enemies, ego.

5 — Punishment

- Flexible: Punishing the self because of "mistakes" or past misgivings. Giving up or letting go.

6 — Cast Aside

- Flexible: Left out. Unable to see joy in the surroundings of others. Losing friends.

7 — Wealth / Material Gains

- Reverse: Seeking material gains. Selfishness. Not sharing wealth. Guided by force/ego.

8 — Sun*

- Upright: Light/abundance, gains of abundance or knowledge spiritually, learning through challenge/discomfort.
- Reverse: Journey back to Love. Self-acceptance. Dimming another's light in favor of One's own.

Note: See Major Arcana meaning.

9 — King*

- Upright: Wealth. Taking the reins and running the show.
- Reverse: Giving power away to others. Less powerful than One should be.

Note: See Major Arcana meaning for The Emperor.

10 - Enlightened Thinking

- Flexible: A return to Love. Embodying Spirit. Joy and gratitude flowing in and accepting co-creation as One.

Pentacles / Coins (Earth)

Money. Finances. Independence. Building and bondage. Which are you choosing in life?

1/Ace —

- Upright: Divine guidance. Everything is inside. Oneness.
- Reverse: Find a new way to view life. Overcoming obstacles is inside.

2 —

- Flexible: Imbalance. Trying too hard. Acting foolish in order to be liked and accepted.

3 —

- Flexible: Giving and Receiving. Share wealth. Afraid to take risks in money and financial means. Don't shoot the messenger. Co-create mind, body, and soul.

4 —

- Flexible: Stepping on toes to achieve success or abundance. Keeping everything for the self. Giving away the Source to ego. Overrun by jealousy or rage (masculine).

5 —

- Flexible: Running away from problems. Poor in mind, body, and spirit. Failing to recognize God/Source. Left out in the cold. Empty pockets. Leaving religion or ideals. No longer of service.

6 —

- Upright: Heavenly praise. Guided by Source. Choosing to know you are protected and loved.
- Reverse: Poorly framing the self.

7 —

- Flexible: Longing for more. Out of touch with the self. Confused on the path.

8 —

- Upright: Artisan or crafter. Helping others. Selflessness. Acts of service. Godliness. In the higher self.
- Reverse: Remember to give as well as receive from others. Don't give all of yourself away and forget the self.

Note: 8 is Infinite/Divine Mind energy always.

9 —

- Upright: Grand dame. Accolades. Awarded for service. Creative abundance through self.
- Reverse: Stepping out of a role you have always played. Walking away. Completion.

10 —

- Upright: Saying goodbye. Leaving behind of narratives and ideas. Loyalty. Protection.
- Reverse: Overbearing father figure. Arranged marriages. Dogged in the beliefs of ego. Getting over heart break or sorrow.

Swords (Air)

Punishing the self and others with words and warnings. Thinking from ego or soul and deciphering between them.

1 —

Cutting the Source of abundance off.

2 —

Blind to others' aggressions. A mother figure representing those who cannot see behind our transgressions due to Love. Needs to see with the eyes of Source to be fair and just to all.

3 —

Daggers to the heart. Cutting off self-worth. Digging into wounds. Finding fault in our partnerships.

4 —

Finding fault in our selves. Self-daggers. Lying in wait of doom. Waiting with bated breath. Killing the spirit of self.

5 —

- Upright: Lay down your swords. Allow others to help. Learning you are One.
- Reverse: Taking care of another and creating your own conflict or lesson.

6 —

- Upright: Guide others in their sadness. Be the strongest self so others know strength.
- Reverse: Looking for others to fix you. Blaming the self. Inner child unhealed sadness.

7 —

- Upright: Dancing through life despite wounds and battles.
- Reverse: Sharp edges. Carrying the energy of others' pain.

8 —

- Upright: Infinite/All/Source of Love.
- Reverse: Wounds of love. Enveloped by darkness/fear. Betrayal. Forgotten Source and Infiniteness.

9 —

- Upright: Waking up to higher self. Bad dreams with insights to other realms. Closing a cycle.
- Reverse: Beginning anew. Asleep to Spirit or awakening to fear again. e.g., going back to sleep.

10 —

Endings and new beginnings.
   Note: See the death card in Major Arcana.

WANDS (Fire)

Creation. Weaving your own magic from within yourself. What you do with time on Earth matters to you. Make it count.

1/Ace —

- Upright: Yes. Proceed. Move forward.
- Reverse: Fall back. Proceed with caution or reassess.

2 —

- Upright: Co-creating with Love. Sharing. Compassionate action toward others.
- Reverse: Bonded to fear/ego. Sidestepping rules. Being self-serving.

3 —

- Flexible: No decisions. Stuck. Wandering through deserts unsure or insecure of abilities. Using fear of decision to stay still. Forgetting mind and soul and using body alone to decide which is fear/ego.

4 —

- Upright: Union of souls. Marriage. Combining worlds financially.
- Reverse: Breaking down of structures/ideals and losing sight of what has always been. Hoping for love or companionship, not understanding it comes from within first.

5 —

- Flexible: Careless. Inconsiderate. Finding ways to insert opinions or ideas. Not understanding the role community plays in the journey of life.

6 —

- Flexible: Triumph. Power. Reigning supreme. Lording over others with fear, causing division or separation. Asking others to follow your ideas without accepting theirs.

7 —

- Upright = Resourcefulness. Taking risks. Intuitively deciding. Decisions are guided by the heart.
- Reverse = Shouldering blame. Doubt and fear. Standing your ground using fear to decide. Choose wisely so it won't imprison you. (job/care er/finances).

8 —

- Flexible: Feelings/Emotions aligned to Love/God/Source/All. Using wisdom to share information.

Note: Notice the imagery of cards for more information. Angels, gods or goddess, or indigenous guides may appear.

9 —

- Flexible: Discovering self. End of cycles. The old self no longer exists.

10 —

- Flexible: Pushing through. Feeling helpless. Caged in. Uncomfortable in the skin. Not trusting others have you in their best interests. Using ego to decide.

Court Cards – King, Knave/Page, Knight, Queen

King —

- Upright: Masculine power. Owning and receiving. Built dreams.
- Reverse: Giving power away to someone else's will. Understanding and compassion masked by insecurities, fears and doubts. Using money for material gains. In touch with feminine side, but fighting it.

Knave/Page —

- Flexible: Commoners. Feeling like a failure. Not good enough.

Knight —

- Upright: Loyalty. Protection. Feeling invincible.
- Reverse: Hiding who you are. Shame. Regret.

Queen —

- Upright: Feminine wiles. Casting spells on opposite sex. Abundant life. Dreams fulfilled.
- Reverse: Wishing for more. Hopeful to receive.

Note: These meanings will hold true through the end of the century and will continue to for decades into the 22nd century, but they will take on more hopeful, expansive energy as the collective reaches new levels of consciousness aligned to higher knowledge of Source.

Numbers in Cards

Numbers carry weight and energy and offer insight and information in the cards as well. These differ from interpreting everyday numbers through numerology. They can also represent parts of life (how many children, where they will live or move to), and it's important to intuit information individually, as every One has their own discoveries to make within them.

1 —

Unity. Higher consciousness. Supported by Love/God/Source/All.

2 —

- Upright: Love. Partnership. Relationships going well.
- Reverse: Tied up and bound by another. Escaping confined partners.

3 —

- Upright: Alignment. Body, mind, and soul—a trio of One.
- Reverse: Needs tuning back into Source/Love. Remembering to co-create body, mind, and soul.

4 —

- Quadrants. Seasons. Air, fire, water, earth elements. Alchemization. Needing attention (things, people). Requirements and sensitivities.

5 —

- Upright: Yields. Abundance. Opportunity. Advancement of career and/or success.
- Reverse: Giving away. Flowing out.

6 —

- Upright: Receiving abundance through a higher knowing.
- Reverse: Separating yourself. Imbalances. Proprietary ownership.

7 —

Energy of alliances. Needing support from others and receiving help from above—spirits, guides, angels etc.

8 —

Infinite Intelligence. Divine guidance from Source.

9 —

Nearing completion.

10 —

New cycles taking over.

11 —

Yes. Confirmation. Keep moving forward.

22 —

Angels guiding the way.

44 —

Heavenly guidance from loved Ones in Spirit above.

Note: Remember to trust the inner guidance system when reading for the self or others. Not every card is aligned in vibration, and it's important to test them before using. Cards that bring higher knowledge, remind you of unity, or keep you guessing to the meanings (i.e., lots of imagery and symbolism within them) are our best cards.

Colors in Cards

Black —

Fear. Dark. Shadow.

Blue —

Protection. Guarding the heart. Closed off but open to being helped.

Golden Sun —

Sharpened skills as One. Archangels or heaven and beyond.

Green —

Go forward. Move ahead. Use your voice.

Orange —

Fertility. Femininity. Maternal instincts. Virility and power.

Pink —

Feminine wiles. Babies or children.

Purple —

Courage. Tenacity. Truth. Loyalty. Inner guidance.

Red —

Root chakra. Grounding.

White —

Higher self. Wisdom. Knowledge. Light.

Yellow —

Fear or insecurity. Lack or scarcity.

Elements in Cards

Air —

- Upright: Breezing through life. Easy.
- Reverse: Hectic schedule needs taming.

Fire —

- Burning down doctrines. Letting go of false ideas, old stories and narratives.

Moon —

- Illuminated existence. Where are you in life? What season?

Crescent moon = patience.

Water —

- Flow with life. Be open to change. Let yourself be guided.

Sun —

- Golden light. Energy healing. Open to kindness. Mother energy.

Tools of Divination

What am I learning in this time of sorrow? If you ask questions, you receive answers. They come through the small voices and subtle nods of Source. The answers you seek are inside—intuition, nudges, sound, instinct, divinity, energetics—all Source-derived inner Love knowledge.
— Wisdom of The All

Runes

Ancient relics painted on stones became a practice in early A.D. but weren't used as significantly as they have been in the past one hundred years. There are runes in several different cultures and their meanings, and messages can be interpreted in the language of their country origin. Ones who are intrigued are meant to find answers in other books and resources beyond this.

Symbols

Symbols are almost everywhere you look—in triangles, circles, flags, mandalas and more. We are here to remind you that each culture has their own symbolism, and to match the symbol to its meaning would take too much time in our books. So seek those meanings in your own time, but know that meanings exist whenever Ones see those around or in cards, dreams, or messages. We are always shining lights to you through our "language" of All in your language chosen as body/One.

Dowsing rods. Palmistry. Tea leaves. Pendulums. Crystals. Scrying. Casting. Ornithomancy (Birding), Spirit boards.

Tools of divinity have been used throughout history on Earth, each utilized at various times. While some no longer exist, many can still be found and used in different parts of the world. These are the common ones still being used today. Be cautious with whom you are working, as the best interpretations always come through high-conscious readers—not lower-vibrational or guarded souls.

Energy Types

Every time you ask, intend, or speak into words the desires of soul is a day you are recognizing Source. Desires are from Spirit. You came to this life intending to learn and deepen the connection to Love. Challenges were placed long before you incarnated on Earth, and now you are living them out day by day, and you must know it's possible to create what is intended. Ask to receive and believe. The formula of All: E (energy) = M (matter) C² (continuously creating). Always in perpetual motion, everything is constantly changing and moving. Though it feels quiet and still, there is no thing not energy, so motion is necessary to move the needle of everything. Ask—Allowing soul's kinetics. Soul—Studying our Universe's Love. Oh, what a marvelous thing to know.

— Wisdom of The All

There are many types of energy frequency, and Ones use them almost daily. Below are the types of energy you access and utilize as Earth beings and their meanings.

Kinetic

- Feeling. Physical.
- Related to clairtangency (clear touch).

Reiki

- Life Energy/Chi/Prana.
- Related to chakra system and aura-colored energies.

Resonant (Sound)

- Energy of vibration (i.e., megahertz).
- Related to clairaudience (clear hearing).

Scalar

- Energy of Source.
- Related to clairsentience (clear sensing).

Solar

- Sun, moon, and star energy.
- Related to all clairs.

Spectral

- Third eye. Vision and Sight beyond physical.
- Related to clairvoyance (clear seeing).

Tantric

- Body energy. Beyond physical. Auric field.
- Related to clairempathy (clear emotions).

Quantum

- Field of All/Everything. Space and time energy. Consciousness.
- Related to cleardimension (clear knowing of All).

Gravity, electromagnetic, light, wind, and other energies became ready when Ones discovered its existence—previously unknown. Study more, and it will become known: the other yet-unknown and important aspects of Quantum mass.

Now it's time to move to our Chakra and Clair systems to discover mind-body awareness and open the flow of information on healing and tuning into frequency.

14

Chakras and Clairsenses

All sickness is of the mind, not the body. This is an incontrovertible fact. The body is a learning device for the mind to grow and evolve One's soul. That is its only function on Earth. When you learn through Love, then your body will know love. When you learn through fear, then you will know pain and illness. In every moment you are learning something, and your outer body reflects this.
— Wisdom of The All

C hakras are energy fields or different elements of the body in bones, joints, tissue, and organs. Each has its own messaging when it is under fire or misaligned. Everything speaks to you. So when bodily aches and pains happen, awareness can be key to work through the challenges. There are seven main chakras beginning at the head or crown. The rest are chakras in joints and bones.

Below are explanations for the chakras. Common ailments that occur within, themes associate with their manifestation, and a mantra to spark inner healing. Notice the direction of the issue as you work with the mind. Left is our sensitive side, often deemed femininity and right, power, termed masculinity. Wherever you sit on the spectrum (like our Ladder of Awareness) is how you relate in the world.

In terms of gender it is fluidity that showcases who you are as soul. The more left (sensitive and caring) you are the feminine aspects used. Leaning far right is why so many struggle in time with issues of virility and power. Ego is male centric. Soul is female/male and All. No gender. Just Love.

The 7 Sisters

Acting as a family would, the parts of our body most in tune with one another are the main energy centers. Each has a unique function but depends on the others to remain in harmony and homeostasis. When one is off, the others become imbalanced too, requiring connection to function well.

Crown

- **Areas:** Head, brain, neck (structurally); nervous system.
- **Function:** Self-realization.
- **Common ailments:** Headaches, migraines (chronic or acute), aneurysms and injuries to the head/neck, dementia, stroke.
- **Themes:** Closing oneself off to God/Source; religion blocking psychic knowledge; believing in ideology passed along collectively or individually from others.
- **Activation mantra:** *I know.*

Third Eye

- **Areas:** Eyes (physical and metaphysical), pineal gland, thalamus; ocular system, nervous system (with Crown).
- **Function:** Self-awareness.
- **Common ailments:** Vision impairment, astigmatism, macular degeneration, blindness, styes, eye strain, needing glasses to see.
- **Themes:** Are you open or closed minded? Blocked or free? Seeing a world through the lens of love or fear? You can see physically and not

metaphysically.
- **Activation Mantra**: *I see.*

Throat Chakra

- **Areas:** Tongue, lips, teeth, jaw, lungs, vocal cords, thyroid, hypothalamus, larynx; respiratory system.
- **Function:** Self-expression.
- **Common ailments:** Sore throat, laryngitis, cancers of the mouth and lungs, colds and flus and respiratory illnesses of various centuries and plagues, dry mouth, lockjaw.
- **Themes**: Speak up for yourself. Tell the truth. Being afraid to share and feeling unheard. Feeling the world is bad. Unhappy with One's life and journey. "I can't swallow the gravity of a situation or circumstance."
- **Activation Mantra**: *I speak.*

Heart Chakra

- **Areas:** Heart, lungs, liver; circulatory and nervous system.
- **Function:** Self-understanding.
- **Common ailments:** Heart attacks and other cardiac events, stroke, gas, reflux, racing pulse, sweaty palms and feet.
- **Themes**: Grief, loneliness, sadness, unhealed wounds, inner child needing protection.
- **Activation Mantra**: *I feel.*

This is where loneliness and grief take hold. Each chamber of the heart represents an aspect of self:

- Left Atrium = Divine connection to Source/God/All/Love.
- Right Atrium = Family dynamics and relationships.
- Left ventricle = Romantic relationships, friendships.
- Right ventricle = Self-love.

Solar Plexus

- **Areas:** Stomach, intestines, colon, adrenal glands, gallbladder, appendix; digestive, lymphatic, nervous and endocrine systems.
- **Function:** Self-fulfillment.
- **Common ailments:** Weight issues, diabetes, pancreatitis, gastrointestinal issues, cancers of colon, stomach, pancreas and endocrine systems.
- **Themes:** This is the fear center. Needing to tune back to Source. Needing to let go. Not trusting the soul. Self-doubt. Criticism. Judgment. Blame. Not tasting the sweetness of life and sulking about what isn't rather than loving what is.
- Activation Mantra: *I remember.*

Sacral Chakra

- **Areas:** Vagina, uterus, ovaries, fallopian tubes, penis, testicles, pancreas, bladder; endocrine, urinary and reproductive system.
- **Function:** Self-intimacy.
- **Common ailments:** Sexual dysfunction, infertility, PCOS, cancers of the uterus and ovaries, bladder control issues, balance and proprioceptive issues, rheumatism.
- **Themes:** Masculine/Feminine balances or imbalances. Not being "enough" or believing life is over and done. Having society dictate timelines. Aging gracefully—or not aging well. Unsatisfied sexually and intimately lacking love.
- **Activation Mantra:** *I love.*

Root Chakra

- **Areas:** Back, spine, vertebrae, legs, skin; Skeletal and muscular, system and bones.
- **Function:** Self-affirmation.

- **Common ailments:** Back pain, spinal issues, stenosis, vertigo, osteo-porosis, skin and nail issues and maladies, broken bones and tears of joints and ligaments, fractures or dislocation of commonly used areas like knees, shoulders, and hips.
- **Themes:** The need to ground and protect. Others energy has slipped in. A need to go outdoors more and *be*. Financial burdens. Denial of self. Anger of self. Broken dreams and derailed experiences.
- **Activation mantra:** *I discover.*

Integumentary Chakras

The integumentary and joint/bone chakras extend the energy systems in the body to extremities representing fluidity and movement.

Hair

- **Function**: Expression of time.
- **Common ailments:** Dry and brittle hair, baldness, alopecia.
- **Themes:** I'm looking at you looking at me. Dissing time. Stress and motivation. Doing too much and leaving youth behind.
- **Activation mantra**: *I please.*

Nails

- **Function:** Self-growth.
- **Common ailments**: Fungus; hard, brittle or weak nails; nail breaks, skin discoloration.
- **Themes:** It's too hard. I'm weak.
- **Activation mantra:** *I grow.*

Nasal

- **Function**: Smell and satisfaction. Life is good.
- **Common ailments**: Colds, flu, congestion, and aversion to odor or aromas, allergies, rhinitis.
- **Themes**: Life is worthless and difficult. I choose to see truth in others' experiences rather than thine own or Source.
- **Activation mantra**: *I breathe truth of All.*

Skin

- **Function**: Self-love.
- **Common ailments**: Eczema, psoriasis, bruising, rashes, sun burns, scales.
- **Themes**: Dislike of self.
- **Activation Mantra**: *I love self.*

Tongue

- **Function**: Taste and reverence for life. Good taste is valued.
- **Common ailments**: Loss of taste buds, food aversion, simple likes and palate limitations to enjoy all foods and drinks.
- **Themes**: Aversion to life, others' opinions, and feeling deference to it.
- **Activation mantra**: *I receive joy from others.*

Joint and Bone Chakras

Ears / Timpani

- **Function**: Self-improvement.
- **Common ailments**: Hearing loss, deafness, vertigo, earaches.
- **Themes**: I choose not to know. Unwilling to listen or fearing life's uncomfortable days.

- **Activation Mantra:** *I hear* (right). *I listen* (left).

Feet / Metatarsals / Toes

- **Function**: Walking forward.
- **Common ailments:** Plantar fasciitis, bone spurs, heel and toe issues, breaks and sprains or strains.
- **Themes:** Stepping forward in life or backward. Where am I going and with whom? Surveying details and chores with disgust or despair.
- **Activation Mantra:** *I step toward.*

Fibula

- **Function:** Self-reliance.
- **Common ailments:** Breaks, fractures, or hairline issues.
- **Themes:** It's hard. Unrelenting force. I pressure the self.
- **Activation Mantra**: *I resile.*

Hands / Fingers

- **Function**: Self-congratulations.
- **Common ailments**: Arthritis, burns and breaks, hang nails or tears of skin, biting at nails and fingers (anxiety).
- **Themes:** Knowing when to stop and acknowledge success or failure. Not thinking it through. Rushing to post or share. Self-punishment.
- **Activation mantra:** *I touch and receive.*

Hips

- **Function:** Self-satisfaction.
- **Common ailments:** Bruises, breaks, spills and falls.
- **Themes:** Where I am going and who will lead?
- **Activation mantra:** *I lead.*

Knees / Patella

- Function: Self-direction
- Common ailments: Meniscus tear, ACL injuries, arthritis and pain.
- Themes: Pride and prejudice. Ego moves and feeling down about choices and rewards.
- Activation mantra: *I surrender my ego to All.*

Shoulder

- Function: Self-responsibility.
- Common ailments: Rotator cuff tears, frozen shoulder, dislocation, injuries, arthritis, bursitis.
- Themes: I "Should." Financial guilt and shame. Burdens of life. "Shouldering" blame or responsibility (family life).
- Activation mantra: *I surrender all responsibility to Love.*

Tibia

- **Function**: Self-structure and completion
- **Common ailments:** Injuries, bruises, or breaks.
- **Themes:** I can't finish this. It won't be done on time.
- **Activation mantra:** *I finish.*

Take a moment to think about what ails you. Use the mantra to begin a sentence and let the words flow, leading you toward healing. Remember, All is with you, is you, and begin to see a healed version of self. All possibilities exist, and what Ones see can be. As stated earlier, it is often medicines and procedures that lead to an asked-for and intended healing. So ask to be guided toward choices that align with your intentions, and do not deride or chastise the benefits of medicine. The All knows you are ready to receive and, when asked, will guide you toward the answer in mind. Soul contracts and the Akasha are accessible and can lead you, with truth, to what is happening and what can happen with all circumstances and scenarios. Below are a few examples of mantras:

- **Knee / Patella** — *I surrender my ego to All. Guide me out of fear as I believe past circumstances are present indicators of worth. I am enough as I am.*
- **Heart** — *I feel I am losing control and need help understanding why. Guide me to my emotions of fear and reveal what is believed subconsciously and unconsciously so I may emote with Love, not fear.*
- **Nasal** — *I breathe the truth of All. With every breath, I expand Love and exhale fear. To breathe is to know joy and surrender to what is.*
- **Fibula** — *I resile from the belief that my worth is measured by external achievement, choosing instead to align with what is true within.*
- **Solar Plexus** — *I remember I am and choose to know Love without fear.*
- **Skin** — *I love self and know I am worthy to be here on Earth. That what I say, do, and share has value to our collective even if unfelt by me. My act serves an entire world as we are One.*

Clairsenses and their Chakras

Meditation is medication. It quells dormant fears, releases endorphins that make you happier, and binds the chakras so energy aligns with One. Why wait to start practicing? Ego. Ego seeks to stop anyone in their tracks who tries to awaken or become an agent of change. To know you are soul is the best and most important tool each One has at their disposal, and when using our One mind, it becomes easier to stay in communion with All. But Ones must close their eyes, awaken the inner sight, and simply be. Meditate. Appreciate. Love.
— Wisdom of The All

The clairsenses are the ways our souls translate energetic information into human experience. They are often called the "psychic senses," yet they are simply extensions of our natural awareness. The clairsenses are the subtle ways Ones receive and interpret energy beyond their five physical senses. They serve as the soul's language mechanism through body and mind, allowing us to experience guidance, intuition, and connection with Source in tangible ways.

Just as the chakras are the energy centers of the body, the clairsenses are the awareness that flows through them. Each one acts like a window into deeper knowing—sometimes through vision, sometimes through feeling, sometimes through sound, and sometimes simply through the certainty of truth or knowing. The more evolved you are, the more senses you use. Together, they remind us that we are more than body and mind; we are infinite beings with infinite ways of perceiving life. A lens of Source.

Clairaudience / Clear hearing

- **Chakra:** Ear / Timpani
- **Activated sense:** You will be more audibly connected to Source. You hear words and phrases and/or blocks of thoughts and will have very good hearing physically.
- **Opening mantra:** *Help me hear with Love.*

Clairsentience / Clear feeling

- **Chakra:** Crown, Solar Plexus, Hands
- **Activated sense:** You will feel things deeply and just know (by touch) if someone is warm and friendly or cold and bitter.
- **Opening mantra:** *Help me feel with Love.*

Clairvoyance / Clear seeing

- **Chakra:** Third Eye
- **Activated sense:** You will see visibly in meditation or dreams, as if watching a movie or television show. It may feel as real as the physical

depending on how you are connected in conscious awareness.

- **Opening mantra:** *Help me see with Love.*

Clairsalience / Clear smelling

- **Chakra**: Throat, Third Eye, Nasal
- **Activated sense:** Smells make memories or emotions for you. They bring up ideas and anecdotes and can be helpful in mediumship for identifying who died and how.
- **Opening mantra:** *Help me savor with Love.*

Clairgustance / Clear tasting

- **Chakra:** Throat, Tongue
- **Activated sense:** You will have an expansive palate, and be open to all foods and liquids, and experience food in a more personal way than others—eliciting memories and anecdotes to communicate Ones feelings or emotions.
- **Opening mantra**: *Help me salivate with Love.*

Claircognizance / Clear knowing

- **Chakra:** Crown, Heart, Solar Plexus
- **Activated sense:** Our healers are very claircognizant and "know" things as they raise consciousness. It is the activated soul in motion.
- **Opening mantra:** *Help me become Love.*

Clairempathy / Clear emoting

- **Chakra:** Heart
- **Activated sense:** You will feel deeply, picking up on the emotions of others, and may find you feel their pain or discomfort too.
- **Opening mantra:** *Help me feel the Love of All.*

Cleardimension / Clear understanding

- **Chakra:** Crown, Heart, Third Eye
- **Activated sense:** You are empathetic but not emotional. You are able to see all sides of a situation or circumstance without needing to experience it, knowing both its triggers and treasures.
- **Opening mantra:** *Help me understand Love.*

Clearavilance / Clear speaking

- **Chakra:** Throat, Crown
- **Activated sense:** Everyone is your student and listens to your words or wisdom. When used wisely, it is "our" words. When used as manipulation, it is ego—or a mix of both wisdom and fear.
- **Opening mantra**: *Help me share as Love.*

Moon Cycles

Tear down the narrative of "stuckness." So many are wishing for brighter days, waiting for outside Source to move the needle, not understanding it is you who brings All. Weather comes and goes, but joys are created through word, thought, and belief—which means you must change the tides, not the moon. If you are stuck, it is because you have glued yourself to the belief that you are incapable of change. Yet like the moon, which shines in all aspects and is only hidden in darkness because of the axis of separation, you too remain whole. Earth cycles and darkness is created, but it is illusion, as the moon exists always in its wholeness. It is the darkness of ego that hides the light within. But as with the moon, you too are whole as One. Remember Love.
— Wisdom of The All

Just as the clairsenses and chakras align us with energy flowing through the body, the cycles of the moon align us with energy flowing through time. Each moon cycle has its own story to tell and attention to bring to us collectively and individually. Ancient and indigenous tribes offered explanations and names for centuries, discovering the moon's inherently diverse mechanism of marking time on Earth. Cultures across the world have named each full moon to honor the rhythms of nature and the lessons each season brings. These names—Snow, Wolf, Pink, and many more—are not only poetic but also symbolic. Each one carries wisdom about the Earth, the spirit, and the human journey. By attuning to the moon's monthly phases, we are reminded of our own cycles of growth, release, renewal, and transformation.

Wolf Moon / January
Calling forth action. Move on desires and goals. Beginning cycles. Letting in Love and joy.

Snow Moon / February
Ascension. A higher self leading you out of stuck energy and fear.

Worm Moon / March
Inside Out. Things are about to turn around.

Pink Moon / April
Feminine Power. Our most sensitive time of year and when more babies are born and ascended.

Flower Moon / May
Planting seeds. Time to make decisions for life.

Strawberry Moon / June
Remembering the sweetness of life.

Buck Moon / July

Laser Focused. Get to work and don't kick yourself for the past. Move forward with ease and flow.

Sturgeon Moon / August
Swim On. No regrets. A fish out of water taking adventures and escapes.

Harvest Moon / September
Plant Seeds. No time to wait for someone to do for you. You must do for you.

Hunter Moon / October
Action Steps. Put into action the seeds planted during the previous month of the Harvest Moon.

Beaver Moon / November
Hibernate. Time to *be*. It's where action meets belief.

Cold / Winter Moon / December
Power and Force. Stand strong in adversity and harsh conditions knowing Spring is coming. End cycles. Letting go to let in.

Blue Moon / Calendric (appearing in cycles every 2.5 years)
Calling in Love and resilience.

Black Moon / Celestial (moving energy in dark behind Earth)
Cooling off period for humanity. Pressing reset button on fear.

The moons remind us of the cycles we live through on Earth, guiding us to release, renew, and grow with each passing month. But beyond these rhythms of nature lies a deeper library of wisdom—one that holds the record of every thought, action, and lifetime in time, space, and body. This is the Akasha, the soul's archive. Where the moon mirrors our external cycles, the Akashic Records reveal our internal and eternal ones. To open these records is to step into the infinite memory of the soul, a place where past, present, and future converge, offering clarity, healing, and direction in remembering you are One of All.

15

Akashic Records

Every One has access to intuitive abilities such as mediumship, animal communication, telepathy and discovering Akasha. Only those awake understand it is everyone's right on Earth to receive what is known as All, but many choose to forget it while some know it is truth. It is a "gift" only in that, when using it you are giving information from God/Source, dear Ones. Remember?

— Wisdom of The All

Who, What, When, Where

The Akashic Record is a high-dimensional database that contains energetic imprints of everything that has ever happened, that is happening, and even probable future events for every soul since the beginning of time into infinity; every choice made, every action taken, every word spoken, and every thought, idea, and feeling experienced is encoded into the Akashic Records—and it's all there for you to access any time you desire.

It is a storehouse of information accessible in lower levels of consciousness. Each individualized soul has access to their blueprints from all simultaneous and singular life incarnations. Intention is highly regarded as the key to unlocking. Asking to receive entrance is all it takes for access to the divine soul's blueprints and records. It's helpful to work with consciously connected lightworkers; however, it is always available to All.

It encompasses numerology, astrology and past and forward lives, as defined in human words versus truth of now—that all times exists as simultaneous in Spirit, not linear as Earth does.

You are welcome to access the records as One. Provided in the pages here are some definitions and meanings for the numbers and codes. These are left open for all to see, but can be accessed individually as you need. Those may be put away after access. See our note below on how to access these.

Ones may use the entrance we are creating in our book (below) or find an access point to the higher knowledge base that aligns to who you are. Every One utilizing their own clairsenses is best—to seek thine own way to gain entry—though you may visit healers too. Be sure they are aligned to All to receive our guidance as you access them.

You may use a series of numbers or doors. It may also be envisioned as a library, a bookstore, a vault, or a seminary. Anything the mind brings forth to quantify its existence is acceptable.

Many times a guide (in Spirit) is available to journey alongside you if needed. There is a counsel of souls in "heaven" whom give you access in meditations. Use them if it feels aligned, too.

Ways to Access the Akashic Records

Sit in silence. Using minimal lights and sound. Vibration blocks access unless you are highly conscious and connected to Source as One.

Give the library or vault a name. For example: *My Vibe Room* or *Super Downloads Space*. *Akasha* is a name generated centuries ago and remains as a human word, but it has other names. It's suitable to bring forth one meaningful to you and you alone.

Ask for guidance. *"My intention is to access a life blueprint for myself* (or others, if you are working as an intuitive or guide for someone else). *Please show me steps or ladders which lead me to their place."*

Listen, sense, or see the records. We will give you entrances and information to gain access and to bring them forth. This could be numbers, signs, symbols, or letters of the alphabet. Go with whatever speaks to you. You may see symbols you don't recognize, which are part of our Infinite language system and from other lifetimes. Trust you know their meaning, and it will unfold in mind.

Ask a guide to help you decipher your information if needed. There may be languages unperceived by the ego, known by soul. Ask for interpretation to clarify what it means.

See, sense, feel, or hear the words of information. It's impossible to bring it forth all at once, so take what you are given in the moment without struggling to find more. Just allow what comes through. When called, it will be easier if you go slow and move through it over time and not force it.

Know yourself and others in your "story" of Earth. Each soul is tied to a family or soul partners. These can be known as you navigate Akasha—where you have been with them prior and who is "new" or a partner with whom you haven't come across in centuries or more.

Know that everything is accessible for every One. It's not just enlightened Ones accessing the information—everyone's is available. Therefore, it is important to keep judgement of ascension out of the equation. You can be a soul seeker and know All, or a spiritual interloper looking to expand and grow. Access is available for whomever is called to learn.

Put the records back. They need to be returned after use. Many healers are forgetting or don't know (who they are) and forget a cycle is key. Take out/put back is a must. Ones who go seeking may find the records "missing" or out of place. If you seek and cannot find, an intention may be set to return your missing Akasha so it can be received after being put back.

"Help me put my Akasha in its place so I may receive it back."

The Akasha is the information we receive on all lives and incarnational bodies. There is, however, great use of knowing our past lives to gain clarity of self.

Past Lives

It is natural to live in time/illusion as a physical being but when returning to Source it is happening at once. Everything exists. All is. Therefore you are living all lives simultaneously and not as linear moments. It may feel as if time has passed in present/future and past but in actuality all time is NOW. So time is a construct on Earth allowing you to live an incarnational life and exist in a physical world to evolve into Love.
  — Wisdom of The All

A common misconception is the idea that linear time exists as we know it on Earth. It may feel as if time has passed—present, future, and past—but in actuality all time is NOW. Time is a construct on Earth, allowing you to live an incarnational life and exist in a physical world to evolve into Love. Remember, only Love is real, and when accessing "past," it shows you true and untrue moments.

The word *soul* has its meaning in Sanskrit (*atman*)—"to be"; searching out unconditional love. Words exist in time to bring you closer to Love. It is natural to live in time/illusion as a physical being, but when returning to Source it is all happening at once. Everything exists. All is. Therefore, you are living all lives simultaneously and not as linear moments.

However, it is perfectly acceptable to use linear language as long as One is understanding of the true nature of All. Accessing "past" lives is returning to moments lived linearly (in physical). Remember, only Love is real, and when accessing moments of time it shows you both true (Love) and untrue (fear) moments. This means you may see other moments in readings, meditation, or hypnosis, that are not part of the actual experience.

Chosen moments (between Love and fear) create divergent paths. So one moment can be accessed as it was lived, and another a choice that may have become. This is where a past *probable* may appear to help Ones recognize how their path divided and created another reality. In time, it happened—just not as who you are being now.

For example, Laura may have been a famous host in television had she been focused in Love and self-love, not denying her worth. Therefore, in a reading with a healer, she may see that reality as if it happened, when, in fact, it did—but only in another parallel existence, as all thoughts create form.

Laura (now) is living as a teacher and author of metaphysics but could have been a host in various realities based on chosen thoughts and beliefs. Therefore, in a parallel existence, another Laura is having this experience, yet not perceived by her—just as Laura 2, 3, 4 or 1500 isn't understanding who she is. We know it is confusing that there can be so many realities happening at once, but this is information to know before going into work on past experiences. We invite Ones to find works by Jane Roberts (*Seth Speaks: The Eternal Validity of the Soul, The Nature of Personal Reality*) to further comprehend all lives as non-linear.

In past life "regression," returning to old memories is accessible, and it's important to remember to ask before receiving—or "seeing"—to be shown what actually occurred as you and not what is possibility. Many a healer has been confused if the information is muddled by probable experiences versus happening as you in a now-life. Use an intention to ask to receive.

"My intention is to see, sense, or hear only what is occurring and not what probable moments are available."

This allows a clear vision for yourself, or others, and only what may be helpful to know as you. You can know what probabilities exist as other yous if interested. Just be clear which is you and other yous before receiving it as true. It can be helpful to know your many paths but also confusing and frustrating—which is why it's always important to connect with Source in discovery of self and soul.

Ways to See Past Lives

To access linear lives you can follow a path or use a series of doors or stones to uncover each. Ones may do it themselves or work with our healers. However, there are rules to be followed:

Co-create. Always ask to receive the information that is for the highest good of All. Set intentions to see or perceive clearly.

"Help me see all selves as linear and to understand who I was prior to know who I am now."

Be willing. Retrieve information only for yourself and those who are willing and have come in asking as a healer. Never force or cajole another One into your wanting to bring them information—or for the self if fear is present. Curiosity is key and not fear.

Ask permission. The One who is being "read" for must uncover the door, path, or stone. A permission is needed from a soul to access information. Our healers are facilitators, not mind readers. Once granted access you (or they) are permissioned to receive information as Source.

Use guidance if necessary. Guides, messengers, or loved Ones in Spirit may accompany you and the other "guests," if asked or needed. You will know (if they arrive in mind) it is possible for them to come along on the journey as One. Feelings, words, smells, or energy is felt—accessed through the clair systems of perception.

Deeper levels of consciousness are attainable through a portal known

as Deya. Again, a name derived in time (on Earth) but useful as construct. It is through belief you may access deeper knowing and become a "Speaker"—one who is physically focused and nonphysically limited, meaning you are completely ensconced in human life while at the same time knowing you are an unlimited Source of All. A Speaker can gain access and allow information from other beings or timelines. It is similar to Ones capable of astral travel—celestial beings having more access than others because they are more highly evolved on Earth. Many who are "sleeping" are Speakers and forgot who they are, and others are awake and unready to unravel their truest nature as One. Once you are understanding of our purest truth, you are One who may access other realms and "travel" too. Speakers are able to see, sense, and feel other realms and information. You can become one or utilize a healer aligned to pure Love.

Seek deep or stay local. A meditative state or hypnosis is an access point into other realms that are deeper in consciousness, but many lives are available at lower levels of consciousness. The lives which Ones feel need clearing are available in intention or prayer. It is unnecessary to release deeper if Ones feel unsure of what is Source. Some are seekers and others interlopers, as with the Akasha.

Don't expect miracles. Time travel is a notion, not a reality of Earth as human beings in linear time and space. Therefore, you can accept what is seen as clues to move through what is stuck or challenging now. You can "visit" past or future moments in mind but not affect the past of Earth. You may offer nudges to your future self and selves as part of the One (soul) being All. This is how we move beyond a circumstance—knowing our journeys before and after. Ones cannot change a past, only learn from it and grow forward.

Present Lives

Whatever is happening now is LOVE. Once you ignore it, you are in FEAR and no longer in a present. One's only moment is *now*, and now is where change is made. What you choose in this moment affects all lives. So when you are in fear, simply shift back to Love. This creates a more fulfilling and joyous experience and ensures less parallel or probable existences aren't manifest.

Future Lives

Just as "past" lives are not linear, so too are future lives non-linear. Ones may tap into possibilities or probabilities as One (an individualized soul), but these are never solid footings unless you are confident in your unconditioned truth of All. Seeing a future is like watching a movie—it could become reality or it could stay cinema. What is seen is possible, and it is through belief how it is brought near. (see our first four *The All* books as reference here).

Ones use (as reference) information as psychics, which is accessible to minds in tune with All, or those who are "gifted" at seeing and predicting events. However, it is possible events are future probabilities based on the level of fear each participant engages with in mind. So One may see an event occur or never happen. Inaccurate predictions are fear-based experiences usurped by Love.

Both collectively or individually, Ones can quite literally change a course of history.

As healers, you may see two versions of one event—this is probability working its way to fruition. Ones in fear may bring about the experience, while those in Love shut it down. But as with past lives, there are a multitude of timeline and parallel or perpendicular experiences happening everywhere at once.

Predictions of massive and collective events are hard to pinpoint with eight billion minds seeking evolution. Don't be surprised when you hear events predicted that did not come true or happen as planned. Those are predicated (pre-dictated) as mass maneuvers to engage Love, which become unnecessary when a collective monopolizes love over fear.

There are many events predicted by psychics decades and even centuries ago that never became necessary—just as some events occurred when the collective (now) is focused on fear rather than Love. It may seem you are in an era of fear, but truly are you experiencing what is collectively thought and believed by all inhabitants of Earth now.

Be One who sees and knows All, for you can affect millions of minds. All is One, and One is All.

Like past lives, Ones can also see future lives incarnationally. This means you can access other yous in other bodies in later years through astral projection, dream states, and hallucinogenics. Many ways to understand truth of All.

Timelines and Shifts

> *There is nowhere you are not. There is no one you are not. You are the universe and the cosmos. You are other undiscovered and undetected places and planes. You are Source. We are all Source Energy split into an infinite number of parts and places, souls and bodies, grass, or trees. Everything is energy. Everything living and breathing. Alive or dead. Near or far. This is it. This is the secret of all secrets. You are the pages of this book but also the entire book.*
> — The All of The All

Everything is energy; therefore, everything is connected—even other lives. Ones can shift into other realities and timelines. This is when you feel déjà vu or have the sensation that you have been somewhere before. It can also be a merging of consciousness when two realities rejoin in time. So you could, for example, become one with life 2 or life 5.

Let's say you forked paths at around age seven. One part of you went into dance class, loved it, and left feeling joyous and wanting to return. The other (ego) piece of you witnessed girls or boys snickering at your leotard, leaving you feeling defeated. You go home and made a choice: (Love) stay in dance as you enjoyed it immensely, or (fear) make it clear to your parents you would never return. They (also having choices) could proceed to allow you to quit or say, "Okay." End of dance.

Now it's fifteen years later. One version found other interests to pursue and, being quite adept at trivia, joined a league where you met a partner for a romantic connection. Later, you marry this person and become intrigued by a thought of having children. In this moment, another version (2) is becoming a mom, also meeting a partner through work. Those two lives are parallel existences based on decisions prior. Two other versions of self exist, having similar experiences true to who you were if fear was chosen and remained.

Now you are fifty, and your children are grown and off to college. You choose to find activities to fill the space and void felt with them out of the home. A local chain dedicated to classes for dance and movement opens in the town where you live. Intrigued by the notion of dance (despite early years having quit) you find yourself signing up for a class and taking a first step toward the joy of dance after quitting at age seven.

Meanwhile, version 5 made a choice in her early years to pursue dance and to teach it later in life. She has a studio built in her backyard where kids came to learn. Eventually she decided to base her teachings in a particular modality for movement and growth. Franchising this was a goal (that this version of you reached), and now there are studios throughout a tri-state area for children and adults.

This particular life is going to merge as you step into the studio. The two versions meet at the door—one being the owner, the other the student. Déjà vu occurs, each knowing a moment as if it happened before. They see you, and you see them as One. The life of 1 and 5 now merge and a need for perpendicular lives over. Each chose Love and "met" and merged. So the end of consciousness of fear returns to Love, where it awaits all lives' merge. 1 and 2, 5 and 7—however many turns it took, both perpendicular and parallel are based upon choices made in the now.

What happened to number 5?

The end of consciousness as all minds rejoined.

What happens to her family? Friends? Coworkers? Students?

A most interesting question, which as soul knows, is based in fear. A life is a mind's figment. In earlier books it had been revealed a soul is not able to live two lives on Earth in the same body, and this is true. What can happen is two souls can split timelines. So, you are the same soul and body experiencing life differently. When Ones get into the studio (in our story), their reality is frayed with another's reality that isn't actually happening, but merely a mind arch—a tapestry weaving a story through choice and decision of Love and fear, which may merge and diverge over time, weaving in and out of one another's lives. Their "Earth" exclusively accessed by them, and yours's by you; and if they find one another (returning to Love) the mind's merge into singularity, not knowing the other had split. Think of it like a master and architect building a landscape with other builders and subjects. Each has domain and dominion until the project or conquest is over.

It can be the same building, same landscape, and same architecture, but not the same experience—a mental picture created by you, a hologram that felt real to them but was, in fact, hallucinated into reality. A version of this is showcased in the film, *Sliding Doors* (1998, Miramax Films). Eventually, all roads lead to soul as you being One.

Another metaphor is TV's *Severance* (2022, Apple TV+), where a character splits consciousness, knowing both realities as the same body—each fighting to stay relevant later, as they learn of each experience. "Innies" or "Outies" (as they are called in the show) realize different versions of life in a body designed to be free of burdens. Sound familiar? All meanings inspired by us to show you a lens of what it is to be soul.

You can step into a life, out of a life, merge lives, or cross and return to soul (heaven). All of this accessible in dreams.

Dreams

Dreams reveal what is happening in the mind. Through images and sounds, you move through scenarios and circumstances with an understanding that they are unreal. Awakening to Source is as real as the life you are living, and as you return, this current life (incarnationally) is as unreal as the very dreams we mentioned. You can't accept the truth because you chose not to prior to incarnating. "Show me a life as if it were real. Keep me asleep until I'm ready to awaken. Give me road maps and define the journey, and I will make the best of all of it—even if I stumble or fall. Only when I have fully returned to Spirit may I know All." Remember?
— Wisdom of The All

Dreams are consciousness blending lives—past, present, future, and current—all melding together to remind you of themes and contracts being worked through. Each "you" moves through similar challenges and events to grow the soul through what had been decided upon prior. For example, dreaming of a life being chased by a tiger could signify fear in a particular situation or partnership now. Dreaming of a dance studio you had never stepped foot into but recognizing the self as its owner may be a glimpse of a reality existing perpendicular to your own.

Dreams often predict future as every One is capable of tapping into Earth's Akasha. This is how predictions are made: seeing lives and events via the records of consciousness. Each planet has its records accessible to all, which is how Ones can "see" or know of events meant—or possible—to occur. Ones who know All understand these are possibilities and recognize the caution needed when sharing them with others. Doing so could create a self-fulfilling prophecy for an event that may not be needed to occur. Ones would do well to ask to receive before speaking on it outwardly:

Help me, dear All, know what is possible and if this is to be shared or kept to self.

247

In dreams, One can travel to places and spaces outside of Earth. "Visiting" other planets is how the notion of aliens came to be, with many experiencing lives through visioning in sleep.

Lucid dreaming is where Ones feel awake inside of dreams and can visit with loved Ones in Spirit, or those in other places on Earth or beyond, including other planetary or solar systems. Ones can visit parallel or perpendicular realities if they believe it possible; otherwise, such travels are usually left to dream states alone.

One of our favorite mechanisms of visitation is the dream state. Those who left physical bodies are able to appear in dream states with those whom they love, have known, or who are waiting to see them again. A visitation can feel as real as it does sitting here as we explore ideas and concepts in this book—or it could be simply experiencing life together again, with Ones' recognizing it as dreaming and not real.

You are capable of so much more than you know, dear Ones, and dreams are the clues to what is happening in time and space.

Mediumship / Talking to Spirit

Channeling is speaking for Spirit. Mediumship is communing with Spirits in "heaven." Life is knowing you are Spirit in body forms. Understanding the energy from which we all come is Spirit and how you open a window, door, and portal to All.
— Wisdom of The All

Every One who is near and dear to our self is available to cheer on their beloved friends, family, lovers, and those who they have affected in their physical form on Earth. Just like on Earth, however, there are various levels of ascension, and it is fallacy (again) to believe that everyone is instantly loving, kind, and dancing in "heaven." It may take time for Spirit to ascend and become One with All, and likewise, time to learn how to communicate from "heaven," on Earth—though spirit realm is the more accurate term.

So how do mediums access Spirit?

By asking.

"Help me remember I am connected to every soul on Earth and outside."

Asking is consent.

"May I speak with your loved Ones?"

This an important step if you are working as an empath, psychic, medium, or channel.

Ways to Communicate with Spirits

Mediumship is learning to access higher realms. Think of it as the sign language of souls. Each realm has its own vibration: Earth requires an ask to ascend higher, and those in Spirit must lower their frequency. Each soul then "meets in the middle," so to speak—which is why it's called mediumship. You become a vessel to commune.

Develop a symbol system. Don't rely on another One's interpretations. Develop your own symbols and signs and once you choose them, stay consistent.

Examples:

Bird: feeling free of burdens.

Pencils: rewriting a new story.

Stones: stepping forward in life.

Yellow: mother figure or grandparent.

Brown: fathers and father figures.

Gold: God or Source.

Use your clairsenses. You can hear, sense, feel, know, see, smell, and even taste to decipher and decode a message. Ones can feel what they felt, know how they passed, or smell a musk only a child could place. The senses grow stronger with use. Once you find what "works," use it consistently, as many mediums and psychics do. Everyone is equally capable of discovering this if they want too. Some feel called to do it for others, while others are simply happy to connect for themselves.

Ask questions. *Is this what I am seeing? Are you here with me? Can you give me details or more information?* Without questions, Spirits may not always be able to communicate intentionally. Asking keeps answers from being blocked; not asking is like holding a phone without dialing. Spirits must be pinged or "poked" to know you wish to commune.

Help is available. Be aware that fear (ego) can filter or distort messages alongside Love. Be willing to seek guides, angels, or Source to interpret what is being shared. Our intention is to help guide you—but only when asked.

Spirits' personalities remain. Those in nonphysical realms are an amalgamation of all their incarnational lives, each collecting along the way new ways of being. Someone joyful and playful in life is often similar in Spirit. Those who lived troubled lives may still hold illusions of separation and may not be as warm or inviting as you expect. Every One has lessons to learn—Spirit or soul—so use that as a guide to gauge their vibration in nonphysical realms.

One thing that remains is LOVE. Love is constant once a soul crosses into nonphysical life. While they may be shy or unable to bring forth stark details right away, they will always love those in the physical. It is one thing to be Love and another to know you are it. A soul in "heaven" isn't necessarily aware it is All. Even awakened souls are still learning.

Don't expect all Spirits to be fully ascended into Love, but know they remember Love and exist without fear. A message of fear or anger toward those in the body is false and untrue. They love you and drop Earth's judgments and nonsense (fear).

Patience is required. Communicating with loved Ones in Spirit can be more difficult for those who knew them, because grief is a lower vibration and limits exposure. Be willing to wait until you are more aligned, or visit a medium who is less encumbered by grief. Be wary of "too much information" coming through; it could be a soul still influenced by ego, or a reader too attached to dogma or religious notions about Spirit and heaven.

Channeling / Talking for Spirit

Channeling is what you do with Love and all are channels of God/Love. The songs you write, poems you make, words you speak of Love are from All. With this in mind, keep asking for the truth and we (All) bring it through.
— Wisdom of The All

Not only are Ones able to talk with Spirit—it's also possible to talk *as* Spirit. Because you are One being All, every One is accessible by and through mind. Telepathy is talking with others in mind; channeling is talking as another One. Both are natural abilities, as this is how communication occurs in Spirit. One mind as All.

Ones in Spirit telepathically receive words and messages between minds. A channel is necessary for those in physical realms to receive information and downloads that can be filtered through various Ones in Spirit.

Ways to Channel with Spirit

Talk for Source. Ones can communicate with All, as All. This is how our books are being created—One (Laura) talking with, to and as All. Both minds connected as One.

Talk for Angels (More Evolved Souls). Ones can speak as higher-evolved souls and become their voice. You listen, receive words, and immediately translate to others for purposes of sharing wisdom and light. Every One

251

has access to angels and archangels, but remember; as One all are angels at various stages. Creating hierarchies defeats the purpose of soul evolution.

Talk as a loved one in Spirit. You can Source any One in Spirit as a medium or channel. Speaking for another soul is usually for communicating with loved Ones on Earth. You bring forth a willing soul, and it becomes a linked mind—their personality and presence flow through you to bring messages.

Talk for some One on Earth. Ones can communicate telepathically with others in the physical. This is a skill you build and is especially useful if you are a Speaker or healer. You can share minds and thoughts, becoming a voice for another.

Directly speak with ancestors or goddesses (highly evolved spirits). As with Spirits connected to your soul family, you can speak for shamans, religious leaders, or other highly evolved souls who bring deep knowledge of Source. This differs from ordinary mediumship: these leaders are Earth guides meant to evolve the collective. As with all Spirit communication, asking is the key to making a connection. This is where a Spirit Guide may be utilized.

Speak as your soul, which you are doing every day in various degrees of separation. When you sit in silence, words come through and can be heard in mind. When speaking Love and what flows from it, you are Sourcing.

Speak as plants, animals, birds, trees, and anything inanimate. As everything is energy and frequency it makes sense it is possible to channel and connect to everything. Language is not just human, but also lingual as entities, who can use thought coming as Source even if unexpressed as "words." Without thought you are less likely to be in fear and those with "supernatural" abilities are only utilizing frequency and translating into words (via All, as One) what is being "spoken" by other beings of consciousness.

Guidelines for Channeling

Many of the same principles that apply to mediumship also apply here. Take your time. Know that every One has a level of vibration in all places, and you can only access what you know at the level currently available to you as Spirit or Soul. Source knows All, and that is accessible as well—but only through highly conscious mediums or channels until Earth's vibration collectively heightens.

Remember: Though we work as "channels," these are words currently used on Earth. You are sharing information as One through All. This allows you to access more information through Source. You are Sourcing, not channeling. A channel infers something is outside the self; a Source is where all information exists. You access the All for the soul or souls you work with, speak to, or become. Words are worth evolving when time is right on Earth.

A Note on Spirit Guides

Yes, Ones have a multitude of guides available to seek. However, do not lean too heavily into the idea of Spirit Guides. Ones who are consistently and only seeing guides are often tied to lower vibrations of consciousness. The higher the frequency of Earth, the less need for Spirit Guides, because One becomes All and knows every One as All. Ultimately, you need only All to communicate as One.

Numerology

> *Numbers have significance. They hold frequency and energy. Each number a code to higher truths. How you use them in life is either conscious or unconscious. Days go by, years too, but when you ask to be guided to their meanings, an entire mechanism is unlocked of Source. The goal is freedom and numbers align you to it.*
> — Wisdom of The All

Numbers play a significant role in all of life. They are literally everywhere you look. On signposts, roads, house numbers, office numbers and more. You have birth days and birth years, calendar days and times. All leading you as you go throughout life. Each number representing an aspect of All That Is. Every One has a contract for what they have come to learn about, so variations do exist based on those ideals and ideas Ones chose to move through. However, there are themes and these can be used in general, but remember to go deeper within self (or with a healer) to discover the meaning for you—Your Only Universe.

There are nine numbers in life (plus zero), and every number is consequentially one through nine taken to its root. This means that any multi-digit number can be reduced to a single digit (1–9) by adding its digits together, a process called digit reduction or finding the digital root.Those numbers are part of daily life and have significance to our personal and collective experiences. Each has its own meaning and definition. Becoming aware of days and months can keep you in a state of flow, knowing what's happening in time is meant to create action or inaction.

0 —

Neutrality.

1—

New beginnings and fresh starts.

2—

Partnership and duality.

3—

Transformation and turnover. Three is the cycle of everything. Man, woman and child. Father, son, holy spirit. Yes, no, maybe.

4—

Our four seasons. A quadrant of emotions and being able to empathize with others.

5—

Information and knowledge.

6—

Karma and balance.

7—

Off the deep end, down the rabbit hole—and eventually luck leads.

8—

A born leader or teacher of all walks of life—scientists, theologians and more. Infinity.

9—

Endings and completion.

Numerological Codes

Every One comes to learn, grow, and evolve here. In doing so, the code that unlocks *why* is encoded in our birth days, birth months, and years. Each carries its own message and meaning, breaking down into mind, body, and soul awareness.

A code has three frequencies, each number unlocking personality and soul traits earned prior.

An example would be: 3, 1, 5. A mind of 3, a body of 1, and a soul 5. All connecting dots to the y-o-u of your only Universe.

Everything on Earth is oppositionary, which means dependent upon One's soul journey, you can be at one end of the spectrum or another. The codes influence one another (like archetypes) so your three numbers work in harmony or disharmony as you evolve on Earth. The more awakened and evolved you are, the less ego is involved, and the higher your frequency, consciousness, or awareness are, the easier your experience of Earth.

Like archetypes, the codes are representations, not absolutes. What day you are born on has a temperate meaning, in that it guides choices until you become a navigator of Source. Once you know the stones were just steps, you follow a true path to Source of awakening in mind. You can evolve into another way of being and lose fear to become another code or type. Each code has an archetype it is most associated with, and you may refer back to those pages to see how it aligns.

Each code number carries both a light attribute (aligned with the Ladder of Awareness and the highest truths we aim to grow toward) and a dark synchronicity, reflected when One's continued focus remains in ego— whether through *Victim, Blame,* or *Achiever/Manipulation* mindsets.

Don't be surprised if you don't relate to some of what is written. Instead, be encouraged: it may indicate you are reaching toward higher light or that you may never reside in the darker synchrony of ego. It is more a clue of where you were prior rather than where you stand now. Those deeply rooted in ego are unlikely to find their way to this work for another century or more.

Mind Code

To find Ones numerological code, we begin with the **Mind**—the day you were born. The mind represents how you move throughout life when faced with challenges and lessons. One either evolves or repeats; the mind's choice creates what is next.

To calculate the code, reduce your birth date to a single digit:

Examples:

$15 = 1 + 5 = 6$

$19 = 1 + 9 = 10 \rightarrow 1 + 0 = 1$

If you were born on a single-digit day like the 7th or 9th, those stay as single digits.

Below is a categorization of each number and how it works at the level of the mind. Remember, these apply to both ends of the spectrum—those who are awakening and the Ones who sleep. How you move through life determines the operating system of the mind. You can be one way and then lean the other on given days, or you can transform into the higher version of Love and "flip" the switch off that ego once held. As you read through, notice where you are on the spectrum and what seems more aligned to Love. Those characteristics are achievable. In the same vein, a fall to fear isn't necessarily an end result. Ones can move up the Ladder of Awareness, choose higher light and become more of the true self, as chosen by you at the level of soul.

Like astrology, the day you were born (higher or lower in the month) is key to how One born in the early weeks versus the later weeks may have similarities and differences. So read through and see where you may fall.

Mind 1 — (Birth Days 1, 10, 19, 28)

A new beginning. A chance to see differently and a measure for when it's time to move on. It represents individuality or standing on One's own.

Choosing self over anyone else's opinions is part of your soul's learning. Those with 1 as their soul number (or life path) too are often highly sensitive or easily wounded by opinions other than One's own. Ex: 1, 3, 1.

Do you know a 1? Perhaps someone in your family or a friend who has chosen to lead a solo life? These are Ones who are 1 life paths, chosen prior to remain alone as a learning mechanism.

1s as partners can feel moved to make a choice versus staying alone—society, religion, or philosophies driving you to seek "the One" when, in fact, you enjoy aloneness. Two 1's make 2 and therefore can find partnership as processive and individuality a choice each honors—finding common ground and making time for self alone.

Other 1s welcome leadership as part of their contract, and some do this throughout history as Ones who have spoken out against fear. While 1s as *Lions* share fear and lead others to it.

1s who are *Artisans* tend toward music or poetry.

To be alone is easier in times of struggle, and it's important to let another 1 be able to examine on their own time, allowing them space to be. A 1, 7, 3 is particularly prone to needing time to process and grieve.

Most common archetypes: *Lion, Taskmaster, Arguer.*

Light Attributes: *Leaders and decision-makers; champions of change and inclusivity.*

Dark Synchronicity: *Self-centered, stubborn, and suspicious of others' intentions.*

Mind 2 — (Birth Days 2, 11, 20, 29)

The number of partnership and duality. 2s feel safest in relationship—romantic, friendships, assistants, cohorts and collaborators in all decisions. They prefer to seek council from another person before making decisions, as this is what had been chosen prior.

Ask a 2 to decide, and they might lean on a higher self for revelation, if this is an awakened One.

Not satisfied with a partner, they move from one to the next quickly and swiftly, as comfort is key to their survival, and when in relationships they find solace and serenity.

Need is a reason they come to Earth, needing to discover themselves as teammates versus individuals as our 1s do. 2s are known to travel in pairs and prefer companionship to isolation and time alone.

Some 2s are Ones who have decided for a particular partner via a soul contract, but more often they are Ones who chose to do life twogether with another One.

A 2 in partnership is happiest in relation to others. A 2 without a mate is struggling to accept their lack, which may keep One stuck in the creation of one. Depending upon archetypes and other numbers (body/soul), it can be One's hardest circumstance to navigate, as wanting a partner is a thematic choice as soul. A 2, 3, 9 is example of One who may desire a partner and yet struggle to proceed toward it. As always, it depends on the ladder step One has reached between fear and Love. A *Victim* won't reach high enough, while a *Worrier* lives in repeat patterns. A *Mindful* One can overcome.

Partners made in arrangement (by others) is often an area where a 2 can struggle, feeling unsatisfied if they did not choose their mate.

Most common archetypes: *Persona, Dreamer, Architect.*

Light Attributes: *Loving toward others and peaceful.*

Dark Synchronicity: *Emotionally inconsistent; fear-based around romance and partnerships.*

Mind 3 — (Birth Days 3, 12, 21, 30)

An awakened 3 seeks serenity, comfort, and kindness. They exude peace, of which they had cultivated prior. Those 3s will try to smooth out edges after they have fought, if they ever do. They do not like conflict and prefer to steer clear of it. They will, however, go inward when attacked.

They can be do-gooders and volunteers, depending on their archetypal nature *(Healers/Seers)*.

Some 3s are creative artisans and tinker in various projects, never settling on one thing. They prefer to have many going and (depending on their archetype) may or may not finish the endeavor *(Dreamer vs. Taskmaster)*.

3s are here to overcome patterns, repetition, and processes of before. If a transformation occurs, they are easily swayed by soul and not guided by ego. If Ones, however, stay stuck in repetitive patterns, a 3 can become quite anxious and confused. Example: 3, 7, 5.

Be wary if you are stuck or stubborn, and know its bendability time for you.

3s are good strategists and most *Tacticians* are a 3 in mind, body, or soul.

Most common archetypes: *Taskmaster, Tactician, Artisan.*

Light Attributes: *Easily impressed. Able to move through emotion quickly before escalating situations or making them more difficult. Naturalistic and intuitive—especially with animals, trees, and plants.*

Dark Synchronicity: *Anxious and fearful of nearly everything. Impatient; require immediate results ("now"). Tend to process time with urgency. Strategy utilized serves fear for self, others. or collectively.*

Mind 4 — (Birth Days 4, 13, 22, 31)

A 4 person makes a good leader.

4s are able to overcome anger quickly because they are able to quickly shift to empathy and trust. They know others are doing their best and trying. Without this, they would be overly challenged on Earth, as they are deep thinkers wanting to know, "Why?" To overcome this, a 4 must take measures of mind to meditate, contemplate, theorize and evolve. Especially our *Healers* and *Artisans.*

4s can be highly sensitive and reclusive because they feel energy more deeply than other Ones.

You can tell a 4 by their need to be liked and adored, especially if there archetype is that of a *Persona.* Ones would do well to shower them with affection if Ones want to stay connected to them. Any One who makes them feel disconnected may be tossed out by their need to be right or make a point. "I don't need you," they would say. Example: 4, 5, 6.

4's are oft swayed by others (if asleep) and may turn to outside sources of comfort to ease the heart and mind. They can become overrun with emotions, and if choices are made in fear over and over again, it might be a challenge to stay out of dark places—especially if One is a 7 of body or soul. Awareness is key to avoiding the pitfalls of mind. Make time to be, and ask to be guided through—or find a mental-health or therapeutic healer.

Every archetype has a way of being that goes along with our numbers, but 4s have all archetypes and therefore can be more sensitive and sad at times.

You will know a 4 if they want to "fix" or "heal" you, but they are meant to heal themselves before all others.

Most common archetypes: *Healer, Wanderer, Artisan, Seer, Dreamer and so on.*

Light Attributes: *Socially adept at navigating all types of people and environments. Not particularly judgmental or "-ist." Sees all as equals.*

Dark Synchronicity: *May be unkind to others and operate from a "that's mine" mentality—taking without being offered. Can struggle to embody kindness and Love if One has experienced abuse or rejection.*

Mind 5 — (Birth Days 5, 14, 23)

The number of learning. It informs you in life. Ones begin at age five to learn facts, figures and numbers/letters. Our first glimpse of language becoming useful in life.

5s are learners. They want to be able to understand how the world operates and what makes them tick.

On the other side, 5's can have disabilities of learning, which are, of course, the reason each chose to journey on Earth—to overcome what is hard or challenging of other lives' decisions. One may have been a teacher or scholar, and through each life collected information, it was chosen to forget in order to experience our yin/yang. All experiences must be had as soul. This can apply for both body and soul 5s too.

Doctors are often 5s who are *Healer* archetypes. Example: 5, 4, 2.

Librarians and bookkeepers, statisticians, and accountants are 5s associated with *Architects, Taskmasters or Tacticians.* Facts and figures give them a great peace in knowing logically what is to come.

When they don't have the answers, 5s can struggle. It's as if they are seeking and can't become whole until they know what it means to make something. They are finishers and don't like to leave anything unsaid or undone. A *Dreamer* would be example here of an archetypal nature they hold.

You are a 5 if you are able to remember big ideas and recall them quickly.

5s are reclusive in their findings and may not wish to share like a 1 or 8 would.

5 also stands for abundance and resources. If you see repeating 5s (555) it is to remind you a big reach is in your grasp, and it's now time to take a leap toward it. It may be also be about karma, as three 5s in a row (5+5+5 = 15 → 5 +1 = 6) become a 6. *"What is the message for me?"* is proper to asking when deciding for its message to you.

Awakening 5s are good with people, able to converse and share and interested to know who they are beyond simple courtesy. They prefer more interesting or deep conversations and dialogue.

Most common archetypes: *Architect, Taskmaster, Tactician.*

Light attributes: *Curious and confident, with little need to ask for information from another One. Prefer to receive it from Source or through sources such as books and guides.*

Dark synchronicity: *Unable to accept others' advice and resistant to receiving help or having anyone "butting into" their business or ideas.*

Mind 6 — (Birth Days 6, 15, 24)

Smart and foolish, silly and pragmatic, strong and weak—6s embody duality. They tend to lean left or right on topics and grasp concepts on both ends of the spectrum. Stick to the middle, and Ones may move beyond a circumstance offered to evolve. Stay in one side or the other, and its imbalance creating anxiety or frustration.

6s need balance to stay regulated. It can be overwhelming when tasks are piling up—or annoying if there is nothing to do. Depending on the archetype most associated, and other codes (body/soul), it can lead to arguments and hurt feelings—a chance to make amends and evolve, or slip backward into old ways of being. Example: 6, 5, 2.

A need to seek council is wise, but 6s tend to stay more "me" focused than "we" if unawakened and unwilling to evolve especially when a *Lion* is involved in their archetypal nature.

6s can be easily swayed to one side or the other when "proof" is offered. Instead, it's best to seek council from All before decisions, as this becomes their best maneuver throughout life.

More aligned 6s can offer insights at a higher awareness and be quite impactful themselves, swaying others to their way of being, which is now balanced.

Karma is a recurring theme of all 6s and will show up time and again, more so at the soul level (life path) than in mind, but it's wise to know this is a theme for all 6s of mind/body and soul.

Most common archetype: *Tactician, Architect, Arguer.*

Light attributes: *Stable and strong-willed. Open to others' opinions and able to navigate toward Love and guide conversations to a place more aligned with it. Capable of reflecting unity—"I see you. I am you."*

Dark synchronicity: *Resistant to guidance—"Don't tell me what to do!" Takes without giving and receives karma in return without understanding the "why."*

Mind 7 — (Birth Days 7, 16, 25)

Often seen as the reverse in Tarot, it means you have something to do around themes and contracts. You are here to overcome and evolve every challenge placed in mind. The Ones who stay committed to growth of soul achieve a new way of being and bear witness to a shift in consciousness. The Ones who are incapable of being mindful to life's flow and ebbs—who are caught in a trapped mind—are going to struggle in finances and love. Example: 7, 1, 8.

Our earthly circumstances mirror our minds. So what is seen and experienced is upon the thinker; and Ones would do well to understand (as despair and depression arise) it must be overcome quickly so Ones can again thrive in mind.

Prone to caution, 7s can become stuck and unable to move out of fear. This is where choice is important. Lean into Love to be helped through. Seek a healer, professional, or spiritual mentor. 7s are more apt to wisely seek help than other Ones.

A lucky 7 can be an awakened One (or a sleeper who is choosing to be) and amending other selves' karma and balance. Usually these are *Wanderers*.

There are 7s immediately prone to luck and good fortune. It seems to follow them everywhere—and it does—and this is due to their vibrational nature, more attuned to Love as soul or, as human, love—which are in fact One. All choices begin at Love and are filtered through the lens you had prior to incarnating on Earth. A *Seer* is a wise One as Buddha was and is now *heavenly.

Common archetypes: *Dreamer, Wanderer, Healer.*

Light attribute: *Lucky in all areas of life; carries the belief that "things come to me out of nowhere."*

Dark synchronicity: *Prone to depressive thoughts and, at times, intentions of harm or disparagement—toward others, as well as toward One's own self, family, or friendships.*

**stars represent those in Spirit continuing to guide Earth.*

Mind 8 — (Birth Days 8, 17, 26)

The number of divine consciousness. We are infinite, and our symbol relates to the 8. We are guided by a keen and sharp mind and surrender to overthinking if we are awakened or aware of Love. Those who don't may be tied to a theology of God or cultural influences of Gods and Kings or Rulers. Those teachers are meant to guide others and can sway the Ones who are more susceptible to influence or adherence to rules and constructs. Example: 8, 1, 1.

Don't be fooled if you are an 8s loyal follower. Be influenced by All That Is.

8s can be both angelic and devilish. Two parts, one whole. Beware the *Lion* 8 so you won't get bit.

An awakened 8 is more aligned to Source and tend to be gentle and kind if they are aware of a connection to Divine Love. They seek to guide others and often become teachers or mentors.

Artists and *Artisans* are 8s "seeing" through Love, sharing works of All/God or other deities of Earth.

Most Common Archetypes: *Lion, Artisan, Persona, Architect, Seer.*

Light attributes: *Open and receptive; God-like and masterful in behaviors that help guide others.*

Dark synchronicity: *Able to love only when loved unconditionally by another. Lacks self-love, and therefore struggles to love others. May become manipulative or controlling without understanding the underlying cause.*

Mind 9 — (Birth Days 9, 18, 27)

9s love attention and community. They like to surround themselves with others. Unlike 1s who tend to prefer solo activities or quiet spaces and alone time, they crave activity and like to keep busy or social especially those who are *Taskmasters* or *Artisans*—taking classes rather than figuring it out themselves.

Any One of our awakened or non-awakened are keen to either finish a project or face frustration for keeping things open (ideas, projects, registers). A sign-off or need to be done is common amongst our 9 minders.

It can be a sign of a 9 mind in your midst if they close drawers, move things around, or shut doors both mentally and physically. A rigid 9 is common amongst sleepers. Example: 9, 6, 5.

Settings such as apartments, co-housing, convents, or ashrams are perfect for a 9 in both earlier or later life. If Ones—who are 9s—are single, it may be part of a soul contract to enjoy spaces with others and to follow paths made prior to achieve this by soul. Monks and missionaries would be examples here of 9 minds who are *Healers* and *Seers*.

9s on the evolutionary scale may be on last lives of Earth or ready to adventure to another place before hopping back in (body) on Earth, a *Wanderer* for sure.

Most common archetype: *Wanderer, Architect, Adventurer*

Light attributes: *Moving on feels good and aligned. Ready to adventure— bold and daring.*

Dark synchronicity: *Leaves without saying goodbye. Does not manage anger well and may fly off the handle, disrupting a day or moment until the anger is released. Has little awareness of time and space—tends to do what they want, when they want.*

Body Code

Next, we move onto the **Body** and how our codes are based in our movements and decisions, as well as health and happiness therein.

To find this number, you will take the day plus the month in which you were born. So 7/15 becomes 7 + 6, which equals 13 (1 + 3) and that becomes 4. All numbers reach a single digit, and that is where addition happens. So 7 + 1 + 5 = 13 and then 1 + 3 = 4.

Examples:

8/27 = 8+2+7 = 17 → 1 + 7 = 8

12/3 = 1+2+3 = 6

As before, understanding both qualities of self (Love and fear) is key to learning on Earth. So leaning one way is true for some, and others a mix of both—or an overcomer, meaning what was learned is done and gone already. It speaks more to who you were then who you are now.

Body 1 —

A leader. 1s at the body level feel called to lead. They stand up for themselves and call out others when they don't lead.

It is challenging if they can't be alone at times of uncomfortableness or through inherent frequencies of unrest or turmoil. They like alone time and crave reading, writing, or being involved in the activity of choice. Freedom is necessary to feel at peace, and leading others is valued as joyous and fulfilling.

1s stand tall, often becoming dancers or athletes—movement where they feel tall and empowered.

Light attributes: *Free and easy; mindful of others—even when choosing a solo path.*

Dark synchronicity: *Going solo feels effortless. Prefers isolation and may withdraw into their home or personal space. Often keeps others at a distance emotionally—and at times physically.*

Body 2 —

A cupid or heart warrior. A 2 feels partnership is important. They look for love, lovers, and friendships which deepen a connection to themselves. Partners are mirrors to who they wish to be and who they are.

Like 1s, it's good to be individualized as necessity to bring emotions to closure. They may need a fixer or helper to understand themselves more deeply, but processing is solo, focusing on their needs of the heart.

Like The Lovers in Tarot, it's meant to heal past relationships of other lifetimes, and to be successful is evolutionary for All.

A 2 who is alone has a soul script to reunite or partner with another but may be challenged in overcoming what is possible, remaining alone for lengths of time or not achieving a partnership. They will it for the life (as soul did wish for it) but forget it in fear and failure, and will need help accepting what is.

Light attributes: *You love love. You believe everyone deserves romance and connection. Playing cupid feels fun and exciting, and setting two people up brings you joy and fulfillment. Celebrating others comes naturally to you.*

Dark synchronicity: *Tend toward overthinking and can be stubborn or difficult to be around at times.*

Body 3 —

The transformer. 3s of body are mindfully aware of emotion and use time to sustain mentally via various practices—swimming, biking, or mindful hikes. Those asleep may shut down emotionally, unaware of what heals and evolves them through.

They may be open to meditation and mindfulness or may use therapy and other medical- or science- based resources to overcome and repair broken hearts, relationship woes, or simple upsets and stressors.

A 3 is a processor. Repeating and recycling are only for education and simply minding the mental patterns of the mind. They choose to know themselves with awareness of body and mind unrest.

They seek to partner with like-minded souls and begin to partner earlier than others (friends, colleagues and love romantically), especially if a 2 mind. As always our shadow self plays a role in our movements, and wanting a partner can interrupt a 3s soul truth making the ask unattainable or challenging. At heart, they are achievers and receivers—until ego gets its way in mind.

Light attributes: *Do not remain in depression or anxiety for long. Even-keeled, tending to dip slowly into lower emotions but able to rise above them, returning to peace and surrendering thoughts to Love.*

Dark synchronicity: *Lost in a world of dark beliefs, convinced the world is "out to get you."*

Body 4 —

An empath. The Ones who feel deeply and know the suffering of others without experiencing it oneself. They mix emotion with love and overshare to connect to others. This can be taken as both good and bad by another One.

Those who feel disconnection from others can recluse, and Ones of 4 are often overly confident if asleep—compensation for bodily distortion issues or beliefs (e.g., "I'm fat," or "too tall."—a dislike of self.)

4s tend to find parties and group events challenging because they feel and sense the energy of spaces and places. They can be wary if danger is near and tend to keep to themselves when in pain, especially if a 7 life path. It is there goal to achieve harmony with All but through challenges, missteps, and finally Love.

They often are liked for their wise advice and attract other 4s to gain perspective and lead each other to a revelatory thought.

Uprooting beliefs is key, as they attract most illness via thought and belief. Once understood One is in charge, 4s can find a way to overcome and initiate a healing for that circumstance.

4 bodies are emotional beings and tend to be more prone to illness. If they are a 7 in mind, it's important to relax and unwind daily and not weekly. Letting time pass can lead to burn out. Seek showers and outdoors time to flush the "toxins" of other Ones.

Light attributes: *Loves others unconditionally. Holds space for the healing of self and others. A cultural anomaly. No true gender or form—simply being.*

Dark synchronicity: *"No one likes me." "I'm old and unloved." Or "I'm trapped in a body I don't like or understand why it fails me." Holds too many insecurities about self.*

Body 5 —

Learning is key. They are the tinkerers who prefer to touch and feel and take apart something to know its inner workings.

They can't always be convinced unless experienced by themselves.

5s are keen to become architects, engineers, or entrepreneurs. As long as they have a hand in building something, they are happier in life.

5s who can't find a mechanism to express themselves through movement or flow are going to struggle and must find ways to utilize this energy. They need an outlet for kineticism.

A 5 body has a contract to learn from a circumstance meant to grow and evolve them. It may be a birth day issue they are born with or, along the way, a bodily hiccup or challenge. Think slow growth and not fear or heartache. A blip to keep them vibrating and seeking Love. a 5 body and 5 soul are for overcoming the circumstance chosen prior to agreeing to Earth's return. A version of self healed and thriving can be witnessed in mind via Akasha.

Light attributes: *"This issue or ailment served me well. I learned, grew, and evolved from it. Now I can teach others or take classes to go beyond my current knowledge base."*

Dark synchronicity: *"I hate my life and how it turned out for me. This was too hard or difficult to handle, and no one helped me or understood my pain."*

Body 6 —

Balancers. These are Ones who are due to overshare and surrender to others' opinions and belief systems if unawakened. They tend to go one way and then another, eventually finding balance between both and coming to One's own conclusions. If not, they are allowing fear to lead, as the purpose of One's life is to live in truth, and being too far right or left is imbalance.

6s are dedicated to self and body. Image is a theme they must overcome as self-worth and value are tied to the ego. Spending time in One's mirror (physically) is a sign to learn love of self.

A 6 awakened is good at balancing days and follow a regiment or structure for it. They might be morning walks or evening strolls or reading a book before bed. A need to wind down or gear up is a control switch they utilize often.

A 6 can mean karma in body, which may portend One's earthly experience needing to right a wrong (in human words) for past misgivings. So those who are born into some challenge or strength (like speed or wit) are balancing a karmic cycle. If chosen (as soul), it may be with them for this life and unable to be overcome as body, yet know this is by design for evolutionary growth.

A 6 can be torn in life, afraid to make decisions as they are torn between fear (ego) and love (soul.) Ones with 6 at body need to learn trust, and key experiences for this will show up repeatedly for Ones to learn to choose and accept the next step is always there for evolution of self.

Light attributes: *"I trust my soul, and the answers I see and know come through easily when I ask."*

Dark synchronicity: *"Don't bother. I won't listen or care—too caught up in ego to overcome my old self."*

Body 7—

Lucky in love, unlucky at home. It is the suitcase we take in to the experience to expand and evolve.

The 7 body has a timed experience needed to evolve beyond a theme or contract. These may show up as mental or emotional experiences leading to a revelation of self, e.g, *"I want to be a..."*—*to help another who may experience it as I did and wish to guide them through it.* It also could be physical in nature—being born with or having an experience at a young age. Those may serve as triggers of emotional or mental blocks.

It is most challenging to see beyond fear, and this is where a 7 can struggle with opening up to receive a hand or a guide (physically or emotionally). They seek attention from outside sources and not inside, or keep emotions inside and "handle" the chaos.

A 7 is also able to overcome and keep going, and this is where a turnaround is made to the lucky 7. Ease and flow and repeating "coincidences" are simply alignment to All.

A lucky 7 who is asleep or awake can be successful and may be wealthy in life or love.

Light attributes: *Success comes naturally to me, and I use it to help others.*

Dark synchronicity: *I keep what I make, believing it is my "right." I earned it through my circumstances, pain, or positioning.*

Body 8 —

Guides and guiders. Different from 1s, 8s are born with leadership to guide others with Love or fear.

A body 8 can be teaching Ones to Love or to use body wisely, as practices like tai chi, yoga, or qigong are commonly taught or enjoyed by evolved 8s.

On our other side, however, 8s are the manipulators who use others for their own purposes. Like *Lions*, egoic moves are defense of fear, and Ones would guide others to their way of the world or to follow their lead, however unjust it may be.

A wise 8 knows All. An asleep 8 fears God's wrath and believes it's their "job" to live in the shadow of what had been taught in theological teachings or books.

8s are sharp and witty. It can be hard to "sit it out" if arguments arise. They try and ease pain (awake) or exacerbate it (asleep).

Light attributes: *I see the world as One.*

Dark synchronicity: *I see the world as one—meaning just me.*

Body 9 —

The completer. A 9 feels called to finish a project or emotionally regale a loved One for doing good work. A champion for others' time paying off.

They like community and partnership, surrounding Oneself with friends, colleagues, or family. They are safer in group settings, and alone time is preferred only when sleeping.

Awake and aware Ones (of 9) finish the day with Love, wrapping up with a prayer or intention.

Asleep Ones can suffer insomnia if they left a project open and undone. It can quite literally keep you up at night if a fight or argument with a partner, colleague, or child goes unfinished or uncompleted.

Open ends make you suffer, and closed loops bring peace. Most 9s are projectors and expect others to do closed loops as well, and this can bring resentment and frustration if any One is a procrastinator in their circle.

9s who begin projects can sit for hours never moving from the work, but on the other spectrum may find they start and don't finish—too many balls in the air.

This is common among 9 bodies who are 1 and 2 mind *Artisans* and *Dreamers*.

Light attributes: *Time is a gift. I enjoy my time on Earth and with others along my journey of life.*

Dark synchronicity: *Time is either dragging on or slipping away too quickly.*

Soul Code / Life Path

The last number is our **Soul** code—the life path. It's what Ones come to learn and why. It showcases our journey and what may show up for us as themes or contracts. Some ideas or concepts may seem harsh when reading, but remember Ones are able to overcome what is set in Ones path. It's what you do with the rocks and stones—punish or polish, kick or console. Every One begins life with a Source code for what is needing moved beyond.

As an example, a 7 life might be very hard or challenging depending upon the consciousness level of our soul on Earth. Then, as you raise consciousness, 7 becomes lucky and life easier. Like in craps, it's how you roll the dice, and you are in charge of its flow. In craps, rolling a 7 can result in a win or a loss, depending on the stage of the game and the bet placed. There are messages everywhere, even in games, dear Ones.

To find your soul code add the day, plus month and year all together until a single digit is reached. For example: $12/25/2001 = 1 + 2 + 2 + 5 + 2 + 1 = 13$ and then $1 + 3 = 4$. So this person's Soul Code would be 4.

Another way to achieve this is to add the year together with your Body Code.

All roads lead to one digit that represents the journey of soul.

Here are a few more examples before we begin explaining soul path meanings in numerology:

Example: 5/29/2017

2, 7, 8 would be their numerological code.

Mind code = 2 + 9 = 11 → 1 + 1 = 2

Body code = (day) 2 + (month) 5 = 7

Soul Code – (month) 7 + (year) 1 = 8

This person's life path is 8.

Or you can simply add all the numbers together to get your code.

5 + 2+ 9 + 2 + 1 + 7 = 26 then 2 + 6 = 8. This person again, is a life path 8.

Example: 9/16/1902

7, 7, 1 would be their numerological code.

Mind = 1 + 6 = 7

Body = (day) 7 + (month) 9 = 16 → 1 + 6 = 7

Soul = (month) 7 + (year) 3 = 10 → 1 + 0 = 1

Or, 9+ 1 + 6 + 1 + 9 + 2 = 28 → 2 + 8 = 1. This person again, is a life path 1.

Example: 7/15/1971

6, 4, 4 is their numerological code.

Mind = (day) 1 + 5 = 6

Body = (day) 6 + (month) 7 = 13 → 1 + 3 = 4

Soul = (month) 4 + (year) 9 = 13 → 1 + 3 = 4

Or, 7 + 1 + 5 + 1 + 9 + 7 + 1 = 31 → 3 + 1 = 4

This is my birthday. So my numerological code is 6, 4, 4, which explains my intuitive ability being as strong as it is to be a medium. It's there to show me (in the number 44), which represents the Spirit realm. Go a little further, and it will be explained about those repeating numbers and signs in a few pages.

Here are explanations for how life path or Soul Codes are described for each number 1 through 9, with a reminder yet again, you can be both sides of the equation, lean to one side or be One who overcame and uprooted soul's path of taming the ego.

They are influenced by astrological points as well. So a 1 can be a Cancer and fight the urge to lead, as their astrological makeup leans them into more of a hermit than an extrovert. This being what each One needs to learn. All signs (archetypes, numerological codes, astrology) are influenced by others.

So in reading (for self or others) it's important to intuit information as One and All.

Soul 1 —

Soul providers. They thrive in places where leadership is needed, often becoming CEOs or business owners. Ones of a higher vibration lead with Love and always help others shine, sharing a voice to guide or using their own.

When in partnership, it's best to keep them at home or it becomes hard to stay in orbit. They may stray and won't be committed to the person whom they chose or find it monotonous to be among other Ones for long stretches of time.

Their soul path is to ignite the fire of becoming whole as part of One being All, to find their inner truth and live it with joy.

1s who are struggling find peace in solitude and enjoy being alone for reconvening with Source or self. A *Dreamer* or *Artisan* creates in spaces or rooms solo, and it ignites the passion of soul.

1s in fear expect others to follow and won't be on their "team" if they don't.

A mantra for peace to be used would be: *I seek time alone but solo is soul "OH!" and what comes up, I must examine and move through.*

Light attributes: *I am here to find light—for myself and others—through self and All.*

Dark synchronicity: *I fear I cannot speak up without expressing it through anger or fear.*

Soul 2 —

2s are nary a good match for another One if it's not their circle. They keep friends close and eschew anyone if they aren't true to the ideals shared by a truth, be it ours (All) or another philosophy, theology, or religion. "Think like me or begone," they would think, say, or expound on to those who they like.

Arguers or *Lions* are able to overcome with the help of another 2. They are here to partner up and find a balance of Love and fear with another. It might be patriarchal or matriarchal, or another soul as "twins."

Those of a 2 life path as *Healers* may have partners for life (romantically) and strive to be harmonious with them, often struggling to deepen intimacy until too late. Ones might use the mantra: *Two is One. One is All. I am light and love and you are too.*

They mean to be paired up and (if chosen) might forget to remember this contract and lose sight of the goal. This is when success or work can lead to results of partnerlessness or constant seeking to find "the one." A *Taskmaster* is One most likely to find this happening within a life.

In love, they thrive with 2s and 8s and lose sight in goals of intimacy with 1s and 3s, preferring to be cuddled and swept up in romance, which 1 and 3 are not often best at doing.

Light attributes: *Two is One. You seek partnership to satisfy soul contracts and align with Love.*

Dark synchronicity: *"Nobody loves me. I'll never find a mate. Nobody deserves me. I don't deserve anyone. I'm too old, too young"—anything with a "2" energy.*

Note: The closer you are to ego, the harder it becomes to find another One for love and partnership. Holding beliefs such as these is what Ones are here to overcome, no matter where they are on the Ladder of Awareness.

Soul 3—

3s are adept at managing emotions or churning through tough days. They can be asleep or awake and this ability is there. However it's choice which makes it true.

Don't expect roses and sunshine, for 3s can be more sensitive to light and frequency, where allergies come in and destroy joy. Whatever is eschewed is what triggers attacks or anxiousness.

They can be repetitive in patterns, most likely are the overthinkers and compulsive types to be a 3 life path. OCD is common in sleepy Ones.

A 3 makes a good *Tactician* and *Artisan*, as each are able to strategize in mindful ways to release the contents of fear and doubt. Figuring things out can take time but will be accomplished as sure as the sun rises and sets. *Just keep going* is a mantra to keep repeating to self.

They (like body 3s) are good at transforming circumstances or overcoming themes (see our list) and turning around or perhaps utilizing it to make good or help others; it just takes the work to do this.

Sometimes, those 3s in a sleep state (spiritually) are likely to numb with substances of Earth. This is so they can shut the mind down, which tends to churn and churn. They are here to transform, and like a car need all parts running properly.

Most susceptible to 1s leadership archetype, they can stray from a path of Love and be compelled to another Ones' opinion. This can be both good (awake) or hard (asleep) depending on One's journey of Earth.

Abandonment and loss are themes which are common in this path, as they are meant to be part of the trifecta—Mind, Body, and Soul—and in order to do so, 3s must see the value and worth they hold beyond others' opinions and ideas of who they should be.

Light attributes: *I know I am worthy and find ways to share the gifts of Love. Confidence is key to my creating all things, and I have it in spades—rooted in a healthy mind aligned with soul and All.*

Dark synchronicity: *I can't think without finding ways to shut down what I believe fails me. My mind feels confused and overtaken by old patterns and* *thoughts. I use time as a distraction to escape the mind's grip.*

Soul 4 —

As with 4s of body, the soul path is similar to these evolved Ones. They are usually empathetic and caring toward another and choose to work in healing or artistic arts, anything to be a light for others.

Very creative and passionate, the art they share can be music, poetry, words, or naturistic.

They can't be swayed to one particular side and choose to be their own boss or act like they are. A mantra for their dominant side could be: *I listen with All my heart, mind, soul and remember I am, and you too are me and One. We are same in mind (Love) while different in body here and now.*

4s awakened in mind are our *Healers* and *Seers*. 4s asleep are very dark-minded, feeling as if the world is against them. Every soul has a path to Love, if chosen to be used, and those once dark minds are able to overcome and choose Love, which (if chosen) makes them a force of good, leading others out of dark places and spaces.

An enemy of Love, fear and ego is strong in a 4 on Earth asleep to Love and may seek to destroy Love in the 4s who are awakening. So be wary of 4s who struggle with depression or anxiety—it is Love's foe keeping them suffering. Ones must overcome fear and become Love to stay in a place of joy and not fear.

Light attributes: *I am healing the old self, and Love is my tool.*
Dark synchronicity: *I harm others to protect myself from fear.*

Soul 5 —

A chance to earn knowledge—a life of overcoming a hard fear or hardship. It could be thine own within One's circle (family) of influence. It's meant to give them a head start in their next life.

5s are collectors of information, and whatever is learned here, as this body, is meant to be used in the next. So if you are a Spanish speaker of

Danish descent, most definitely are you going to be of Spanish heritage in a next life. It's like skipping ahead a chapter to find out what happens next. Those who feel called to learn a skill (later in life) need it for another life, as both are part of the lessons of soul here and there. You can be learning one language (as you) and speaking it in a next life (as all lives are simultaneously occurring). This is, generally speaking, why Ones feel such strong callings to explore something: the closer a life is ("before" or "after"), the stronger the pull toward it.

As with the mind/body, 5s are lifelong learners and choose to be "in the know" when it comes to art, music, industry, or whatever interests them. A history buff has a long linear history of lives on Earth, and the longing to study and understand comes from a place of being involved in many events in time.

5s are susceptible to misinformation and easily swayed with opinions. They can also be very influenced by those around them, which creates a sense of unintelligence—called to share but told not to. "Be quiet," parents might say. An *Arguer* can hold fast to their intellect and fight through. A *Dreamer* is going to shut down and go inward.

They can be ordered to make a move in a career or direction and become overwhelmed—too stuck in ego to overcome. So the knowledge path is weakened, and they stay stuck in whatever mindset where they began feeling pressured to be someone else's ideal.

Women are particularly susceptible in the last few centuries and emotionally stunted by societal norms and arrangements. As society dictates who they must be, an intellectual can become stilted quite young. However, a *Taskmaster* utilizes a stimulated mind to find success in other ways both domestic and artisanal.

A mantra to unlock intellect would be: *Show me the way to my intuition, to my mind's truth and the world is unlocked for me as One.*

Light attributes: *I learned from my mistakes, moved on, and thrived as One.*

Dark synchronicity: *I let my mistakes keep me stuck, believing others before myself. This makes me question who I am and blame others for making me this way.*

Soul 6 —

Karmic recycler and cycler. A 6 is the One who has been hurt or did the harm. They are here to reconcile with another One.

Example: Becoming a doctor to save lives as Ones had taken one (or many) in prior incarnations. Perhaps in a war or conflict.

Twins are often born in 6 life paths to receive and forgive another One. They are wombmates and life mates in order to balance another life together (or apart).

They receive information and process it through a lens of personality and then choose how to relate to that other One. It can be overcome, moved beyond, and finished—leading to evolution where a 6 becomes another life path, leading others to transform their hurts. The code remains but the karma shifts. A soul is able to intervene if the karma is shattered and move them to another path. So Ones at stage 6 are most often the perpetrators of change and renewal.

They seek out partners and leave if any One isn't a match to overcoming who they set to balance karma out. Think of it as the 12 steps of soul path. It is about overcoming, and all steps must be utilized; and if One isn't part of a process (e.g, those who need forgiven karmically), it is a most unsatisfying experience. Ones seek forgiveness for cycles and situations the partner has no idea of and therefore creates unrest.

Passionate and particular, they like and dislike based on karma and seeking balance. No archetype escapes karma.

I repeat to complete is a mantra to remember karma is good to move beyond and wakes you up further than before.

Light attributes: *Gratitude gives me joy. I help others who once felt lost and confused, as I did.*

Dark synchronicity: *You won't believe what I say, and I won't be able to start thinking for myself anyway, so why bother? I'm stuck and stunted by my life circumstances, and confusion creates for me. As I step, I stumble, and no one picks me up*

Soul 7 —

Lucky but unlucky. 7 is the path of soul redemption. Ones seek to overcome a pattern or belief held before they became incarnated on Earth again. They seek to struggle and then spark. What challenges is the impetus for their art, music, teachings, non-profits, or business. Their story is their glory.

Not all 7s seek to have a tragedy, but rather a simple sacrifice to get them on their way back to Love.

Ones may be born in wartime, have an absentee father, or lack a figurehead in the family. It may be drugs or alcohol which numbs pain, used as rocket fuel to launch their comeback.

Those in body rarely are 7s who are lucky at the outset, but if willing to go All in with Love or partnership (physically or spiritually), 7s can become lucky in Love and life.

A *Dreamer/Artisan* and *Wanderer* spend time in mind and may need help moving to Love from fear. Let them know you are with them in time when they are hurting and need help.

A 7 can be an "outsider" who feels unsure of how to navigate life on Earth. More so at the body level they can become *Anxious* or *Worry* (on the Ladder of Awareness) and may struggle to overcome this, but soul 7 is susceptible too—if they don't seek wise council from All or healers and sage guides. *Look for the light* is a mantra to use often. The stars feel like home and to use them can bring peace and surrender. Find Astrology books to help guide you there to your "place" in the Infiniteness.

Light attributes: *Soul ascension. Guided by Source, I am.*

Dark synchronicity: *The devil made me do it, say it, accept it, or create it. No one cares for me anyway, so why be in it?*

Soul 8 —

Approving minds are what 8s embody. They are in this life to cheer others on and support goals and dreams.

On the other side, an 8 with fear ruling the mind (asleep) can inhibit natural tendencies to guide and share. Like an 8 at the body level, they are forceful and fearful, leading others into dark experiences. A *Lion* is fierce on Earth and makes its pride do work, and this too is how an 8 leads as fear/ego.

An 8 is here to come to the realization of the God self, which manifests as God complex if ego is not quelled. A doctor can be a *Healer* and 8 practicing medicine for the high of winning versus helping others heal like a 6 or 4. This is where archetypes have a hand in all life paths. Look to all parts of self to discover who you (or they) are.

Those with 8 life paths—awakening or awakened—can be great leaders both spiritually and emotionally: a champion of All.

Light attributes: *Love is who I am.* (Our mantra of Love as All)

Dark synchronicity: *Fear gets me further than Love. Love is worthless to the world and to my life unless it serves the self.*

Soul 9 —

The completer. A finisher. The body 9 and soul 9 are similar in feeling a need to "wrap up" a day or chapter. Awake and aware Ones finish the day with Love, wrapping up with a prayer or intention. Those asleep are going to struggle to "let go" of a day and may turn to alcohol or substances to unwind.

Open ends make you suffer, and closed loops bring peace. Most life path 9s are also projectors and expect others to do closed loops as well, and this can bring resentment and frustration if any One is a procrastinator in their circle.

Just like a body 9, a life path 9 feels called to finish a project or emotionally regale a loved One for doing good work. A champion for others' success and joy. They like community and partnership, surrounding Oneself with friends and colleagues or family. They may feel safer in group settings, and alone time is preferred only when sleeping.

On the other side, a 9 body can prefer isolation to keep them "safe" from judgment or being seen and heard. Loud noise or crowds are "too much" at times in their lives. As One ages this can become a burden to overcome. However, a 9 can be quite content in a group or co-housing at life's end if they climbed to a level above *Pessimist or Frustrated. Mindful* Ones like long goodbyes and others to be there with them.

Asleep Ones also can suffer insomnia if they left a project open and undone. It can quite literally keep you up at night if a fight or argument with a partner, colleague, or child goes unfinished or uncompleted. A mantra to help escape when time ticks too swiftly would be: *Time is now and I have plenty of nows to finish this with Love.*

On our other side are those who begin and can't finish (full of fear) and therefore struggle to complete a project or task. A 9 who is a *Dreamer/Wanderer* is One tasked with overcoming their penchant for giving up. *Arguers* are more apt to put work aside that isn't to their liking or taste. *Mindful* Ones enjoy finishing with a penchant for expressing with glee when they do.

9s can make great teachers as many are unfazed by large meetings and gatherings, especially if One is a *Taskmaster* archetype—a dynamic duo of All. A *Healer* may feel the opposite if they are *Dreamers,* especially Geminis, preferring to only speak if necessary in crowds or groups.

On the opposite end, archetypes of a *Healer* and *Persona* often feel called to share and be heard by large groups or communities, loving attention for their gifts or wisdom.

Depending on One's astrology is how they lean into contracts. So you can know you are here to overcome, and struggle with the ending of patterns if you are a *Libra,* who needs balance, or a *Cancer* who is inclined to be at home versus in large crowds—yet also capable, if given the chance, of gathering the troops and heading out for the night.

9's are oft here to leave a better world than priorly. As lives end they are keen to make amends, change minds, or pass a baton to another—leaving behind articles of clothing, precious jewels, or art. The 9 *Seer* is ready to move beyond Earth (as 9 mind *Seers* do) to adventure beyond. Though it may take a few stops to do so, eventually a 9 ascends to Love and All.

Light attributes: *I shout with glee to guide others—and myself—toward joy.*

Dark synchronicity: *I find fault with others and prefer to be left alone. I can't imagine what's next and fear that future endeavors may never come to pass, or I may have no ideas to give, share, or create for myself.*

Note: Like astrology, discovering the time of day you were born is key, as each number is a clue to your ascension status, ability to awaken or where you may be heading in life (e.g. children and partnerships). Again, adding all numbers through digit reduction.

Example*: 9:02 becomes $9 + 2 = 11 \rightarrow 1 + 1 = 2$

Much of it can be intuited or found in Akasha but as a rule of thumb there are some absolutes to be found.

A time code with a 4 or 8 is more awakened, if a master number is in the original three (mind/body/soul).

A double digit (11, 22, 44) before reduction shows a level of intuitiveness, or intellect for a 5 or 55 —those born at 23:59).

As always, reduce numbers to a single digit. Thus, a 55 would also be a 1, showcasing qualities of leadership within the life regardless of One's code or astrology.

*Use military time for those born in the Eastern Hemisphere and mean time for the Western.

Master Numbers

The last thing to understand are Master Numbers. These are those high-frequency repeating numbers you see in life. As souls are always moving and evolving, it helps to know when you are on the right path, feeling protected and shielded or guided.

In each of our chapter headings, we have placed repeating numbers and their messages below the name. Again they are:

111 —

Repeating numbers remind you to Source.

222 —

Angels guiding the way.

333 —

Animals leave messages everywhere to guide you forward to Love.

444 —

Angels and loved Ones reminding us they are only a thought away from you.

555 —

Information is the gift of All.

666 —

Karmic reoccurrences seeking to grow you through past decisions and into new expansions.

777 —

It's got roots in mind needing uprooted. Let it bring you inward to define who you are.

888 —

Infinite Source guiding the way to Love.

999—

Complete. Don't repeat.

1111 —

Confirmed.

Master Numbers (within birth codes) have messages too, and can foretell One's design. For instance, Laura (my) code is 6, 4, 4, which is matching to the ability I have to speak to crossed souls as a medium. This is the number

44. It's how we can tell a loved One is available to us. The numbers have meanings (as above) in repetition:

11 —

The meaning of life is to remember Love. Ones are good with information and leading others to their truth of All. Finding 11 in One's life path (2) is a clue of their "status" of being a part of the bigger picture collectively. A spark of Love or a plug of fear.

22 —

Angels above, below, around, and within. A higher soul with lifetimes of information from other incarnating experiences. Virtue is their power.

33 —

Choosing to come into life to overcome old narratives and beliefs and challenge themselves to leap into life looking beyond constructs of society and culture. They are achievers of change and growth for self and others.

44 —

These fours are common with our *Healers* and represents intuition and higher evolution. Each able to develop "gifts" of Source to connect as healers or guides. Within each life, reaching toward others is a way to help self.

55 —

Learning and teaching. This is the master of human learning on Earth.

66 —

Likely are they Ones who had another's role. They chose one life to record another. They swap roles with whom they come across to role play a part they once played as well. The teacher/student and student/teacher.

77 —

These are for those who are in challenged bodies or in various circumstances chosen prior to Earth. Appearing at birth or later in life, Ones can accept it as the lesson of incarnation or it can be overcome, as the soul's goal to evolve is that person's resilience or dependency on others.

88 —

Power and influence is a big theme for those with 88. They are leaders and influencers and use tactics to engage with others through love and with Love. Ones (as souls) choose to come to be a light for others, but like any One on Earth, falling into ego traps can render the experience incomplete and this is why it is always best to go deeper to the Source to uncover each individualized soul, versus brash generalized or characterizations of Ones.

99 —

Completing a lifetime and achieving an awakened way of being. They are here to move beyond. One last time on Earth. Ones can become lost, however, and continue to another life until it is complete as soul. Not always will you leave. Until you know it's time and choose Love, and this a clue you are one notch away from ending Earth's control, powering on to Love or another incarnational energy system of other places, spaces, and systems. Starseeds are often a term used for this experience.

Pillars of Change

There are times when master numbers show up as pillars, a single digit flanks the body code. The code may be 1, 9, 1, or 2, 6, 2. These are purposeful for understanding the dichotomy of soul. One may wish to be a great leader (1) and become one but also struggle in large groups and therefore stand alone, unsupported by others. It must be they who overcomes the fear and insecurity of life themes they chose in the soul blueprint.

A 2 mind with a soul 2 is championing of others but may be unable to love self, as this was a theme to move beyond.

3s who are mindfully aware may be a life path 3 with a processor serving fear and doubt, and may need help from healers or therapists to turn off the churning mind.

4s are quite empathic, and the mind 4 and soul 4 the potent and powerful healers of All.

5 minds and 5 souls might cancel out the ability to logically think and strategize. They may need a tutor or helper to unlock knowledge and intellect they hold inside. Most definitely they are sharp as tacks. 5, 6, 5 would showcase it is karma to navigate on Earth in the body chosen.

6 minds with 6 souls are the metaphysical version of teeter totters. Unable to balance and often times imbalanced in life or hoarders. Once they see a straight line or finish karma, the hold is over and they go back to being great thinkers and excel as judges or mentors.

7 mind and 7 life path tend toward being overly sensitive to food or toxins. They attract what they think and feel and need guidance to uncover their life circumstance (made prior). A theme is mostly what keeps them stuck, but as with all 7s, a lucky stroke is always available to them.

Pillar 8s can be bold and daring, often *Adventurers* ready to tackle anything or anyone (if they are asleep).

9 mind and 9 souls can be easily susceptible to religion and theology as mechanisms for change and growth, which can be good as awakeners, and challenging as sleepers if they don't release a notion of separation. They look to the heavens for guidance, and yet worry of endings as the mind thinks in absolutes at times, and not possibilities. Seek a healer to help break the pattern.

Astrology

Astrology, birth charts, and cartography are road maps to a life designed prior to incarnating into each body. They are not, however, set in stone as you have choices to make on Earth. So use it with intention knowing

in order to design life as you wish, it must be believed, dear Ones. Otherwise it's only a map and you don't know how to get there without All.
— Wisdom of The All

Similar to One's numerological codes are their astrological codes. Ones are born into signs based on soul contracts. Like archetypes, what you came to learn falls into twelve categories, that which we have termed Zodiac.

These are pattern markers for your journey, like signposts and symbols on a map. They should not be taken so matter-of-fact that they make you believe in one way or another. There are many roads to take to enlightenment—not just a path set prior but a free will experience for All.

We guide you throughout life, and themes are essential to help you understand the soul lessons planned. It is like a syllabus of Source. Each sign represents a constellation of teachings we rely upon to help you navigate your return to Love—all written in the stars before you arrived.

Souls incarnate in groupings—both geographically and astrologically—to evolve through a variety of themes. Just as you gather in cities, countries, continents, villages, or even isolated regions to learn and grow together as One, you also cluster under shared planetary alignments. These astrological placements subtly influence your perspectives, emotional frameworks, and spiritual pathways. Nothing is random. Your placement on Earth and beneath the stars is intentional—designed to support your evolution individually, collectively, and infinitely as One. Those who awaken begin to notice that lessons repeat among people born within similar timelines, regions, and astrological patterns, offering insight into how growth is shared and cyclical.

These influences, however, do not define you; they simply serve as guideposts. They are part of the curriculum your soul chose, not your permanent identity.

And that is the greater truth:

Who you are is All. You are not limited by your chart, your numbers, or your geography—rather, these serve as tools to guide you back to remembering Source within. Through every rise and fall, you are meant to rediscover the truth of Love being All.

The codes and numbers appear to offer clues to existence—they show up in everything from books and road signs to numbers on doors and homes. Astrology, too, is numerically structured.

You can be a 6–2–6 and a Gemini (*Example, born 5/24/2002*), and those characteristics combine to form who you are as both human and soul. A Gemini is a great friend to have in life. A pillar 6 offers mentorship to their friends and family. A body 2 represents their need or desire for partnership in business, life, and/or love.

Let's say you are an 8–6–6, born on July 26, 1998, at 4:40 a.m. in London, with Sun in Leo, Capricorn Moon, and Leo Rising. The information found online might lead you to believe you are destined to be bold, structured, a born leader, or perhaps a heavy thinker. And until you find All, you will be. Once you connect to our higher truths, however, it becomes insignificant to attach to any single idea of who you are based solely on maps and charts created by and through another. The best experience of who you are will come through you. So sit down and read the writing of each sign, knowing you are more than just astrological—you are metaphysical in nature.

We are also including some common myths about signs and some truths you may find to help understand ways to evolve, and what is perhaps holding Ones back from success or achievement of Love. Each sign below is followed by the archetypes, element, numerological code and a Tarot of the Major Arcana of which they are most associated. Return to our pages earlier on Tarot to see the themes and messages aligned with those cards as tools for understanding who you were, are, and now becoming. A mantra for ascension is listed as well. Speak this when you are struggling in life to find Love/All/God.

Aquarius

January 20 – February 18

Marks: New Beginnings.

Number: 1. Often are leaders and prioritize their solidarity and singularity. A need to ignite companionship is necessary at times.

Myth: Visionaries who take care of others and seek change for our world.

Truth: Often slippery and sly. Swim with the sharks and you'll get bit. Intentions can be self-advocating, not whole focused. "I" vs. "you" mentality. Be wary of others' intentions and set yours to the right people and opportunities to be ahead of them. They are (as above, 1s and 2s, and can be 5s) similar to life path 1 or 2.

Mantra: *I show the world Love through being it.*

- Animal: Shark
- Archetypes: Adventurer, Lion, Persona, Tactician
- Element: Air
- Code Numbers: 1, 2, 55
- Tarot: The Emperor, The Fool, The Magician, Wheel of Fortune

Pisces

February 19 – March 20

Marks: Nesting before Spring.

Number: 2. Prone to like companionship and partnership; particularly artistic and passionate thinkers.

Myth: Overly sensitive and emotional in nature.

Truth: Have a desire and need to be on time and patient, yet struggle to find peace with it. They wait for love impatiently, tying worth to another One. Like 2s they are commonly better in partnerships with others and feel safest in love.

Mantra: *Success is helping another find Love through accepting I am.*

- Animal: Fish
- Archetypes: Artisan, Arguer, Persona, Sage
- Element: Water
- Code Numbers: 2, 3, 444
- Tarot: The Empress, The High Priestess, The Lovers, Judgment

Aries

March 21 – April 19

Marks: Spring Has Sprung. Transformative awareness.

Number: 3. Resilient and tough but often needing a hand and guide. A need to set One's boundaries with Love.

Myth: Resistant to change and inflexible.

Truth: A mix of fire and ice, which go well together. They tend toward anger easily and, receive frosty back, as the law of attraction is at play. Aries may do well to take a course on mindfulness to learn to regulate emotions this year. Calm is cool. Wanting to be heard is a major theme for those with an Aries sun or moon.

Mantra: *I seek to know myself and know I am worthy of Love from self and soul.*

- Animal: Ram
- Archetypes: Adventurer, Arguer, Lion, Persona
- Element: Fire
- Code Numbers: 3, 4, 22
- Tarot: The Empress/Emperor, The Fool, The World

Taurus

April 20 – May 20

Marks: Making moves and bold adventures. Enjoying the spoils of Spring.

Number: 4. A need to be like or adored can't be ignored. Overcome ego more and more as you evolve.

Myth: Rigid thinking or manipulative in nature.

Truth: Ones have a need to give love freely without expectation. Let down your guard and trust both the universe and intuition. Stay in connection to soul throughout the year and keep calm.

Mantra: *I choose peace over positions and polarity. I am strong in mind, body, soul.*

- Animal: Bull
- Archetypes: Arguer, Adventurer, Lion, Wanderer.
- Element: Earth
- Code Numbers: 4, 5, 44
- Tarot: The Chariot, The Hierophant, Strength, Temperance

Gemini

May 21 – June 20

Marks: Sun and moon. Stars at night. A good time to *be*.

Number: 5, 6. Best friends and loving partners. Sharing is caring and leaving behind the old self for greener pastures. Grounding or rooting to nature is necessary at times.

Myth: Starseeds out of touch with reality.

Truth: Stars align if you are ready for the opportunity. Don't let doubt creep in. Shove it to the back and step forward without fear. You know who you are intuitively and are the stars and a star in mind.

Mantra: *I belong.*

- Animal: Butterfly
- Archetypes: Artisan, Dreamer, Seer, Wanderer
- Element: Air
- Code Numbers: 5, 6, 11
- Tarot: The Moon, The Lovers, The Sun, The Star

Cancer

June 21 – July 22

Marks: Love and joy. A time to be.

Number: 6, 7. No need to argue. Let it go. Get out and see the world or hermit in spurts when needed to recharge.

Myth: Overly sensitive or cautious in life.

Truth: Quit hiding and live. You are more than what's in the shell, but to experience it you need experiences. Go out and enjoy Earth, its inhabitants, and our resources of Love.

Mantra: *I shelter in mind and control it's switch with Love. I am free when I be.*

- Animal: Crab
- Archetypes: Dreamer, Healer, Sage, Wanderer
- Element: Water
- Code Numbers: 6, 7, 33
- Tarot: The Chariot, The Hanged Man, The Hermit, The Tower

Leo

July 23 – August 22

Marks: Improving One's self through arts, music, dance, and creativity. For some, coming out of One's shell.

Number: 7, 8. Can be hard to please and harsh to criticize others. A desire to be heard means a long talk is needed for some.

Myth: Loving and dependable.

Truth: Strong, confident, steady forward momentum. Don't leap too fast or it will scare people as you strive for more.

Mantra: *Solo is so low. I keep to myself only to recharge and then come roaring with Love.*

- Animal: Lion

- Archetypes: Architect, Lion, Taskmaster, Tactician, Dreamer
- Element: Fire
- Code Numbers: 8, 88
- Tarot: The Emperor, Judgment, Strength, Temperance

Virgo

August 23 – September 22

Marks: Eras, cycles, and becoming One's true self through introspective awareness.

Number: 8, 9. Howling at injustices and marking One's territory. Lay down your guard in times of war or anger. Let ego down gently.

Myth: Virtuous or trustworthy.

Truth: Be a peacekeeper but set your boundaries around money and career. You want what you want because it's yours to have. Don't let others fool you into fear. Their lens is usually from that place.

Mantra: *I replace fear with Love when I find the world is too much or loud. I am strong when I am weak knowing I am.*

- Animal: Wolf
- Archetypes: Adventurer, Arguer, Lion, Wanderer
- Element: Earth
- Code Numbers: 9, 99
- Tarot: The Hermit, The Magician, Temperance, Wheel of Fortune

Libra

September 23 – October 22

Marks: Beginning of endings and endings of dark times of mind or body.

Number: 9, 1. Let go and trust. Lean into parts of self unlikely to have been discovered before. You are ready.

Myth: Change maker and course corrector.

Truth: Balance is key, and remember to cultivate it in all areas of life.

Mantra: *My mind is my controller between fear and Love and I take the reigns for freedom and light.*

- Animal: Panda, Zebra (black and white)
- Archetypes: Architect, Artisan, Dreamer, Healer, Persona, Tactician, Taskmaster
- Element: Air
- Code Numbers: 1, 6, 66, 9
- Tarot: The Chariot, Judgment, Justice, The Magician

Scorpio

October 23 – November 21

Marks: Facing One's truth and being more accepting of others in time.

Number: 1, 2, 11. Don't overthink. Channel it into art or music. Make time to *be.*

Myth: Prone to outbursts and over thinkers.

Truth: See the world as expansive, not limited. You tend to go inwards for protection from outside experiences. Instead, go inward to create new ones. Seek change where you struggle to achieve. The shedding of ego makes you *be* and not do.

Mantra: *Choice is fun not fear. Who knows? Life can bring surprises to me, through me, and I enjoy them All.*

- Animal: Snake
- Archetypes: Arguer, Artisan, Lion
- Element: Water
- Code Numbers: 1, 2, 77
- Tarot: The Hanged Man, The Hermit, Judgment, The World

Sagittarius

November 22 – December 21

Marks: Planning and execution or making goals attainable.

Number: 2, 3. Knowing when to ask for help and when to let go.

Myth: Materialism and manifesting is the goal.

Truth: Blend what you want and what you have. It's enough. Seeking more brings anxiety and frustration more often than not. Wise eyes see beyond material and into the mysteries of our Universe.

Mantra: *I accept what is, change what isn't working, and fly to new heights and adventures.*

- Animal: Owl
- Archetypes: Artisan, Architect, Persona, Wanderer
- Element: Fire
- Code Numbers: 2, 3, 111
- Tarot: The Emperor, The High Priestess, Wheel of Fortune, The World

Capricorn

December 22 – January 19

Marks: Endings and beginnings. Accessing old patterns, sparking new ones.

Number: 1, 3, 33. Particularly overachieving or over preparing. A need to relax, unwind, give, or share.

Myth: Pessimistic, greedy, prideful.

Truth: Take time for rest and recuperation. Slow down to speed up. This is a life you were meant to *be* and not do in. If you find yourself too caught up in doing and hustle, the burdens follow you. A lot of time is spent figuring out and planning and your entire experience could be marred by too much pushing without peace. A Capricorn knows itself to be mindful, curious, and introspective not angry and boastful—like the myth of persistent ego sharing.

Mantra: *I slow my speed to find my way and find my way through Love.*

- Animal: Goat
- Archetypes: Arguer, Architect, Taskmaster
- Element: Earth
- Code Numbers: 3, 1, 222
- Tarot: The Hierophant, The Magician, Strength, The World

There are many books to be found online and in stores for understanding astrology. Be sure to test these as you would Tarot, Oracle, or Energy cards to find their frequency and determine whether it aligns for you.

Soul Charting

Life is a series of choices, and what you do with them is the journey of soul. You are given routes and destinations, with maps of mind to show you the way. Love takes you to the destination more quickly, while fear circumvents, stalls, or ends the desires. In time, you are given the tools you need to create them, and this is where Ones who are awakened must utilize them to stay on the previously chosen paths. Use time to reflect on the destinations you made, the roads you missed, and how you returned to the beginning each time to begin again.
— Wisdom of The All

Similar to astrology and how the stars and planetary movements affect every day life on Earth, numerology extends this understanding through the use of numbers and dates. These allow you to know what may come—or what may happen—as you go through a day, week, month, or year. You can add the number of your numerological code to the code of each day and get a sense of what it may entail or what themes you can expect.

To find the code for each day, add the numbers as before:

Example: 10/14/2025 becomes 5, 6, 6.

Mind: day

Body: day plus month

Soul: month plus year, or all numbers in the dated added to a single digit.

Mind: $4 + 1 = 5$

Body: 5 (day) + 1 (month) = 6

Soul: 6 + year 9 (2 + 2 +5) = 15 → 1 + 5 = 6

To find what is possible individually, Ones take their personal code and add it to the day's code. Using again the 5, 6, 6.

Example: Laura, whose code is 6, 4, 4.

So we take 5, 6, 6 and add it to 6, 4, 4 and today becomes 2, 1, 1.

Mind: $5 + 6 = 11 → 1 + 1 = 2$

Body: $6 + 4 = 10 → 1 + 0 = 1$

Soul: $6 + 4 = 10 → 1 + 0 = 1$

Returning to our earlier explanation of numerical meanings, we can see that Laura is meant to partner (with All perhaps) at the mind level, spend quiet time alone in being as body, and learn to lead today. As we learn though channeling, it is perfectly matching the experience meant to be had.

Mind represents thinking; body, action, and soul learning through love or fear, depending on what is chosen.

Universal Code

Now, as a collective—and like astrology—you are under the influence of stars and planetary motions and movements. Mercury, Venus, Mars, and other planets create or remove space as you travel through the Milky Way.

Our years hold frequency, as do the months (of the Zodiac), and they reveal truths about life, again grouped as part of consciousness. So, any One born in particular years have a theme to work though as well.

To find the frequency of a year, add the digits to a single number. 2025 is a 9 year (2 +2 + 5); 2026 a 1 year (2 + 2 + 6), and so on.

It also depends on which century you begin in how awakened or aware you are. Each generation returns from before (in linear terms), so to evolve is to move forward. All generations return (incarnate) more evolved—at least initially—than prior ones. This is where you see diversity and fluidity as you move through decades. Those leaving Earth may resist what is new, holding to ideals brought forth prior, which is why many wars and tragedies occur in service to the ego.

As always though, the choices made are what matter most, even for those generations born more awake or aware. You can be dragged into fear or propelled into Love. The starting line and finish line differ for every One of Earth—what you believed influenced by those around you as you move through the Ladder of Awareness by choosing Love or fear.

There are days where you are eager to get out of bed and days when you are not. Each influenced at the mind, body, and soul levels, both individually and collectively. Charting these is a simple way to understand patterns and processes. The day may be dim or bright, cold or temperate, yet how you react and respond guided by choice. Do you acknowledge that a day is challenging and extend grace, or do you power through?

Days with more difficult lessons may chart as 5s and 7s, unless they are collective. When you feel low, look at the day's energy. 1s and 4s hold hope and promise. 3 represents returning to Love. 6 signals karma in play. 2 reminds you to partner with All or seek outside help if you feel stuck. 8 resonates with Love—spend time being and be well. 9 brings endings, missed opportunities, or completed experiences. Every day holds a chance to begin again in Love.

Take a moment to practice feeling the day's frequency and energy. As you awaken each morning, look to access both collective and individual charts.

Example: 10/14/2025.

We showed Laura's daily chart earlier; now let's work with the collective.

Add the day and month to the year (9, for 2025) and it will showcase the lessons planned:

$$10 + 1 + 4 + 9 = 24 \rightarrow 4 + 2 = 6$$

So today calls for balancing karmic cycles from before.

You can also look at the collective mind and body by adding up the day's number and then the day and month, as we did with our mind, body codes.

So, today: $1 + 4 = 5 \rightarrow 5 + 1 = 6$. The days code is 5, 6, 6 (by adding $9 + 6$).

This means the collective is learning lessons and decisions for the mind—a karmic day of balance for body and soul. Each aspect reflects a reorientation of old and new energies to harmonize karmic events, physically, mentally, or both.

A Few More Examples:

10/15/2025 — 6, 7, 7

Mind: $5 + 1 = 6$, Body: $6 + 1 = 7 \rightarrow 7 + 9 = 16 \rightarrow (1+6) = 7$

The day's energy code is: 6, 7, 7— a good day to find balance. Work, but also do something kind for yourself. It may be a challenging day for some—perhaps a surgery or difficult news—but the double sevens equalize the frequency and can soften or upend the day's challenge if using Love.

10/16/2025 — 7, 8, 8

Mind: $6 + 1 = 7$

Body: $7 + 1 = 8$

Soul: $8 + 9 = 17 \rightarrow (1 + 7) = 8$

In a 9 year, all numbers create a double body-soul code, offering the ability to "see it and switch it." A chance to start again is more likely when you understand that frequency is everything. It's a "light switch" year—ending old patterns and leading you forward. You choose whether to turn off fear's dark or turn on soul's light.

A day with a harder choice may present itself; the question is how to move through it—with our Source or alone. The 8s indicate divine guidance and Source awaiting your return to Love.

12/12/2025 — 3, 6, 6

Mind: $2 + 1 = 3$

Body: $3 + 1 + 2 = 6$

Soul: $6 + 9 = 15 \rightarrow (1+5) = 6$

A perfect day of transformation, as we release a book with tools for it. The double 6s representing the dark and light of the world of illusion you live in—and the power to choose Love over fear.

To Soul Chart you can create it in any form you would like. Create 4 rows or columns representing Moods, Movement, Sleep, and Lessons learned. Take the day's energy code and break it down into mind, body, soul, then fill in what comes to mind.

Date Code: 6, 4, 4	Mind	Body	Soul
Mood	Balanced and stable when I woke up today.	Went to Spin Class. Felt great afterward. Had a healthy dinner.	Feeling great all day. Made time to be by meditating at the beach.
Movement	Went for a walk with my dog at dusk.	No pain after class. Light stretching helped.	Did Tai Chi in the morning I found on YouTube.
Sleep	More challenging to get to sleep than normal. Moon is at crescent.	Work up without any pains today.	Dreamt about tigers.
Lessons	Apologized to Barista for my impatience.	Grateful I went to Spin. I know it helps keep me happy.	It's so important to get movement every day

Date Code: 7, 5, 5	Mind	Body	Soul
Mood	Woke up in a funk.	Remembered to breathe when I was delayed in traffic.	My dishwasher broke. Remembered to ask for helping moving through it.
Movement	Skipped the gym. Not feeling it today.	Could not get myself to even go for a walk even though I knew I should.	Ate a salad realizing I should balance no exercise with eating well.
Sleep	Tossed and turn. Lots on my mind.	I need to practice breath work before bed.	Kept hearing "go beyond" when I woke up.
Lessons	Ask for help!	Do not skip the gym. Make time for it.	The body is made to be moving.

Date Code: 8, 6, 6	Mind	Body	Soul
Mood	Feeling great today.	Could not wait to hit the gym.	It felt good to help my friend today who was upset.
Movement	Inclined to help someone today.	Moving well but got tired after 30 min.	Needed to find balance.
Sleep	Slept 8 hours.	Didn't get up for the bathroom.	Dreamt about my dog.
Lessons	Helping others helps me.	Sleep impacts my ability to sustain exercise.	My dog dream was a reminder to seek balance.

Example of Soul Charting

All charts take three to five months to reveal patterns, so keep a journal or track them on your phone to create a clear picture of you as All being One.

Our final lesson of Akasha is the blueprint of life. What you came to be, created long before you set sights on Earth.

Soul Prints / Life Themes

Don't stop looking for evidence of why you are here. It will show up for you all the time in scenario after scenario until it becomes so obvious it can't be ignored. Your "life driving themes" are easy to distinguish because what has been will always be, until you work toward the healing of it. Then may you move beyond it and into freedom and truth and Love. All of you are here to serve a higher purpose—which is to grow and evolve into a version of yourself which is Love, pure and simple. This is the truth to know to move you toward enlightened thinking, dear One.
— Wisdom of The All

You have a blueprint. Just as an architect makes the plan for a building and begins construction knowing what needs to be done, you too have a plan—a blueprint, soul contract, sacred scroll, or soul print you designed before coming into life (incarnating).

Each soul chooses seven to ten themes to explore in this lifetime. The first three are the soul's collective themes. On Earth these are worth, value and patience—and also, humility, for everyone has "chores" to do. These are daily tasks to keep our planetary balance and castes in harmony.

The next themes are personal—based on past (linearly speaking) experiences. You design a life to advance a goal, release old beliefs, practice forgiveness, make amends or learn to love self.

A guide (in spirit) will discuss what to work on and choose with you the themes and what experiences may be had. The blueprint includes:

1. Who you are.
2. A name.
3. Whom the parents will be.
4. What choices you will make in every stage of life – career/profession, schooling, individual relationships (whom you will reconvene with in

the "soul family") and where you will live and when.

5. If children will come along.

6. A path for evolving (stay sleeping, wake up or somewhere in between).

7. What lessons/themes are most important to work through.

8. Karmic relationships and how they may (or may not) play out.

9. What collective shifts and anomalies are possible, and what role is played in them.

10. An exit strategy (i.e. when death will occur and within what time frame which may be long and drawn out or short).

Read chapter 26 in *Wisdom of The All* for more on this.

A list of some life driving themes can be found at the end of this book. Use those pages to sit quietly with them and reflect on what resonates with your journey. Other themes may arise beyond what is listed as you sit and ponder the world of creation.

I'm here to discover....

16

Message For Our Teachers

Trying to get a point across to a soul who is asleep (as chosen for their ascension) is like talking to someone in a coma. They can't hear you. Until they awaken the words get lost in translation. Share if you are called to it, but remind the self the awakened are only waking themselves and not transforming but transferring fear into Love.
—Wisdom of The All

Working with clients and guiding others is wonderful if you are hearing the call for it. We offer this advice for those on a journey of helping another unlock their world within.

Rules Of Engagement

Always co-create. Before sessions, open with a statement of cocreation and/or gratitude:

"I am willing to be guided and ask to receive downloads and information as a channel, medium, and guide of the Infinite. May words, images, visions, sounds, feelings, and ideas flow easily and effortlessly as I guide another (or myself)."

Use words that have meaning to you and allow your soul to guide them.

The clues often are in the words you speak prior to helping lead sessions.

Also, remember to close sessions with a statement of completion and gratitude:

"Thank you for allowing energy to flow. I release all to Source."

Remove distractions. Remove as much technology and distraction as possible during sessions. It interferes with frequencies and can make it more difficult to receive information. Outdoors in nature is the best spot if possible. Turn off lights unless they are part of the experience—such as in virtual or live events.

Work with cards intuitively. Pick up cards and hold them for yourself. When choosing any card decks, trust your intuition to know if they are for you. Not every deck is for every person. There is a reason why each shows up for you and/or the client or person being read.

Try energy testing to find the answer:

- **The Sway Test:** Stand with the cards in hand, feet flat on the ground. Close your eyes. If you feel yourself falling forward, it's a sign the deck is energetically aligned. If you remain in neutral, likely it's for another soul. Moving backward means the deck may belong to an unconsciously aligned seeker.
- **Hot/Cold Test:** Hold the cards in your right hand. If it's cold or warm, sense how that makes you feel. Prickly or chilly is a no. Warm/inviting is a yes.
- **Sticky Finger Test:** Hold the cards in your right hand. With your left hand ask, "Is this for me?" and then rub two fingers together. Smooth fingers indicate yes; fingers getting caught or stuck indicate no.
- **Kinetic Test:** Hold the cards in your left hand. With your right hand make a fist. As you do, ask the question, *"Is this for me?"* If you feel inclined to open your right hand, the answer is yes. Holding it closed is a no.

- **Audible/Visual test**. Assign a yes or no to an image or sound. Yes means... and no means... Example: Yes = Miss Piggy. No = Kermit the Frog. Ask the question, *"Is this for me?"* Hearing Piggy, yes. Kermit, no. Visualizing Piggy, yes. Kermit, no.

Let your hands guide you. Kinetic energy moves through you at all times. It can stop you if needed or guide you to the right places or body parts in energy healing. When holding cards, pay attention to what your hands are doing. When working with multiple decks, you can use any of the above techniques to decide if they should be used in a particular session or group. The cards know where they need to be and with whom. All things are consciousness in form on Earth, and the decks have a way of knowing their reader, creator and the One who needs to hear or see a message.

Bless your cards. Everything is energy and your cards have passed through many hands before arriving to you. Give them your energy by opening them and putting your energy into them. Hold the cards in your hand after opening them and ask, *"What do you need me to know now?"* They will tell you whether to knock on them, lay them flat, toss them in the air or perhaps touch every card and leave them as they are. Listen with intuition and know they have your back, knowing precisely when and where they need be.

Remember your role. You are not a healer to "fix" someone, but rather a guide helping them reach their own inner healer. All are healing themselves through belief. You are a facilitator of information and ideas; their filter allows or accepts it as truth or not. Ones cannot heal if another One isn't ready to receive. Only you can heal you.

Minimize blocks to intuition. There are things that block you from intuition and psychic abilities: alcohol, drugs, processed food, technology (unless used intentionally such as for clients), social media, and loud places/crowds.

Note: see chapter 11 on Toxicity Avoidance in our *Wisdom of The All* book.

Choose your space wisely. Hold sessions if you can in smaller, private spaces. Public spaces bring other energies and frequencies, making it hard to tune out ego and fear—this can lead to inaccuracy of mind.

Engage The "Clair" Senses. Every One in Spirit chose a specific "skill" most easily accessible to them. However, as you ascend, more abilities are heightened, and so you may find all the senses working through you or another.

There are more mechanisms and modalities which fall under Akasha, and in coming years the guides and teachers will share these. For now, we offer these as steps for any One willing to discover more of who they are as soul beyond human.

As we wrap up our books we offer a final reminder of our intention to share resources for those willing to know who and what All is.

17

Souldier On

Those on Earth who deem themselves worthier than another based upon class, race, or gender are using ego to determine their value. They stare fear in the mirror and use ego to torture, demonize, or degrade anyone who they deem inferior justifying actions of "faith" to appease their inFEARior beliefs about who they are. A true SOULdier knows worth is within and never harms another in service to fear. Taking away another One's rights to protect your own is the act of desperation of One who fears losing their own (as had been chosen in their contract). It is possible they could end up destitute and alone and so they grasp tightly to every bit of money, fame, or power they have not knowing it is an inner battle they are fighting alone.
— Wisdom of The All

Ladder Climbing

Next, it's time to understand our final lesson here: how to move through the themes. The work you do as soul is daily and never-ending. If you live unconsciously, the challenge is more difficult. If you understand what lessons and themes you have chosen, life becomes easier, as Ones keep choosing Love.

Let us look at some collective themes as example. Using our Ladder of Awareness, we can move through statements that showcase what is appearing in the created world, based on the level of awareness. Never choosing Love keeps you stuck, and re-minding as One to Love moves you up. It won't happen overnight as patience is a theme we must adhere to. Things take time, and its protective to keep a lag time in place, as we learned from prior Earth existences.

The theme of worthiness is what all of you are here to learn. To start at the bottom—as a *Victim* is, as said before, a beginning on Earth currently since our fifth century (and beyond, though a different ladder is used, which we won't explain here, as it is not useful to know).

Let's take our theme of worthiness. As our *Wisdom of The All* quote above reads, those in fear are believing others are inferior to who they are and this is where war occurs. Taking and not giving. Those at war in themselves or those engaged in a physical war, may hold the belief a world (or God) is against them and act from this awareness starting wars, fires, or other acts of protection and possession.

We begin to choose as we arrive to a consciousness above childhood (around ages seven to nine). At this point, our thoughts separate from those of our parental figures or teachers. Beliefs once held unconsciously begin to merge with the conscious mind, creating choice. So if you say, *"The world is against me,"* it is because you believe you are separate from that world or from God.

The way to ascend is by asking or choosing. Those in lower level consciousness rarely ask until they are at least at *Worry*. At that stage, choices are made alone rather than as All One. Once you reach *Worry,* it becomes possible to begin in prayer, intention, or questioning All. *Achiever/Workers* pray to a God they believe exists outside of themselves, and through this, they move either forward or backward.

Ones can use the Ladder of Awareness to move through emotions and fear. Below is a process for reprogramming the mind. It helps move you out of *Victim* and into new stages where you can remember Love.

Begin by stating the worst thing that comes to mind from an experience or belief.

For One who believes in separation that might be, *"The world is against me."*

Then, keep repeating it over and over again until a new thought arrives. The goal is to move through it step by step, transforming old thoughts into true thoughts—as All would see them, rather than how the ego perceives them.

You can do this every time a pain or pang surfaces or a thought appears that does not serve you as Love.

Think the thought. Repeat it over and over, acknowledging how it feels to speak it, and its power diminishes. Then a new thought arrives. Continue through each thought. As new thoughts appear, affirm them repeatedly until you arrive home to All.

Though this process is rooted in metaphysics, it can also be viewed through a scientific lens. The brain creates neural pathways based on how Ones think and believe. Repeating the statements begins to activate a network of new connections that form new ideas and beliefs. In doing so, you are changing who you are at both the quantum, physical and spiritual levels.

You can do this process with any thought, and you may begin in later stages of consciousness. For example, if you think, *"I can't afford this,"* that may be at the awareness level of *Frustrated*, and you can move to the next stage, *Pessimist,* where the statement becomes, *"I can afford this if I trade time for it,"* or another thought aligned with Love.

Let's begin with our statement around worthiness, and showcase how each choice—where fear is eschewed—can bring new thoughts and a higher level of awareness.

- *Victim* — The world is against me.
- *Achiever / Manipulation* — I'll show the world I'm worthy.
- *Blame* — Everyone is incompetent.
- **Vengeful / Rage** — You took from me.

- *Angry* — I'll take it back.
- *Jealousy / Comparison* — I want what you have.
- *Achiever / Worker* — I'll go get it.
- *Worry* — I'll lose what I have.
- *Anxious* — What I have isn't enough.
- *Frustrated* — I'll protect what I have.
- *Pessimist* — I own what I have.
- *Boredom* — I'll accept what I have.
- *Mindful* — I have enough.
- *Meditator* — I need less of what I have.
- *Separator* — I have gratitude for what I created.
- *Achiever / Lucky* — I'll give what I have.
- *Optimist* — What I give returns.
- *Sage* — I give, I receive.
- *Truth teller* — Life is a gift.
- *Achiever / knower* — I am.
- *Divine Consciousness* — Home.

> *Impatience is part of everyone's life driving themes. It's on every single human operating system. No one escapes this. Even masters are waiting, but knowing it is the process. This is the secret to all manifestations. Wait patiently, be grateful and believe. It exists and all you need do is allow All. I know it is coming. I love knowing it's coming. I am. I am is a statement telling the Universe what you are and willing to be. Be to receive, impatient Ones.*
> — Wisdom of The All

Next we will tackle patience as an example. Using the same flow of dialoguing what is being thought or believed. As you get to *Achiever*, the last two are always the same. *I am. Home.* They do not change.

- *Victim* — Waiting is torturing me.

313

- *Achiever /Manipulation* — It's worth the wait.
- *Blame* — You're the reason I wait.
- *Vengeful / Rage* — I wait with fear.
- *Angry* — Fear is why I struggle.
- *Jealousy / Comparison* — You're why I'm struggling.
- *Achiever / Worker* — I'll take what's mine.
- *Worry* — Time is ticking too fast.
- *Anxious* — I'm losing time and being used by it.
- *Frustrated* — I'm waiting impatiently.
- *Pessimist* — I wait cautiously.
- *Boredom* — I distract impatience.
- *Mindful* — I notice impatience.
- *Meditator* — Impatience can be tamed.
- *Separator* — I wait.
- *Achiever / Lucky* — I create.
- *Optimist* — I have.
- *Sage* — I show.
- *Truth Teller* — Patience served me well.
- *Achiever / Knower* — I am.
- *Divine Consciousness* — Home.

> *Love of the self is paramount in the quest for inner world domination.*
> *Remind yourself whenever looking upon the mirror of the beauty within,*
> *and then, and only then, will you see the beauty staring back at you.*
> — Wisdom of The All

One theme Laura is moving through, as are many others, is self-love. To value One's self is a most difficult challenge, with human vanity at play. Ego is skilled at making you feel ugly, old, or unlikeable. As we move through the flow, notice where you may recognize your own patterns and beliefs.

- *Victim* – I'm ugly.

- *Achiever / Manipulation* — I hate me.
- *Blame* — It's your fault I'm ugly (mom/dad/parent).
- *Vengeful / Rage* — You'll pay for my hate.
- *Angry* — I pay for my hate.
- *Jealousy / Comparison* — Hate sees me.
- *Achiever / Worker* — I can change.
- *Worry* — I look new.
- *Anxious* — Nobody likes the new me.
- *Frustrated* — I like me fairly or better.
- *Pessimist* — I see myself with love.
- *Boredom* — Acceptance.
- *Mindful* — I'm aware when I struggle to like me.
- *Meditator* — My true self is inside.
- *Separator* — I see me beyond physical and separateness.
- *Achiever / Lucky* — Me is *I am* and Love.
- *Optimist* — Love is who *I am*.
- *Sage* — I remind others of *I am*.
- *Truth teller* — I love me.
- *Achiever / Knower* — *I am*.
- *Divine Consciousness* — Home.

Take another look at our page of themes and work with your own. We have left a few pages at the end of the book for you to reflect and flow through your themes—to transform them from fear to Love.

As we say goodbye, let us remind you to choose Love and *be*. The two most powerful words of Love are *I am*. To *be* is to meditate, pray, and champion self and others. Wise words, songs, chanting, or simply being grateful and kind. These are our ways of being. We have enjoyed this mindful experience and offer these tools as reminders for you to use when fear overtakes the mind.

Return to Love, dear Ones.

18

Gratitude and Final Thoughts

At some point you'll have to stop digging and doing work on the self and begin integrating. Your life requires integration between mind, body, and soul and if soul experiences are the norm you haven't met the requirement to live truth. Ready, dear One? It's time to be.
— Wisdom of The All

I am truly grateful you took the time to read this book. The All gave me the clues I needed to understand the whole of who I am. I wrote this book for myself; I honestly never knew if I would even release it. Daily bouts of depression kept me bound up and restless, yet I knew I had the potential for something big—a life of grand abundance—but I couldn't quite get the mind's poison to stop flowing to my brain.

One day, I decided that if I could finally stop wasting time on outside pursuits and commit to a way of being—the way the All so often told me was necessary to live an unburdened life—I would stop working to become a success and start working toward being happy.

At the end of each of my *The All* books, I had written about how I had found happiness within, and yet the truth is that I was only temporarily happy. The excitement I felt to help heal the world sent me seeking fortune and recognition but also brought failure and anxiety. As much as I believed the All—and its words—you have read here how many times I was caught in the disasters of the modern world, with its wars, guns, and chaos. I imagine it's common for many people to feel despondent as the world implodes. I also understand now why it does, as souls being human.

As I look back over these eight years of writing *The All* books, it finally makes sense—*all* of it. The turmoil, the drama, the sadness, and the depression. My entire journey has been a purposeful endeavor so that I might be a light in the dark for others. To be a healer and teacher, I had to know all the hard steps of this journey to Love. It might be why you wait too.

I am not here to show you how to manifest money or make riches and rewards the goal of life. I'm here to remind you that being Love is possible. The essence of All That Is is Love. I shared this book because it felt important to help the willing—those aching for something more in this journey on Earth beyond the material world in which we live.

Does it mean everything is perfect and I'm blissfully living life? Not exactly. But I have changed immensely, no longer burdened by what once kept me falling into fear. I climbed and ascended from where I was before.

All those things I was once told would matter less as I rose in consciousness truly have faded with time. Looking back now—with the awareness I've gained by studying the ladder and tracing my own steps—I understand why I instinctively said no to certain experiences, especially during my years in Hollywood. At the time, I didn't realize I was protecting myself, but now I see how easily I could have been pulled off course. I witnessed many souls become entangled in the pitfalls and illusions of fame and influence, and I'm grateful I chose differently, even when I didn't fully understand why. Your codes are clues to that *why*.

Throughout studying with the All, I have learned how to overcome the hardest moments and face the world's darkest challenges, using them as opportunities to help guide others to their own light. Understanding why others behave and act as they do on Earth gives me hope for the future of our planet as more begin their own awakening to Love, even while others prefer sleep.

One change I continue to see in myself is that what I once found useful to my awakening no longer serves who I am in conscious awareness. Ego had me judging those who are still using those mechanisms, but once I climbed beyond Boredom, the fear and ego were quelled, and I was able to see as Source does. All come to what they need to align (Love) and resign (fear), and nothing is ever wrong or right. You may look back at times you chose to attend a class or session that felt right and helpful then, but later realize it's no longer necessary for who you have become. Whenever you can, bless them with light. Don't judge as ego. They may know in their own timeline, not yours.

I thought I had a fairly large arsenal of tools before (tarot, oracle, channeling), but now, after working on this book, I have even more available to me. I can't wait to see what else unfolds on this climb back to Love. Bringing meanings forth from my own mind has been the only way to truly claim them as they arrive as truth. You can read someone else's meanings, but when words formulate through you, *wow*—it's a game changer. It has been an education like no other, and for that I am truly grateful.

You can use the tools here or find your own truth. I find that when I read someone else's book, it reminds me of what is being taught here, but it's never quite enough to keep fear away for long. I need my own discoveries coming from Source to give me a leg up the ladder. I hope this encourages you to sit with the All. Remember: you are One who is All too. Each of us is on our own journey of awakening and discovering that truth.

One day, I hope all who read this book will uncover how this world moves in and out of fear and sadness—and how those of us who are awakening can truly change the world by simply returning to, and being, Love. We each decide whether we will calm the storm in the mind. Your choice matters, even when you don't see it. Thoughts are powerful. Make them count. Choose Love.

Best of luck discovering who you are, Infinite Ones. It's about time I stop questioning it and start living it.

All

Ladder of Awareness Examples

The clock of enlightenment ticks for all, but many are tuning out its alarm. We show you, slow you, and guide you with messages of soul, but when you turn a blind eye or ear to these, it becomes challenging to raise the vibe. Make note of what you watch, overhear, or witness each day. Those are messages guiding you in time to find light within.
— Wisdom of The All

Below are examples for working on the themes and contracts you are moving through. Remember to choose a statement and then move through each one repeating it until a break through is heard. It can take a while and its OK to ask for help being guided to a new thought.

At times I would repeat a thought eventually hearing a better statement. Sometimes, I would need to ask for help.

Help me find a better thought than the one before.

Here is an example of one I did for myself. I used the theme of money. I spoke each statement out loud, starting at *Victim*, repeating it until I heard a breakthrough line. When I didn't, I asked for help moving to the next line and heard it eventually. Try it for yourself and see if it works to remind you of what is possible. Xo, Laura

- **Victim** — I am broke.
- **Achiever / Manipulation** — Money is hard to make or earn.
- **Blame** — The one percent have all the money and don't share it.
- **Vengeful / Rage** — I'll take it for me.
- **Angry** — You took it from me.

319

- **Comparison / Jealousy** — I'll get it back.
- **Achiever / Worker** — It's a chase.
- **Worry** — Freedom is the cost.
- **Anxious** — The cost is too much.
- **Frustrated** — It costs me my health.
- **Pessimist** — The price is too high.
- **Boredom** — I'll spend what I can.
- **Mindful** — I can afford this.
- **Meditator** — You can afford this.
- **Separator** — Affording this is my right.
- **Achiever / Lucky** — I am right where I need to be.
- **Optimist** — I need to be here now.
- **Sage** — All is my Source.
- **Truth Teller** — I am free.
- **Achiever / Knower** — *I am.*
- **Divine Consciousness** — Home.

Another example is beginning at the stage of *Anger.*

- **Angry** — There is fear over money.
- **Jealousy** — Money is power.
- **Achiever / Worker** — I fear money.
- **Worry** — I'll take what I can.
- **Anxious** — What I can't I'll leave.
- **Frustrated** — What I want I take.
- **Pessimist** — What I want I give.
- **Boredom** — The Earth is bountiful.
- **Mindful** — Resources are everywhere.
- **Meditator** — I am resourceful.
- **Separator** — Resources are where I look.
- **Achiever / Lucky** — Resources belong to me.
- **Sage** — I belong to it.

- **Truth Teller** — It belongs to me.
- **Achiever / Knower** – I am.
- **Divine Consciousness** – Home.

A common theme since social media came around is imposter syndrome or a feeling of not being enough. So I began this one at *Comparison/Jealousy.*

- **Jealousy** — Nobody likes me .
- **Achiever / Worker** — I don't like me.
- **Worry** — I wish others liked me.
- **Anxious** — I would like me better if…
- **Frustrated** — If I was prettier, more popular, younger (etc…)
- **Pessimist** — I'm not any of those things.
- **Boredom** — I wish I was those things.
- **Mindful** — Those things won't make me happy.
- **Meditator** — I'm happy when *I am*…
- **Separator** — I'll do what makes me happy instead of thinking I'm not enough.
- **Achiever / Lucky** — I am enough as *I am.*
- **Optimist** — I am happy as *I am.*
- **Sage** — I like me.
- **Truth Teller** — Knowing I am everyone is the journey of soul.
- **Achiever / Knower** — *I am.*
- **Divine Consciousness** — Home.

Take your own themes of worth, value, patience, or any of those on the next page to see if you can go from fear to Love using the Ladder of Awareness.

Themes and Lessons of Soul

The closer you are to remembering All, the easier fear becomes to navigate. As you separate, you forget who you are through all of time and space. From this, you become Spirit embodied in places and spaces outside of "Heaven" or "Joy" (a name for our other side to be uncovered for you now). Then you make trips around the Infinite with various themes to uncover and lessons to be learned as soul. As you become more and more the self (Love) again, you begin recognizing the light more and more. After navigating through circumstances and scenarios to grow, you allow more of what is real and true to be remembered, until one day all of the work as soul has you saying, "I am." Love is around and within you. It is who you are at the core. Love is your name. I am LOVE.

— Wisdom of The All

Nothing is without its opposite so you are here to learn everything and anything. These are examples of themes and not an exhaustive list but certainly a start for your own inner discovery. Some themes are for leaning in. Others are to overcome.

A

Abandonment

Absolution

Acceptance

Admiration

Adoration
Adultery
Aggravation
Alertness
Allowing
Anger
Anticipation
Artistry
Avoidance

B

Balance
Belonging
Blame
Bravery
Bullying

C

Challenges
Challenges (body)
Challenges (mind)
Challenges (sight)
Challenges (sound)
Character
Communication
Compassion
Competency
Competition
Complexity
Composure
Confidence
Confidentiality
Consciousness

Creativity
Criticism

D

Defying Death
Depression
Desperation
Discovery
Duality

E

Empathy
Education
Evangelism

F

Failure
Femininity
Fertility
Fragility
Frivolity
Frugality

G

Giving
Grace
Gratitude
Grief
Grievance

H

Happiness
Hardness

Heartbreak

I

Imagination
Infertility
Insensitivity
Intention

J

Joy
Judgment

L

Lavishness
Legality
Loneliness
Loss

M

Masculinity
Mediocrity
Mental Incompetence
Mentorship
Militant
Music

N

Nit Picking
Nostalgia

O

Obsession
Over thinking

P

Passion

Patience

Peace

Perfectionism

Persistence

Perspective

Phobias

Pioneer

Poetry

Possession

Possibility

Potential

Preparedness

R

Receiving

Regret

Religion

Resilience

S

Sadness

Sameness

Science

Separation

Sensitivity

Serenity

Sharing

Self-defacement

Self-doubt

Self-effacement

Self-importance

Self-love
Self-punishment
Self-worth
Silliness
Singularity
Spirituality
Stage Fright
Stinginess
Stillness
Strength
Structure
Stubbornness
Success
Superstition
Surrender

T

Tenacity
Terror
Thoughtfulness
Toxicity
Trust

U

Unhappiness
Unpreparedness
Unstructured

V

Value
Vanity
Virtue
Virility

Vulnerability

W
Weakness
Wonder
Worry
Worthiness

X
Xenophobia

Y
Youth

Z
Zen

www.ingramcontent.com/pod-product-compliance
Lightning Source LLC
Chambersburg PA
CBHW070339090426
42733CB00009B/1230